P
c
1o
Y

How to Produce Comedy Bronze

How to Produce Comedy Bronze

Jon Plowman

Published by 535
An imprint of Blink Publishing
2.25 The Plaza
535 Kings Road,
Chelsea Harbour,
London, SW10 0SZ
www.blinkpublishing.co.uk

facebook.com/blinkpublishing
twitter.com/blinkpublishing

Hardback – 978-1-78870-039-9
Ebook – 978-1-78870-040-5

A CIP catalogue of this book is available from the British Library.

Typset by Envy Design Ltd
Printed and bound in Great Britain by Clays Ltd, Elcograf S.p.A.

1 3 5 7 9 10 8 6 4 2

Blink Publishing is an imprint of Bonnier Books UK
www.bonnierbooks.co.uk

To Francis

I owe you everything, far more than I can say

Contents

Foreword
by
Dawn French

'Jon Plowman is a total twat.'

Ah yes, the familiar sentiment I've heard about him over and over again in the 40 or so years I've known and worked with the said twat. Very often, the various folk who utter the above truism, are people who inevitably request to work with him repeatedly, and who also become lifelong pals. Like me.

Y'see, Jon Plowman is no stranger to straight-talking. Although his job requires that on occasion it might serve him well to massage the truth a tad, he actually prefers to say exactly what he's thinking rather than filter his thoughts through any kind of subtlety or sensitivity mesh. This means that what you often get is raw Jon. Jon concentrate, so to speak. Full on, honest and in yer face, he will tell you *precisely* what he thinks. Luckily, with years of experience, Fatty Saunders and I have learnt to completely ignore him.

How to Produce Comedy Bronze

'Plowbags', as we know him, is someone you want on your team. He is one of the few producers who will champion your script/treatment/idea from its very birth all the way through to its production and transmission…or, in a few sorry cases, to its extinction and guillotine-style execution. He genuinely cares that good comedy is properly produced. He will lie, cheat, steal and bite to make it happen. He is that little terrier who won't stop humping your leg until you are forced to club him to death, however cute and furry and googly-eyed he is. No sorry, that last bit's *not* Jon. That's Wayne Sleep…

For hundreds of years, he was our 'key man' at the BBC, and because of him, *French and Saunders*, *Absolutely Fabulous*, *The Vicar of Dibley*, *Murder Most Horrid* and tons of other shows that I'm not in, so frankly can't be arsed to mention, plopped into people's front rooms. He has always been a ferocious advocate (not advocaat, silly, that's entirely different). By 'ferocious', I don't mean that he has fangs and would scare children…although…in a certain light…

No, I mean that if Jon believes in what you've created, he will stop at nothing to make sure it is realised *In the Way You Intended*. He is risk-interested. He creates the firewall between the creatives and the suits which ensures you have the right environment to experiment and be silly and make mistakes and get better at what you do.

Fatty and I always found the business end of making telly utterly deathly. All good ideas die right there if you allow them to, if you give in or get distracted. Jon is the Cerberus of comedy. He guards the gates of broadcasting Hades to keep the naysayers and spoilsports in, so that your idea is free to develop and grow without too much attack.

This book, whilst very funny and informative, (dare I say, I genuinely think it even properly TEACHES, whether you want to learn or not!) will most definitely offend plenty of people.

Foreword

It's full of lies and exaggeration, but then Jon is a PRODUCER and has never been one to let a silly little fact get in the way of a hilarious anecdote. He lied to get his first job in telly, and he hasn't stopped since...thank goodness.

BAD Things About Jon: moans quite a bit
pisses off extras
driving skills (NIL)
can't eat without spitting
  or burping
massive gossiper
can't learn lines for cameo roles
has a monstrous leg injury
  (ask to see it)
has had brain removed through
  nose (fact).

GOOD Things About Jon: mighty swearing skills
is deliciously indiscreet
is hilariously rude
tells funny stories
is hands-down the best audience
is a mensch
has great taste in husbands
is bulletproof
is calm
loves writers/actors
is a loyal friend
will lend you his house
is the *best* guy for the job,
  every time
collects cuddly toy rabbits
makes no apologies for the above.

Above all, Jon has never forgotten that we all need to *play*. He is a child in a man's body, a person who hasn't quite grown up. With any luck, he never will, and he will continue to defend the right for all of us to have a bloody good, quality laugh, however childish or un-PC.

Working with him is the best of times, he's someone you want to raise your bar for, someone you long to make laugh And for me, the most satisfying thing about this book is that finally…he has had to sit down…and know what writing feels like.

Excuse my schadenfreude, but honestly, that in itself is *fabulous*.

Enjoy the book.

Enjoy this lovely, clever man.

1

Beginning

Before I start this is really just to give you, the reader, a bit of background about the whens and whats and wheres of me, the writer.

I was born and brought up in Welwyn Garden City, which is not the funniest place ever, but not the grimmest either. My first encounter with comedy, apart from watching it on TV, was when I appeared in an amateur production of *An Italian Straw Hat* for the Welwyn Folk Players. I played a smallish boy, which was good casting because I was one.

I left school and went to university, where I appeared in a variety of productions but also directed a few. This gave me my first experience of being a producer, because directing plays at college involves convincing people to give you money, then motivating actors to turn up for rehearsals and, finally, persuading an audience to sit down and watch.

In my first term, I directed a three-man one-act play for a university freshmen competition. I did it largely because no one else wanted to. It was called *Oldenburg*. Mel Smith, also a newbie at another college, directed an all-singing, all-dancing half-hour distillation of *Marat/Sade*, by Peter Weiss with a cast of thousands. And won. Bastard. Later on I directed a production of *West Side Story* in which the leading man committed suicide halfway through rehearsals, poor chap, and the guy I was directing it with had to take his place.

At the end of my time at university I wrote and directed a play at the Edinburgh Festival, which starred an actor who subsequently became my lifelong partner. This received very nice reviews, so finally my career was kicking off because something had worked out *for itself*, rather than because of either apathy or death.

The play came down to the King's Head theatre in Islington and it was from there that I wrote to the Royal Court Theatre in Sloane Square and asked for a job. As you may know the King's Head is a pub with a theatre out the back. I wasn't earning any real money from the play so I was working behind the bar of the pub to make some cash. It was up to this bar that a woman walked one night and said that she was PA to the then artistic director of the Royal Court, Oscar Lewenstein.

'Oscar got your letter and he was wondering whether you might be able to come in maybe next Thursday for a chat with him and Albert.'

'Albert who?'

'Albert Finney. He's directing *Loot* for us soon.'

> *'Barely a page into the book and he's name-dropping away like a mad thing.'*
>
> *'Now he's showing us he's aware of his name-dropping and wants to do it, but not be thought the worse of for doing it.'*

> *'Well, I guess…it wouldn't be so interesting if he didn't tell us who he was dishing the dirt on…I mean "the disgusting toilet habits of Cyril Pratweasel" isn't as interesting as the disgusting toilet habits of….'*
>
> Me: Well, if you're not keen on name-dropping, I suggest you put the book down now and just walk out of Waterstones, because it's going to get worse, I warn you. Actually, if you don't mind it too much, buy the damn thing! Please! It's not that expensive!

I did go along and I did meet Albert and I did get a job as an assistant director. Not with him though. I lucked out and got a job as assistant director to Lindsay Anderson who was about to direct another Joe Orton play, *What the Butler Saw.* This was in 1975.

Lindsay was a genius and I was very lucky to have worked with him. He was probably best known for his films *If...*, *This Sporting Life*, *O Lucky Man*, and *Britannia Hospital.* His work at the Royal Court Theatre (which he ran with Anthony Page in the early seventies) included a lot of plays by David Storey, such as *The Contractor* and *The Changing Room*, plays set in and about the north of England. He directed *Home*, which starred Ralph Richardson and John Gielgud conversing and reminiscing in a large house, which little by little we realise is actually a mental institution.

He was usually described as a prickly man, but that's not really the point. He was very bright and did not suffer fools. He was a man who knew what he wanted to achieve and was going to achieve it. He was a director who believed that a big part of his job was to make the team into a coherent unit. I agreed. He thought that the job of director and cast was to find out how to 'do' a play, then get the wagons in a circle and fire at any Indians who might be on the attack. The Indians could be the audience or critics or people who had other ways of doing things. He and the cast were *right*, and this had to be accepted. He was kind and loyal once he knew that you were working with him not against him.

I worked with him both at the Court and on a season of plays in the West End. It was there that I saw him in the company of Arthur Cantor, an American who was one of the producers of the season. Arthur was a perfectly decent chap but not the sharpest knife in the canteen. Lindsay was trying to write some notes in the office one day, and Arthur was in gossipy mood.

Eventually Arthur said,'Lindsay, you should write your autobiography.'

There was an impatient grunt.

'What would you call it?'

Lindsay looked over his glasses at Arthur and after a pause said, '*Surrounded by Idiots*.'

Lindsay's collected writings were in fact called, rather appropriately, *Never Apologise*. I recommend them to you.

From working in the theatre, I went to the Arts Council and from there on to a tour of America and thence to a 'crammers' in Sloane Square to earn some cash. It was from the crammers that I was sucked (*no, no, no, stop it*) into the world of Film and TV.

2

Absolution (of a Kind)

So there I am, 23 – a neglected showbiz talent – teaching Middle Eastern girls how to part with their money, or more accurately, English as a Foreign Language. What they really want to know is the quickest route from the crammers (intensive educational facility), to the handbag and cosmetics departments at Harrods. My students have very, *very* small attention spans and I find that I'm teaching by telling jokes, just to amuse myself.

'Today, let us consider the subjunctive. Were my dog to have no nose, how would he smell? Answer – bloody awful.'

One day, as I reach for the joke book, there's a knock on the door.

'Sorry to interrupt but there's a phone call for you in the office, Mr Plowman,' says the school secretary. 'It's 20th Century Fox.'

This is one of those occasions when you wish that the BBC, ITN, Fox News, Al Jazeera and half a dozen international news outlets were present with camera crews to record the moment. It was also one of those occasions when I wished that my teaching skills had been better, so that the group of would-be Iranian fashionistas could have grasped the full significance of the secretary's message. So they could fall back in amazement at the circles in which their fast-departing teacher was evidently moving. This is (and there is *no* question about it) the equivalent of the secretary at the Château d'If knocking on a cell door and saying, 'Oh, Mr Count of Monte Cristo, there's a limo and a crowd of whooping journalists and supporters just outside the gates. Could you spare them a few minutes?'

It was ESCAPE and it was a huge movie organisation showing enough interest to track me down. Interest in *me*. ME, here.

'Mr Plowman, Celestia Fox was wondering if you might pop in for a chat.'

Clearly international stardom beckons. I'm out of that school faster than my students on the first day of the new season sale at Burberry. It turns out that Celestia Fox is a very well-known casting director.

I'm told that she's casting a film by Anthony Shaffer the writer of *Sleuth*, to be directed by Anthony Page, who used to run the Royal Court with Lindsay Anderson. The film is being produced by Elliott Kastner, and it will star Richard Burton, currently going through a sober patch and recently married to Suzy Hunt (who, it turns out, is never anywhere but by his side…better safe than sorry.).

The film is to be called *Absolution*.

It takes place in a boys' public school, so quite a few boys need to be auditioned and cast. Celestia needs some help. Evidently, Lindsay has suggested that I might be the man for the job, not least because he knows that I'd appreciate a leg up. So I swap Sloane Square for Soho Square where 20th

Absolution (of a Kind)

Century Fox, who are making the movie, are based. I've joined the film industry.

My job is to help audition a large number of child actors, and older actors who might pass for 14, 15 or 16. We meet them singly and then in groups, to see if they might be part of the 'dorm' where actors Dai Bradley and Dominic Guard are resident. These two are playing the main schoolboy characters even though Dom is already 20 and Dai is 24. The camera* never tells the truth.

Celestia is a canny caster and I like her a lot. Once she sees that I more or less know what I'm doing, we begin to discuss the adult casting as well. I learn that the producer wouldn't say no to another star or two around Mr Burton. The other role that might attract a 'name' is that of the long-haired gypsy, Blakey, who haunts the woods and fields near the school and is important to the plot.

Various names are mentioned like Roger Daltrey and David Essex, who would lend the film a whiff of sex, drugs and rock 'n' roll (it *was* a long time ago). Then the name of Billy Connolly pops up. He's only recently become a star as a result of his appearances with chat-show host, Michael Parkinson. His 'look' and heavy Glasgow accent won't be a problem, indeed he looks like a gypsy without any help from us. The only obstacle is that Anthony Page hasn't heard of him. He's been in the US until recently on his film, *I Never Promised You a Rose Garden* and he hasn't been watching much British TV. He doesn't know who Billy is, or why he's famous. So Celestia rings Billy's manager and invites Billy in to meet Anthony. Then she does a very canny thing.

'No worries, darling. We're at 20 Century in the far corner of Soho Square, but you can't easily drive round the square

---

* With a bit of help from makeup.

at the moment, so get his driver to drop him at the top of the square and then he can just walk across to us. No distance at all. It'll be fine, let me know when he's on his way and I'll come down to meet him.'

She knows that there is a young hip crowd in Soho Square. Paul McCartney's company MPL is moving in on one side and there are media and advertising companies on the other. People here will recognise Mr Connolly. So the next part of the plan is to get Anthony Page to the window of our fifth-floor office.

'Oh look, Tony, here comes Billy. You'd spot him a mile away.'

As the Big Yin walks across Soho Square he attracts a good deal of attention. Autographs are requested and pictures are taken, even in these pre-smartphone days. He makes his way, rather slowly, across the square. Anthony Page observes all this. By the time he arrives at Fox, it is clear to Anthony that Billy is a star, the part is his for the playing, and play it he did.

So the film (which you may never have seen, few have) stars Richard Burton, playing one of the many Catholic priests that dotted his long and illustrious career. Burton liked playing Catholic priests, not least because when he is in the confessional he can have all the pages of the script stuck to the wall behind the camera. If the priest happens to be a teacher, then even better, because there are books to be marked and handed out, and the script can always be taped inside one of these. Burton is rarely without a book in this film. He's no fool.

In *Absolution*, he is Father Goddard. All around him is an impenetrable plot, through which he has to navigate as well as he can. Gypsies turn up, gypsies are murdered. Boys disappear. One boy is good at mimicking another. One boy in calipers is resentful at the cruelty he thinks Father G has inflicted on him. Confessions are made. Father G is bound by the sanctity of the confessional. Spades are wielded in anger. Bodies fall to the forest floor. And suicide is a mortal sin. Father Goddard is trapped.

Confused? Download it.

It's a dark and gothic thriller. Indeed, its darkness may have been a handicap at the box office, but we don't know that yet. For now there are classroom scenes that need pupils, cricket matches that need players and dormitories that need testosterone-packed schoolboys, even if they come from stage schools. This was my job. They are my responsibility. All for one and one for all! Play up, play up and play the game!

We didn't do too badly, when I come to look at what happened to these fledgling actors. I mean, only a few of them even had lines in *Absolution*, but one of them went on to play Tony Blair's aide in *The Queen*, one of them played Mordred in *Excalibur* and Guy of Gisborne in *Robin of Sherwood,* and one of them is now a rather good film and TV writer. I'm proud of my brood. Well done, boys.

Did they send me 'Thank you for my career' cards? Did they beeswax.

I learned early on that the film industry in those pre-Thatcher days was what we used to call 'a closed shop'. As time passed, I became quite friendly with Anthony Page and was invited to work with him, not just on the auditions but on the film itself. I would be an assistant to the director and help look after my dormitory-load of actors on the job. No. That sounds very bad. I mean – part of my job would be to look after these young actors during their working hours. Yes. That's better.

However, it turned out that I couldn't be credited as an 'assistant director', a far more prestigious job. My position as 'assistant *to the* director' didn't really exist at that time in the movies. But eventually a solution was found. I was given a part in the film. Fame at last! I was to play Father Piers, a young postulant (look it up), and a character who only appears for a second, running down some stairs in a cassock (I *know*, stairs are rarely seen in a cassock) as International Superstar and Welshman Richard Burton rushes up. I was to be contracted for the whole shoot, even though I occupied maybe 15 seconds of screen time. After all, Piers *might* be needed on *any* day of filming, any time Mr Burton was ascending a staircase. It was only logical to pay me for the whole shoot. Thereby Father Piers was on hand to help Anthony and the boys.

I found that mine was not the only anomalously contracted cassock-wearer. There was also the odd case of Father Clarence, another character seen rarely but contracted for the duration. He was played by Brook Williams, son of eminent playwright and actor Emlyn Williams. He can also be seen in *Cleopatra, Equus, Villain, The Wild Geese, The Medusa Touch* and many other movies in which Burton had a starring role. He was, quite simply, someone who Richard had befriended as a child, and who Richard liked to have around the set. And so there he was, available to join Burton for a chat or a drink between takes. Not that new bride Suzy ever let Burton escape her gaze, so it was chats only for Brook and maybe a double Ovaltine.

The other person who never left Richard's side was a tall, quiet black gentleman, Mr Wilson. I think in earlier days he may have been his bodyguard, he had that look about him. We learnt more about his duties one afternoon when Richard was kept waiting for a few minutes on set.

'This is not at all like the old days,' he said in that rumbling voice from the valleys. 'I remember when we made *Becket* at Shepperton. At the end of the shoot I sent Mr Wilson to settle up at the local hostelry and he came back looking worried and said, "Richard I think you and Peter [O'Toole] must have had a very good time. I settled the bill and it was £32,000!'"

Burton paused for the enormity to sink in. It had been 1963 when the film was made and this was a huge amount of dosh.

He topped it off with, 'And do you know, getting the 16,000 out of Peter was like getting blood out of a stone.'

It must have been quite a lengthy shoot, but Burton's view was that clearly every unemployed actor who'd ever worked with either him or O'Toole had popped down to Shepperton and put a bottle or two of vodka on the slate.

No such behaviour at Ellesmere School, where we filmed our exteriors. I had to look after the boys and rehearse them in their scenes. Sometimes, though, I was beside Anthony Page for the filming and observed how things could go adrift. On the first day of shooting the producer, Elliott Kastner did something I've never seen a producer do before or since: he ripped a scene out of the script in front of the director and crew. It was a cricket match, which I can see that Kastner thought was going to take too long to set up and shoot, but it would have provided useful air and light in the movie, and we weren't behind on our schedule. Yet. That's producers for you – anything to save money. Old-fashioned producers. With fangs. He was American, maybe he just didn't understand cricket.

There wasn't much that Anthony could do, the money had spoken.

Once the shoot moved to Pinewood Studios, my job changed somewhat, and among other tasks, I found myself going to Richard's hotel room and putting rewrites of the following day's scenes under his door. Please don't tell anybody, but Anthony Shaffer hadn't spent a lot of time on the dialogue, so there was another writer working day and night to make it say-able. This was all very cloak and dagger. Nobody was supposed to know. *Richard* wasn't meant to know (of course he did), and so Anthony S took the credit for somebody else's work (did he ever realise?). It also meant me furtively negotiating the corridors of Claridge's in the middle of the night. Ah! the glamour and intrigue.

The film came out in 1978 and won an award at the Miami Film Festival. Critics were complimentary about Burton's performance, though, surprisingly, I didn't get a mention.

A footnote. Around the time the film came out, there was a revolution in Iran. As a result, most of the girls I'd been teaching at the crammers, ended up *working* in Harrods rather than shopping there.

3

No News is
No News

> •
> •
> • **LESSON: Know your limits even when you're**
> • **way beyond them.**
> •
> •

My television career began with a lie.

After *Absolution*, I was working for the Arts Council of Great Britain looking after some theatres on behalf of you, the taxpayer.

Truthfully, I wasn't doing much at the Arts Council – where it was really quite easy to do not very much. So, thinking that none of the theatres I 'looked after' seemed very likely to offer me a job, and that teaching English as a foreign language was not my destiny, I applied to a Granada TV scheme for theatre directors who wanted to train as TV directors. This looked like a good gig, *except* that it was in Manchester, another country, a *long* way from my comfy digs in Notting Hill – well, north of Watford. But I filled in a form, I was offered an interview, I did the interview, I got a second interview. Then I received a phone call from an enthusiastic Scot named Steve Morrison.

'Hi, well we liked you a lot [surely a lie] and you got into the last six, but we think you're a bit too young [the big lie] so we'd like to offer you a job as a researcher.'

'Well, I'm not sure. I mean, I really have my heart in the theatre [I lied], and I have this job at the Arts Council, and…'

Then he told me what the money was and I said 'Yes.'

The first show I worked on was misnamed *Fun Factory*. It was a two-hour Saturday morning show for kids, and a summer fill-in for the much more anarchic *Tiswas*. My job was to produce short items and to dress up every Saturday morning in a brightly coloured boiler suit, in which I prevented those kids unlucky enough to be invited to the studio floor from being run over by cameras. The other brightly clad researchers included Trish Kinane, who went on to produce *America's Got Talent*; Sarah Harding, a future director of *Marple*, *Poirot*, and *Coronation Street*; and, perhaps oddest of all, the guy who wrote the definitive history of punk, Jon Savage. As you can see, we were a wildly overqualified bunch. *Worse* – this was the show that first put Jeremy Beadle on TV. May we all rot in hell! *Beadle's About* need never have happened. (Ask your parents.)

After that came the ordeal that every researcher had to go through: a stint working on the local news show, *Granada Reports*. It was at this point that both I, and the organisation for which I worked, came to see that I lacked even the most basic instincts of a newshound. There is (apparently) an art to making news for local TV. Yes. Really. I was surprised too. And you know? I was a stranger to the subtle magic of that art, and remain so to this day.

No News is No News

Cut to a Friday on the Granada News desk.

News editors dreaded Fridays. By Friday, proper news reporters and crews had used up all their working hours, so it would now be a *Golden Friday* when everyone had to be paid at least 8T in overtime. That is *eight times* their normal rate. Result: the editor would pray that nothing happened in Manchester and its environs at the end of the week, because it would cost a fortune. They would be prepared with something made earlier in the week but not too time specific. Gardening tips, say, or a consumer piece. Something not good enough for Wednesdays…a few soft studio items…maybe five minutes of local football league speculation. *Anything.*

Cut to one particular Friday in the GTV Newsroom (oh, we've cut already, sorry…you see how bad I am at local news?). By now, the editor has me down as a bit of a current affairs numpty.

'Go to Liverpool,' he commands, 'and make us a "What's on at the Weekend" piece. Three minutes, no more. Lots of graphics, a bit of archive if you have to.'

Not too bad. We're based in Manchester so at least I get a nice day out. Except that when I arrive in Liverpool I discover that there is yet another strike at the Halewood car factory and negotiations are happening *now*. These facts probably don't mean much to you – they meant *nothing* to me.

But the news editor is very excited.

'There's a crew downstairs, each of them earning enough to settle the whole strike, Take this cutting from today's *Times*.'

He hands me a scrap of newspaper, no, *smaller* than a scrap, a *scrp* of paper.

'This'll get you up to speed. I need a minute and a half for the one o'clock that will also serve the 6.30. Get up there [wherever "there" was] cos I hear it may be all done and dusted by 12.'

Whether it was either done or dusted by 12, I can't remember.

I do know that this was *exactly* what I hated about news. The idea that, armed only with this *scrp* and my very tiny abilities as a newshound, I was expected to become the definitive expert on Ford's industrial relations policy for the whole of north-west England and beyond. All this in the time it was going to take me to walk downstairs to a film crew who couldn't believe how much overtime they were about to earn.

It was terrifying! In my head, car workers were already saying, 'Now, lads, OK – we're stayin' out cos that bloke on ITV telly said we're getting an extra 26p a shift when the shop steward just told us it's 26p less! That's it! Every-body out!'

This is my terror. This is why, when I turn up to the editorial meeting at 9 a.m. every morning, I'm terrified at what I'll need to be a world authority on by the end of the day. It's the reason I end up doing fluffy items on the role of St Helens in the gobstopper industry now that the last factory is about to close with the loss of 180,000 gobs unstopped.

Any road up, imagine a large building on a hill in Liverpool, and a whole claque of journalists elbowing each other out of the way to catch the first words uttered by the union chap from Ford. 'What's the news?' 'Back to work on Monday?' 'Accommodation reached with management?'

On the edge of the melee stands one relatively disinterested arts graduate from Granada Reports. I've never been good in crowds, here or anywhere else. So I sidle up to a grey-looking chap who might be the main chap's assistant. None of the claque are interested in this guy.

'Hi, I'm from Granada TV. I wonder if, when your man has finished, you might ask him if he wouldn't mind giving us a few words around the corner here. It won't take awfully long and I think if we angle it right we can get both the cathedrals in shot which would look nice, wouldn't it?'

No News is No News

I appeal to his aesthetic side. Even now, 40 years later, I'm rather pleased with this strategy. And yes, a few minutes later the main man plays ball, and I find myself coming out with the most clichéd question imaginable.

'So, does this mean an end to strikes at Halewood as we know them?'

What a zinger. What does it mean?

It's all I have at my fingertips after casually watching years of news and current affairs.

He's a bit taken aback by this question or perhaps just by its banality, but eventually he manages to respond with a halting reply. And *I'm* thinking – 'What on earth did I just say? Does it mean anything? Do I get overtime? What shall I have for supper?' But isn't this exactly what journos are paid for? Jeremy Paxman, Hugh Edwards, John Craven. I began to see why they might deserve 8T. I certainly did.

The interview is urgently despatched to Manchester and edited for the one o'clock bulletin, and I get working on the much more vital 'What's on at the Weekend?' piece.

The only comment I received from the man who sent me on this mission, worthy of Orla Guerin or Kate Adie or Jon Snow (not that one) at their height, is,'You made it look too much like lunchtime.' This from the editor of the *evening* bulletin, who also wants to broadcast my feat of reporting brilliance, made originally for the lunchtime news.

What the hell does that mean!? What was I supposed to do? Edit in some shots of dusk over the Mersey, or ask the question in some past and future tense as yet un-invented? Or ask the chief union negotiator at Halewood if he was off for his supper?

Hey ho, a journo's life is not for me. David Dimbleby I'm not.

4

Séance and Sinatra

JON'S CONSCIENCE:	You *failed!*
JON:	No, no…
JON'S CONSCIENCE:	Dismally, woefully!
JON:	Don't hit me…
JON'S CONSCIENCE:	You let *everybody* down…
JON:	It was only journalism…
JON'S CONSCIENCE:	Appalling, arrogant, amateur…
JON:	STOP!
JON'S CONSCIENCE:	I'm still on the A's…

Not having made journalism my home, I was next inflicted on Local Arts and Features. I know what you're thinking. Films about clog-dancing in the Wirral, searing exposés of whippet sexing in Oswaltwhistle? No. Nothing that good. Local Arts and Features covered whatever people threw at it. The 'local' specification described the region the programmes were *shown in* (roughly from Stafford to the Lakes).

How to Produce Comedy Bronze

I began by working on a half-hour arts programme called *Celebration*. We made a film about Arnold Bennett, with a budget so small the researcher (me) had to hold a boiling kettle in front of the camera to transform AB's arrival in Stoke from a diesel into a steam train.

It was at this time that I met and began to work with the future head of ITV, David Liddiment. He was a very good director and, just as importantly, he knew the system. David and I had lots of fun with local arts. We staged a reunion concert with Fairport Convention on the very slim pretext that they were important and had once played at a local folk club. We got into hot water when we put together a show featuring Loudon Wainwright III, a great folk singer and satirist who had included the north-west in his tour schedule. He slipped in a song called 'Vampire Blues'. It contained the line 'I love you when you're rough and ready on the rag'. *Apparently*, this was a reference to his girlfriend's *period*. Who knew? I have to say I didn't, until the day after transmission when a disapproving note from the programme controller arrived.

Somehow, *Celebration* also became the series that allowed us to make a half-hour show with comedian Alexei Sayle. The notion was that Alexei was part of a cultural exchange with Albania. It involved him having to perform stand-up in a bleak deserted shopping precinct in Wythenshawe to absolutely no reaction. It allowed him to do his famed Berthold Brecht impersonation, and it climaxed with him performing as Adam Ant in a spoof video filmed in a children's playground in New Brighton.

It was a rare privilege about which we thought very little: a half-hour slot on ITV with no strings attached. The slot gave those who worked on it a huge amount of leeway. It was a great way to learn and in public.

Séance and Sinatra

On the slimmest of pretexts, namely that we liked her style, we made a show with model, fashion icon and chantooze, Grace Jones. Yes – for Local Arts and Features. The pretext was that we would – in her company – examine the similarities between club life in New York and nightlife in Liverpool. Of *course* we would! We started filming on the day after she hit chat-show host Russell Harty live on air (she claimed that he was ignoring her). This meant that we were followed everywhere by members of the press pack; followed, that is, once we'd managed to prise Ms Jones from the Atlantic Towers hotel, three hours after her agreed call time.

This unlikely half-hour film *also* featured Grace meeting writer and critic George Melly, boxer John Conteh and punk housewife Margox. It may not have told the viewer much about New York or Liverpool but it was definitely – er – different. And that's good, isn't it?

JON'S CONSCIENCE:	Wayward, worthless, wasteful...
JON:	You've missed out a few letters there...
JON'S CONSCIENCE:	You haven't been listening...

It may have been the Grace Jones encounter which set me on the road to what used to be called Light Entertainment. At this point in Granada's history, the department was run by the ebullient Johnny Hamp (*ebullient* – from the Latin, to boil, nothing to do with bullies or ebola). It was Johnny who brought viewers *Wheeltappers and Shunters Social Club* and *The Comedians* (you know how to use Google, right?). His background was club comedy and variety for which the north was famous, and which provided him with local stars. Result – he didn't spend pointless hours trying to lure the likes of Morecambe and Wise or Nana

Mouskouri up from London or Athens and away from the BBC, but he was the first guy to get the Beatles on TV and Frank Carson.

Johnny needed a young producer for a late-night strand that was going to be edgy and real and hip and groovy. Well, within reason. I put myself forward and got the job. Although I may not have been 'hip' or 'edgy' or 'groovy', I was incontrovertibly 'real'.

LESSON: When in doubt, get banned.

The first show that I made for this late-night strand fell into none of the categories mentioned above. It was *An Evening with Doris Stokes* and if she's hovering around out there in the ether, I'd just like to say 'sorry'.

Doris Stokes was a clairaudient. In other words, the dead spoke to her and she relayed their messages back to the living. And as far as livings are concerned, she made a good one. People *flocked* to hear news from 'the other side', desperate for word from their dearest and most deceased. Doris was a lady of mature years, early seventies, I would guess, and she could have been your gran. Well, probably not *your* gran, but mine certainly. She had a husband 'who had a plate in his head – from the war' and he didn't say much. But she made up for that.

I got to know her because a friend from university (André Ptaszynski – now executive producer of *Matilda*) was touring her round the country (I think he was as amazed as anyone by her popularity). She gave her audiences a show, and if they were lucky a 'visitation'.

Séance and Sinatra

I catch her at the Forum, Wythenshawe. It's packed. She says things like: 'Oh, they're coming through with so much love. Now I've got a Nor...man?, Nor...een? – from the other side... Nor...Norma...Robert? Can anybody take that?'

(Meaning does anybody have a relative with that name who can get me out of this hole?)

'Oh, they're coming through with so much love, and they're saying that there's a blue carpet...'

(No response.)

'Oh, it's not Robert, it's Doreen! Doreen from Heaton Chapel.'

(Quite nearby.)

'Yes, was that your mum, darling?'

(Someone has 'taken', thank God.)

'Yes, I can see a little light above your head. Yes, it's your mum, isn't it, and she's coming through with so much love. Did she go over recently? Yes, yes – she says yes she did...'

(Doris is now in contact with the dead spirit.)

'She says it's all going to be all right with the grandchildren and the court case, and she likes the new wallpaper.'

That's the world. It's quite tabloid: lino gets mentioned a lot and sometimes there's a cashbox under the floorboards. Occasionally, John Lennon pops by and asks for Elton, but it's never Sir John Barbirolli asking to speak to Arvo Pärt, and that's *fine* because she knows her audience.

So we meet and we talk about doing a late-night show for Granada. She's thrilled. So thrilled that she says I must come to a private session she's doing. It's with the parents of a girl who's recently been murdered. The police have drawn a blank and so the parents have asked for a meeting. It's very difficult and I'm sure that I shouldn't be there, but the parents have been consulted, and they don't seem to mind. I think *I* would mind, but they don't.

Doris begins with: 'Now, is it a drug-related slaying?'

The parents nod very slowly.

'Oh dear, I can see a lot of blood...'

(Unsurprising – there's been a murder.)

'...I can see a kitchen table and I can see a knife...'

There's quite a lot of this vague stuff, and Doris eventually informs the bereaved parents that the assassin may have been a red-headed man, or perhaps a number of men from the Middle East. To call this random speculation is to overestimate its place in the rational scheme of things, but it *genuinely* seems to be of some comfort to the parents. I think that's why they came, so they feel that they've left no stone unturned in their grief and in pursuit of closure. They leave happier than when they arrived.

As they go, Doris says to the father, entirely out of the blue: 'You've been for tests at the hospital, haven't you?'

He nods.

'You didn't tell me,' his wife says – a little bit anxious, a little bit annoyed.

'Don't worry,' says Doris, 'It's all going to be fine, you're going to be all right.'

They leave. But scarcely has the door closed behind them before Doris turns to me and says, 'He's not long for this world.'

In many ways, she's a monster.

We construct a format for the programme. There will be Doris, and her audience – 25 spiritualists, 25 punters and 25 psychology students from the University of Manchester. A balanced crowd. Views from all sides. I hope that some of them will give Doris a hard time. The host and mediator will be a Church of England vicar, Roger Royle. He is a man of camp but kindly demeanour, known for his cheery appearances on Terry Wogan's *Pause for Thought*.

Doris does her stuff. The dead leave that undiscovered

country from whose bourn (at least as far as Hamlet was concerned) no traveller returns, and so does a dead budgerigar called Denis. Rather annoyingly, the psychology students – brought in to wither Doris with their scepticism – are hugely keen to catch up with their own dead relatives, so the spiritualists and punters hardly get a look in. Roger Royle is kindly and giggly and not quite the stern religious balance I was looking for, but hey-ho, the programme is only regional (you patronising git, Plowman) and late night. So what can go wrong?

Plenty.

First of all, *The Sun* rings me (at this time not quite the Murdoch torch of truth that it became, but nevertheless, *The Sun*).

'Hi, this is Derek from the TV section, we may not be able to do very much about your programme because it's late night and regional but just tell me about it, Jon.'

Remember, this is my first programme, and I'm just thrilled that anyone wants to write anything. Publicity! My pulse quickens and I spiel as follows.

'Well, it's really interesting because Doris brings back the dead, and they talk to the audience, so that's exciting, but it's only regional and late night.'

'Well, I'm not promising but I'll see if we can give it a mention on the day.'

Derek is as good as his word. Better. Worse. A couple of weeks before the show is due to go out, the TV Section of *The Sun* yells: 'HORROR CHAT SHOW STORM, THE DEAD RETURN'

Well, it's publicity.

It seems that what dear Derek did after my chat, was call Doris. He told her that Granada were very worried about her show, so Doris gives him a few, 'I don't mean no harm to nobody, I'm-a-good-girl-I-am' quotes and then Derek rings a well-known anti-spiritualist priest who says: 'If Jesus were going to bring back the dead he certainly wouldn't do it on a chat show.'

Actually, I disagree, but by now my phone is ringing.

The first people up in arms are the northern branch of the religious programmes department of the IBA (Independent Broadcasting Authority). They get hold of a copy of the show and can't make up their minds whether it should be broadcast, so they send it to the IBA in London. The big boys. They look at it and also can't reach a decision, so they send it to the head of the IBA and he says 'No, it shouldn't be broadcast.' Wow. Thanks

I think that the big cheese dumped on us because the programme was made by the Entertainment Department and must therefore have been frivolous. It turned out the big cheese had also been the chairman of Capital Radio in London who used to broadcast Doris every Tuesday night. Mike Scott – controller of programmes at Granada – rang me up afterwards and said that he'd been dealing with the IBA about a particular edition of *World in Action* and that my programme had just been a bargaining chip. Perhaps he was being nice, which is a rare trait in television. He also said, 'If your first programme gets banned by the IBA, you'll do all right'. I suppose I did do all right, but it still seems a bit odd.

By the way, I have a VHS of the programme should anyone be interested.

Perhaps the most curious aspect of the whole affair was that no one on the other side had warned Doris this would happen. Strange.

After we recorded the programme, Doris and the director and I had dinner at the Palace Hotel in Manchester. She tried a bit of 'her stuff' on us during the evening, just for fun. She told the director, Lorne Magory, that 'someone on the other side' was hinting that he had connections in Canada. Since he had a fairly strong Canadian accent this wasn't necessarily the greatest mystic revelation. Turning to me she said, 'Now I'm getting someone over there, on the other side telling me there's a "Peter" who's very important in your life.'

I racked my brains and found that, curiously, I didn't know many people called Peter and certainly none that were important to me, unless you counted a cousin in Chester who I'd hardly met. At that moment, the boy pushing the sweet trolley arrived. He was wearing a name badge. And of course, she was right. Without Peter, there would have been no sherry trifle.

LESSON: Never pass up a freebie.

After Doris, I was edged towards safer ground: an early evening show called *The Video Entertainers*. This was much less contentious. It was an ITV variety show consisting of various acts linked by Johnny Hamp. The *Video* bit of the title was inserted to make the programme sound hip and modern. I did my best to book people who would make it at least tolerable to the under-thirties. I brought the Tom Robinson Band in to perform *War Baby*, I got a dance group to perform a Peter Gabriel number, I booked a guy called Christopher Cross to stand in the studio on the prow of a large yacht to sing a number called 'Sailing'. The record company seemed a bit surprised that I was booking Cross because, and they put this much more tactfully, he wasn't the best-looking guy ever. I recall that they suggested employing (and may even have provided) a curvaceous young female model to appear in the number with him, so the camera had something lovely to cut away to.

Video Entertainers was chiefly memorable (at least as far as I was concerned) for one happy event. When we were setting up the series, I went to see a potential booking at Caesar's Palace in Luton. Yes – there was a Caesar's Palace in Luton. Honest. While I was there I met the manager of the place, who gathered that after the series, I was going to California for what I thought was a richly deserved holiday.

'Well, Jon, you've got to pay a visit to Caesar's in Vegas. I'll give you my card. Tell them Richard from Luton sent you, they'll look after you.'

I couldn't quite imagine myself saying to anyone 'Richard from Luton sent me', so I thought no more of it until I realised that I was in Las Vegas and that I still had his card in my wallet. So I stomped up to the reception desk and said, sounding very like a twat, 'Hello, I'm from England and I was wondering if you had any rooms left for my partner and me. We'll probably be here until Monday. [It was Thursday.] Now this may sound stupid, but I was at your sister establishment in Luton, England a while ago and Richard there said I should mention his name if I was over here. I think I have his card if it's of any interest at all…'

They look at the card, then at me, and there is a muttered exchange with senior management.

'Yes, indeed sir, we know Richard. How is he? Can we offer you a penthouse suite at a premium discount and also two line passes to see Mr Sinatra this evening?'

Bloody hell! Yes, *of course* they can, and thank the Lord I kept Richard's card, and that it wasn't all the bull that I'd first thought it was.

Yes, thank you, the room was *very* nice and the complimentary line passes were one of the great treats of my life. A line pass is what it says. It means you pass the line and don't have to queue to see Big Frank. And you don't pay! Yippee. As it happened, Mr Sinatra was only 98 per cent sold out on the Thursday so he refused to perform. Well, you wouldn't, would you? He did perform on the Friday night though, and bloody brilliant he was too, even though his support act – daughter Nancy – didn't necessarily sing in tune as much as she might have done.

So, thanks, Richard, wherever you are! If you're on the other side, give my regards to Doris.

5

Break a Leg, Russel₇

'**I**f you don't give me something more interesting to do, I'll just have to go home and bottle jam.'

So said a very un-meedja-savvy lady researcher during my time at local programmes Granada. And she meant it. Her name was Susan Brookes and she later became the cookery guru on *This Morning,* during the Richard and Judy years. She came from Giggleswick in the Yorkshire Dales, which at the time was also home to the extraordinary Russell Harty, soon to be my employer.

Russell Harty had been a teacher at Giggleswick School. He then rose fairly smartly to become a talk show host, firstly at LWT with a show called *Russell Harty Plus,* and later for BBC2 without the *Plus.* His was a twice-weekly show: from Manchester on a Tuesday (with real people) and London on Thursday (with stars). He had started at the Beeb on a show called *Monitor,* a renowned series of arts documentaries, which also featured a young Melvyn Bragg, Ken Russell and a really quite old Huw Wheldon. Russell H always implied that those were his 'high art' days where he really belonged, and that he'd been lured away by the siren voice of showbiz. He wanted to interview Jacob Bronowski, but could see that Rita Hayworth had more glamour and wore frocks that sparkled more

Russell was looking for a producer for a new BBC1 twice-weekly early-evening show. Here the frocks would be *incredibly* sparkly. It was suggested by Susan B, I think in the Stables Bar next to Granada TV, that I should apply for the job. I did, and this led to an interview with Richard Somerset-Ward, then head of music and arts at the BBC. It was perhaps the strangest interview I've ever had.

It took place in a nice but cramped office at the back of Kensington House, just behind Shepherd's Bush Green. 'KenHouse' was the home of all things Arts and Docs at the BBC. You arrived off the street at a front door/reception, which was actually on the second floor. Below were film editing rooms housing men, and a few women, all distinguished by a uniform of cord trousers, pipes and beards. They were the stewards of countless cans of film out of which they were constructing indictments of post-war government housing policy to be shown on BBC2, just after indictments of Henry VII's foreign policy, complete with battle reconstructions also on BBC2. There were larger editing caves for landmark series like the *Ascent of Man* or *Floyd on Fish*. Higher up the building, beyond reception, were production offices for all manner of serious arts programmes, and beyond them at the top of the building were the offices of the top brass, and also the offices of Russell and his production team. So high up that they were almost invisible, hidden away, their very existence denied by the rest of 'Music 'n' arts'. We were the programme equivalents of Grace Poole, looking after Russell Harty, the madwoman in the attic. So high up because we were so low brow.

Break a Leg, Russell

We were on BBC1, for heaven's sake!

It quickly became clear that this was to be more of a chat than an interview, since somebody had assumed that I was already doing the job, whatever it was. Across the desk sat Somerset-Ward, a perfectly nice middle-aged man asking me what sort of show I thought it should be. I was surprised, but I did what you do on these occasions, I made stuff up. 'Well, it could be topical stuff and maybe some less topical stuff, then some current affairs stuff and finally the big showbiz interview that Russell is *so* good at.'

The great Fred De Cordova, producer of the *Tonight Show with Johnny Carson*, said that there are very few decisions to be made about talk shows: chair or desk for the host, guests all on together or one at a time. That's it. So I'm maundering on to no great effect when I notice that most of Mr Somerset-Ward's questions are somehow being pitched over my right shoulder. A quick glance tells me that this is because the women's semi-finals at Wimbledon are on a television just behind me. I am interrupting the BBC head of music and arts as he admires a short-skirted Chris Evert-Lloyd at 6–1, 5–1, just recovering from a careless double fault. But she's winning, even if I'm not. It seemed to me that my interviewer was much more interested in her than in me

Anyway, I got the job. Hooray.

Whilst my younger self is off celebrating, let me tell you a probably untrue story about a BBC head of department who was so diverted by a member of the fairer sex that he was tempted at a Proms Concert to beat out the rhythm of the 1812 overture on her bottom whilst in a box at the Royal Albert Hall. Now, of course, this would lead to a huge furore. Rightly so. Then he was simply told by his neighbour that he was slightly out of time and should listen to the piece more carefully. Times change.

How to Produce Comedy Bronze

To begin with, producing the *Harty* show was rather odd. I was too inexperienced to do the job well so I had to learn as I went along. I learned that unknown men and women made better guests for Russell on an *early* evening show than the stars who were just there to flog a film or a book. So the production team spent all their time trying to find good, lucid, 'real' people with a story to tell. Not easy. The most memorable guests we ever had in my run were three guys who'd been through terrible deprivations as prisoners and slave labour on the Burma railway. They brought tears to the eyes of both audience and host when they sang a couple of the songs that had helped them get through.

I must say that I liked Russell enormously. He was very good at his job. He cared about so-called 'ordinary people' (he wouldn't have considered anybody 'ordinary') and had a way of talking with them that brought out the best. He was funny and camp and kind, and generous. He was certainly generous to me. When I was knocked off my motorbike in the middle of a series, and ended up in Guy's Hospital with a broken leg, he was the first person who came up to see me bearing grapes and a copy of Barbara Cartland's latest. Bless him, but it's still unread. The executive producer – I must point out – never undertook the five-minute journey to do the same. He just tried to get a phone line installed next to my bed so that I could carry on producing the show whilst recovering. It would save him having to do it. Thanks.

So what else did I learn?

I learned that Russell's questioning technique was often baroque. He would put em-*phas*-es all over the place and start questions with things like: 'So was it after or before your second or third *die*-vorce that you first took up market gardening?' He said that he did this partly to unsettle certain guests and relax others, so a question that began, 'So I have heard, that when you're in bed...'

(Interviewee is unsettled and doesn't know where this is leading.)

'...you are *in*clined, at least so I've heard, to...'

(Interviewee gasps.)

'...not wear any pyjamas.'

The guest immediately relaxes, and proceeds to tell us about the time they were in bed with the prime minister, who commented favourably on their striking nightwear and how it matched the auburn curls of the foreign secretary's boyfriend.

That was his theory, at least, and clearly where I'd gone wrong at Halewood car plant.

I learned that Russell really only wanted to talk to the people he wanted to talk to.

'We thought we might get Clement Freud on, to talk about the election and food.'

There would be a pause. Then: 'Who are you going to get to interview him?'

Sometimes he might come around, but not always. This was where his brilliant secretary/right-hand woman Pat Heald came in. She would tell me quietly whether this was a real or a fake sulk. She was truly wonderful, and when Russell died many years later of hepatitis, Alan Bennett mentioned Pat at his funeral. Apparently, when Russell needed a new kidney and one could not be found, he had said to Alan, 'It'll be OK though, because Pat's on the case.' She probably was. A remarkable man helped by an even more remarkable woman.

I also learned that it's not the greatest idea to have your production office on one side of London (Shepherd's Bush), and your studio on the other, near London Bridge. Not least because it meant that the producer, me, is tempted to drive across London twice a week on a motorbike, at a period of maximum stress and maximum traffic. I've already described how this ended up. My publisher's budget does not run to including a photograph of the sensational scar left on my left calf by the accident. The scar arose from unfinished surgery to treat 'lateral compartment syndrome', and it can still clear beaches to my left when I go down to the sea wearing shorts.

Guy's Hospital was great, and once it became clear that I was going to get visits not just from Russell himself but also from people like Alan Bates and Rik Mayall, I quickly got a room to myself and *devoted* nursing attention, especially during visiting hours. There was sometimes a queue to take in my meds.

I got better, and went back to the show in a cast.

Talk shows are not as easy as they look. They're difficult to produce because they're difficult 'to book'. The people you want on the show often don't want you. They want that show with better ratings on the other channel, or the one that's hosted by someone funnier or prettier. I still have anxiety dreams in which I've been invited back to produce a chat show and THERE ARE NO GUESTS. Except maybe a once famous, briefly jailed ex-politician with a book out, a minor soap actress who's launching a donkey sanctuary, and the act that came third on *Britain's Got Talent* three or four years ago. The researchers seem to have been slacking. I wake up in a cold sweat.

On the subject of researchers, I've never quite worked out how one of ours on *Harty* ended up as chief defence correspondent on *Newsnight*. Was it something I said that led to his interest in intercontinental confrontation and strategic ground-to-air missiles? I take it back, whatever it was. Another researcher, Kevin Lygo, ended up as head of ITV. It was the training I gave that led them all to seek for other work.

Talk shows are the easiest shows in the world to slag off

in print. This is good news if you're a columnist out of ideas (not an unheard of phenomenon) but it's less fun if you're the producer, or one of the team of people who work their socks off to get the shows on air.

One such columnist was a man called D— F—, the 'TV critic' of a newspaper known as *The M on S*. Week after week, he would end his column with a little swipe at us, detailing how trivial, worthless and generally pointless we were, how bad Russell was at his job, and how he and we should be fired *immediately*. We were an easy target, and occasionally we deserved it, but nevertheless it would quite often ruin my Sunday – the one day of the week when you can't book guests or make the show any better, much as you might want to.

'Get over yourself!' you cry, and rightly so – it's only a bloody chat show. But this did not stop me from holding a grudge. Hard cut (as we say in film and TV) to a few years later when I was producing the *Wogan* show – same sort of show, different accent – and a pile of mail landed on my desk. It was the usual collection of hate mail, vile abuse and requests to appear on the show. Among them was a letter along these lines:

Dear Mr Plowman,
I have long admired your work in the chat-show arena
and I was wondering if Mr Wogan might like to talk
to me in a few weeks when I have a show opening
at a small theatre in Hampstead about the music
hall queen Marie Lloyd? Terry Wogan is such a good
interviewer and it would be wonderful if you could fit
me onto the show one Monday, Wednesday or Friday.
Many thanks, D— F—

I gasped with delight. Yes. Revenge! Within my grasp! At least two or three years had passed since *Harty*, and I really *really* should not have looked at this letter as a golden opportunity to get my own back. I was wrong to so see it that way and I should have risen above it. But I didn't. To my eternal shame, I wrote back:

> Dear Mr F—,
> How extraordinary. You seem to share both a Christian name and surname with a man who used to make my life a misery every Sunday by writing facile abuse about the *Harty* show, which I also produced. Sadly, we are fully booked with guests on the *Wogan* show for the next six months, otherwise I'm sure that Terry would love to talk to you about Marie Lloyd.
> Sincere apologies, Jon Plowman.

Obviously, I'm ashamed and would like to take this opportunity to say how sorry I am that this letter was ever sent. Honest.

The thing is – it mattered. It was a good time and a good show. And, as I say, I learned a lot but perhaps not to let things go

> **LESSON: Any chat show will deal with three types of guests: a) the ones you want but who don't want you; b) the ones you don't want but who are desperate to appear; c) the third group are the ones not good enough for (a) nor bad enough for (b). These are the ones who get on the air.**

I was about to do another one…

6

Terry on Tranquillisers

'**A**-ha, another new producer! The more the merrier, jolly good.' (Terry Wogan's first words to me.)

'Ah Johnnie, so they haven't found you out yet.' (Sir Terry Wogan's last words to me.)

The jocular Irishman greeted me like this because, when his three-times-a-week show started on BBC1, he got through three producers in about as many months. That's not quite fair, it was the organisation that got through them.

After my time with Russell I produced *Pop Quiz,* including a mostly inaudible contest between Spandau Ballet and Duran Duran, but when that finished I went to see Jim Moir, the legendary BBC head of light entertainment and variety. My contract still had some time to run so I offered myself to Jim for free.

JIM: Dear boy, I could offer you a job as a researcher
        with Geoff Posner, the esteemed and highly talented
        comedy producer and director, and his boys on

Terry Wogan's Saturday night fun fest.

ME: *(plaintively)* But I've just been *producing* Russell
        Harty's show for BBC1 and I've been doing—
JIM: *(grandly)* But you haven't worked for this
        department, lad. Take it or leave it. It's all I've got.

I left it.

Cut to four months later. I've filled in my time changing the Spanish format *Tutto Secondo Counteth* into the wittily titled *Every Second Counts* for the department that made *Pop Quiz*, *The Old Grey Whistle Test* and *Great Railway Journeys*. Network Features was a sort of catch-all BBC department which made shows that didn't fit in elsewhere. I turned *Every Second Counts* from a 21-minute commercial format to a 29-minute show for the BBC, hosted by Russell Grant with notional celebrities playing for charity. We made a non-TX pilot (TX stands for 'transmission' in TV parlance, and should not be confused with T-Rex, which is a fierce dinosaur with big nibbly teeth who won't stand for *anything*).

Every Second Counts seemed to work, and Network Features duly sold the new format to Jim Moir who was trying to find a vehicle for Paul Daniels. (I suggested a Ford Cortina leaving Television Centre as soon as possible, but no one listened.)

Three months later, I'm asked to see Jim Moir again, and this time the conversation goes: 'Now, I'll cut to the chase. We need you to help produce young Terry Wogan's chat show. Are you up for it?'

I said that I was and didn't remind Jim that three months ago he'd thought that I wasn't.

'Obviously, you'll have your way of doing things, but Frances Whitaker is running a pretty tight ship, and you'll be just the man to help her. You'd better get over there and introduce yourself.'

Terry on Tranquillisers

That was how things were done back then.

Frances Whitaker was the executive producer of the three-times-a-week *Wogan* show, and she enjoyed a good relationship with Terry because they'd worked together on the gone but not forgotten *Friday Night, Saturday Morning*. This was a gab-fest with a different host each week; one week it would be Harold Wilson, the following week Terry Wogan. She was, and is, a woman of serious mind but cheery disposition. Her job and her relations with Jim Moir occupied less cheery, sometimes tricky ground.

When this iteration of *Wogan* began three months earlier, it was part of a spring clean around the schedules by Michael Grade, the newly appointed controller of BBC1. He wanted to keep the audience watching from seven o'clock through the evening and through the week. He knew that a goodly number of viewers were going to leave at 7:30 to visit *Coronation Street* on ITV, but a man has to do what a man's paid to do. So he launched his own new soap, *EastEnders* and brought in *Wogan*. On Monday, Wednesday and Friday it was Terry; Tuesdays and Thursdays it was Angie and Dirty Den. In a way, Albert Square residents had it easy – not something you hear very often – because they knew what they were. They were part of a soap, where people went in and out of one another's houses to stab each other in the back or borrow a cup of money and then headed on down to the Queen Vic for a pint and a fight.

Wogan, in its early days, had a bit more of an identity crisis. Was it a variety show with lots of glitz and showbiz, as Jim Moir would have liked? Was it a tight early evening show, that made the news and had people from the news in it (this is what Brian Wenham favoured, and he was managing director of BBC Television at the time)? Was it a big ratings grabber which was what Michael Grade wanted and needed?

41

How to Produce Comedy Bronze

Frances had to try to keep all these people happy *and* keep Terry onside. And what was Mr Wogan's view of the show? Remarkably sane. He knew that the show had to be 'part of the television furniture' and that while the higher echelons of the BBC might be arguing about it and the critics might be writing about it, 'It just has to be one of the shows that *only the public like*. It just has to be "on".' His words.

It was an odd brief. Most chat shows (Johnny Carson or Stephen Colbert in the US; Michael Parkinson or Graham Norton in the UK) are late night, not early evening. Most US talk shows are led by comedians. They start with a monologue on the day's events, then, after a commercial break, they do 'the desk' section. This inclines towards sitting-down comedy, maybe using a 'second banana' or sidekick (well, you wouldn't use a real banana, would you?). Then there are more ads, then back for a handful of guests who are usually there to sell their film, book or album. They are interviewed in decreasing order of fame because of the lateness of the hour. So – Matt Damon first, Olympic bronze medallist second, woman with hamster that looks like Donald Trump third.

In the UK, most interview shows up to this point had been hosted by journalists or chaps from public life; Michael Parkinson had started as a journalist at Granada TV, Russell Harty had been an arts journalist, John Freeman had been British ambassador to the US and high commissioner to India before he made *Face to Face*, the first rather serious talk show. Terry Wogan had worked in a bank and been a daily radio DJ, and he was the funniest of the lot. But he wasn't a comedian.

I observed at close quarters when Joan Rivers came over to do a chat show for the BBC. This was the American format trying to fit into the British slot. Joan had been queen stand-in host for Johnny Carson, and she knew how to do the US model with commercial breaks – and that was what she was going to do for the BBC, whether they had ad breaks or not. So the recording went like this. Joan did her monologue and then, 'OK, so we'll be right back with Roger Moore, Candice Bergan and Rupert Everett, and my good friend Peter Cook.'

These were words that would never be broadcast. But nonetheless the show would take a recording break while Joan looked at her notes for the next interview. This was presumably what she did on the *Tonight Show* which was recorded 'as live', so she had two or three minutes to 'revise' her questions while the ads were on. In the UK, all the breaks would be edited out, leaving one seamless, commercial-free show.

Her 'second banana' on the BBC show was 'my good friend, Peter Cook'. He appeared on all the shows to 'explain English people and manners to Joan', and to do 'a bit' with her after her monologue. An unhappier pairing has rarely been seen this side of a royal marriage. Her style was very feisty and Jewish, his was intelligent, surreal and Cambridge. I've never seen anyone as miscast or downright unhappy on a TV show as Peter Cook was then. To make matters worse, everything that was recorded had to be approved by Joan's husband – an Austrian dentist called Edgar. No interview was finished unless Edgar *said* it was finished, and only then could things move on. This was irritating to say the least.

There's a footnote to this story. Fifteen years later I had the weirdest phone call from Joan's manager.

'Hi Jon, this is Billy Sammeth phoning from LA.'

I'd met him once or twice with Joan, and liked him, but we'd spoken maybe three times about work and that was it.

'Hi, Billy, how are you?'

'Hey, Jon, good news, Edgar's *dead*!'

Clearly Billy had had a tricky time with Joan's husband and

was phoning everyone on his Rolodex to tell them the glad tidings. The passing of an Austrian dentist.

Back to Terry.

The *Wogan* show was broadcast at seven. In his ideal world, Terry would have arrived with us at about 6.55 p.m., he would have been told who the guests were, and then stepped in front of the cameras. He was a broadcaster who believed in 'winging it'. He thought he should find out about the guests by – well – asking them some questions on air. His team and producers were much too neurotic for that. We wanted to know in advance which questions would elicit *good and funny* answers. Peter Estell, the other producer, and I each had a team of four researchers who would go to meet the guests in advance, tell us if they had anything of interest to say, write up the interview they'd conducted, and give us a copy of their research on the evening before the show. They did the hard work. I would then write Terry a letter. Essentially, I tried to make this sound like something he might say at the top of the show which sometimes he did. For legal reasons, I've changed the names of some of the guests.

Dear Terry,
Well, Wednesday's show seemed to go well despite
that moment with the marmoset. Tonight is an array
of talent the like of which has not been seen this side
of Bertram Mills Circus. Best say nothing of world
events and the spat/spit between Mrs Thatcher
and the guide dog. Also, least said about bovine
spongiform encephalopathy the better, largely because
I'm not able to say it twice in one day. Tonight, we
have music from Los Angeles' finest, The Bangles,
who for some reason believe it's 'Just Another Manic

Terry on Tranquillisers

*Monday'. Now I know it's Friday (despite being here
at the BBC where you just can't get a decent calendar
for love nor money) – but The Bangles say they can
cope. We are also joined tonight by the redoubtable
Karl Marx whose trademark beard and bow tie have
made him beloved of millions, and he's here to talk
about his new book on Russian cookery. Moses
should be dropping by, fresh from his mountaineering
adventures, to talk to us about talking to God, and
Geoffrey Smith will be along with some planting tips
for autumn. But first, you'll be welcoming a man who's
never without a good yarn, Edward the Confessor.*

Obviously, we never did this show. We couldn't get Moses out
of his ITV contract.

The letter would continue with a summary of each of the
researchers' notes on the guests and a few thoughts about
likely questions and areas for chat. For example: *Moses is
good on Egypt – experiences in; has a funny story about the
Red Sea; might be good on his relationship with his brother;
has a nice story about bullrushes. Might lay down the law a bit,
but otherwise chatty.*

On the afternoon of the show I would give Terry a general
brief and then the researchers would come in one at a
time and tell him about their meeting with the guests and
go through a suggested list of questions. Once these were
agreed they would go to our chap who did 'the cards', Chris
Winn. The cards were question prompts for Terry during the
show and would occasionally have 'CUT GUEST' or 'SHUT
UP' written on them, but more normally – 'FUNNY NAME –
WHERE FROM?' or 'DOG STORY?' or 'TIME WITH MUPPETS?'
Chris Winn subsequently wrote a string of best-selling books
which each had the title *I Never Knew That...* I think it may

have been based on things he never knew till he had to write a card about them for Wogan.

The cards rose to fame (briefly) when the Duke of Edinburgh was on the show. He was available because he was taking part in a two-in-hand or possibly four-in-hand festival. This is in fact a horse-carriage racing event. The Duke wasn't the world's *greatest* interviewee because horse-carriage races were *all* the Queen's Consort was willing to talk about. In the end, he took to making fun of Terry and the cards.

'Why do you need these cards here, being held up by this chap? Is it because you can't think up your own questions? Need someone else to help?'

I'm sure he felt that he was being funny and for a second he possibly was, but then the mood shifted, and there was a slight feeling in the audience that he should 'Stop turning on our chap, Terry'. If it had gone on much longer – who knows, there might have been a violent republican revolution beginning at Television Theatre, Shepherd's Bush Green. Amazingly there wasn't. I can't wait for Peter Morgan to cover this incident in future episodes of *The Crown*.

LESSON: You have to remember that *Wogan* was live. No, not as in 'alive' (though guests like the Duke of Edinburgh sometimes made me wonder), but as in '5 million people are watching this *as it happens*' 'Aaaahhh!' 'pressure, tension, ulcers'. No second chances, no brilliant work in the editing suite, no clever removal of long pauses. LIVE. Like theatre. Or sex. The joy of 'live' TV is that a) you never have to watch it again, b) when it's done, it's done. There should be more of it!

Terry on Tranquillisers

There was another evening when I particularly remember the cards coming into their own. It was the night of the tranquilliser victims. One of Terry's great skills was chatting to his audience. He did it every morning to about 6 million listeners on the radio. But the TV show was very different: much shorter, and you could see the guests up close. Terry would tell us of the moment when he could see a look come into the eyes of a non-celebrity guest, that said, 'Somebody more interesting is going to come on in a minute, I know they are, because I've seen this show on the telly.'

They were usually rather bad guests.

We were going through a phase when the Warm Human Story was king. One of the researchers had met up with four people who'd been to hell and back 'coming off' tranquillisers.

PLOWMAN: Perfect, book 'em.

RESEARCHER: The only thing is, Jon, they need to be handled sympathetically and they need a bit of time to tell their story. But they're really good and interesting.

PLOWMAN: They can have time. We'll give them the last 12 minutes of the show, I promise. Should be more than enough for anybody, as long as they're awake.

If this makes me sound like Walter Burns talking to Hildy Johnson in *The Front Page*, I'm sorry. Cos I'm not like that, honest. I'm not that considerate. (*The Front Page* is a brilliant play and a wonderful film. Go get the DVD NOW.)

These poor people who had genuinely been through a VERY difficult time, were booked for the last part of the show. This was the section after the audience had mostly flipped over to watch *Coronation Street* on ITV. The withers of any remaining audience members would be well and truly wrung. We hoped.

The night of their appearance also coincided with the arrival of a new executive producer, a man called Peter Weill, who was a newshound with an impressive track record but no great sense of showbiz. He'd exposed the misdeeds of dignitaries up and down the land, but didn't really know one end of a boy band from a hole in the wall. He didn't understand how the show worked, but was perfectly happy to learn.

It went something like this.

TERRY: I know that some of you think that one of this
          show's main aims is to help the nation sleep,
          but my next guests know, in all seriousness, that
          there is something far more dangerous which
          does that for real, and can have very harmful
          and addictive effects. Tranquillisers. They may
          look useful and worth trying when you're going
          through a difficult patch, but these people
          know that they have a much darker side. Please
          welcome Patrick, Trisha, Graham and Louise.

APPLAUSE

On walked the four people who were to constitute the last 12 minutes of the show. I was in the gallery, as was the researcher whose guests they were, and the new exec, Peter. I had contact via an earpiece with Chris the card guy, but not with Terry, who wouldn't wear such a thing. He had a dedicated camera and could always communicate with us via a raised eyebrow or a shake of the head.

We had a list of questions which we had been through

Terry on Tranquillisers

earlier with Terry, but this was one of those interviews where his native wit and sympathy would be the main elements in a good, warm and informative conversation.

TERRY: So tell me, Patrick, how did this all start?

PATRICK: Well, I suppose it started when the doctor put us all on tranquillisers.

TERRY: And why was that?

PATRICK: Oh, it was a personal thing.

TERRY: *(after a moment)* Louise?

LOUISE: Oh, much the same, really.

TERRY: *(a slightly longer beat)* So, Graham, what was it like when you came off them?

GRAHAM: Oh, it was terrible, but I don't want to go into details.

PLOWMAN: *(in gallery)* GO INTO bloody details, that's why you're here!!

This was not going well. Loquacious, they weren't. Reticent on camera, they were.

We got through the list of questions rather quickly and before long, Terry was sweating slightly on his upper lip. By now I had the researcher by my side and I was asking her for more questions for the card guy, who was writing with one hand and holding the cards with the other. In retrospect, I might have been holding the researcher's throat just *a little bit* tightly and shouting down Chris's ear *a tiny bit* loudly.

'Where did you all meet first?'

'Are the effects long term or short term?'

'Can anybody get these pills?'

'Should the NHS be doing something about this?'

'How bad was it?'

'Favourite colour of pill?'

How to Produce Comedy Bronze

The more urgent question seemed to me, 'Were they still on tranx, and COULD I HAVE SOME?'

By now, thanks to the native wit of our host, we were maybe six or seven minutes into the interview, though it felt like six or seven days. The new executive, possibly sensing an air of panic, offered to go to help Chris with the cards. I was more than happy that he should. He left the gallery without owning up that he'd never been in the place before. The Television Theatre where we did the show was an odd building, part auditorium, part TV studio bolted on to the side. The gallery didn't lead to the stage, it led to the dressing rooms and the make-up area. It was a maze. Needless to say – the exec producer did not find the auditorium or the card guy until we were off air and fighting for breath in the hospitality area.

But before that blessed moment of relief, we had had to get off air. One of the decisions that had to be made on every show was how to end it. We had three versions of pre-recorded credits that played us off the air after our time slot – each one a different length. These gave the presentation desk (or 'Pres', as the people who play the trails and link all shows on the BBC are known) warning that we were coming off air, or in *some* cases, falling off air. There was the 'crash' credit (just a card with producer and director on it), there were the 'short' credits (20 seconds of guest and production names) and then the 'long' version (hardly ever used – this included the names of *everyone* who was to blame for the show). Tonight, the guilty might *all* be revealed. We might even show a list of people in the studio audience.

In the gallery, as well as making up inane questions for Terry, I can hear the PA on the phone to Pres: 'Can you take us early, Pres? Well, how long do you need? OK, we'll "fill", but please hurry. *Please.* We'll be playing the "long credits" tonight.'

Terry on Tranquillisers

Pres were desperately trying to find that really long trail for next week's dramas, and the very, very long version of that week's *EastEnders* story catch-up, and of *course* the phone number for tranquilliser sufferers to ring 'in case you have been affected by issues raised in tonight's programme'.

What about the people suffering from high-blood pressure in the gallery? Spare a thought for us!

'OK take us, Pres. Coming to you in five, four, three, two, one...'

Sigh of relief and off for a drink with Terry who says, by way of farewell, 'Well. I think that went OK tonight!'

You see? He was a decent bloke. He didn't come off the set waving an angry ego at us. He didn't pick up chairs and throw them at secretaries. He coped. He understood that the problems of a chat show host talking to four secretive tranquilliser addicts didn't amount to a hill of beans in this crazy world.

Most of our shows were much less eventful. Film stars, ex-politicians, authors, actors and comedians came and went without problem. Actually, Terry wasn't entirely enamoured of comedians...

'A light comes into their eyes, and I have the feeling that they might drag their own mothers out of the front row and chop their heads off, if they thought it would get them a bigger laugh.'

Comedians were fine in their place and their place was sitting in for Terry when he had a holiday. Ronnie Corbett did it with his usual meticulous approach, and Bruce Forsyth did it, aided by Moira Stuart reading a 'good news bulletin' (stories that ended happily and hadn't made the *proper* news at six o'clock).

There were weeks when it seemed that the stream of celebrity guests (or people we'd even heard of) had dried up.

And there were nasty surprises, like the night I had to knock on the dressing room door of drummer and now theatre producer Dave Clark and tell him that although he had already been to make-up and the show was about to 'go live', he was not about to 'go live' on it, indeed, he was about to go home

Mr Clark was the producer of a 'musical' called *Time* starring Cliff Richard (apparently alive) and a hologram of Sir Laurence Olivier, who didn't know how lucky he was not to be there. Mr C (once famous as the leader of the Dave Clark Five) was appearing on *Wogan* to talk about his musical, but he or his marketing people had made the mistake of taking a full-page advert in that night's *London Evening Standard* to announce his appearance. Now the BBC's charter expressly forbids heralding appearances on telly for 'strict commercial gain'. In other words, none of the guests on our show who mentioned they were in a movie or had a book coming out, had taken out huge ads *in advance* to say that they were there to speak of absolutely nothing else. An eagle-eyed BBC lawyer who had been sitting at his desk perusing the *Standard* at the end of a busy day rang us at once. So it was that I found myself knocking on the door of Dave Clark's dressing room to impart the bad news.

'What d'ya mean? This is out of order. I know people, I know Alan Yentob. Get me a phone. You haven't heard the last of this.'

He was really annoyed and I don't blame him, but he had a genuine problem showing it. He'd had cheekbone implants, and, sadly for him, they'd somehow melted into his face. Rumour blamed a sunbed. The result was that he seemed to be permanently smiling. So he was threatening litigation and revenge while simultaneously looking quite pleased with how things had turned out. Odd.

Terry on Tranquillisers

We had him back a few weeks later, unheralded in the *Standard*. He could take out as many ads as he liked *afterwards* but not before.

One guest who went that route was diminutive ageing juvenile Mickey Rooney. He was in London, appearing in *Sugar Babies* – a musical. He took a full-page ad in *Variety*, the US show-business newspaper, linking his appearance on *Wogan* and the success of his show: '*Sugar Babies* breaks box office records after Mickey Rooney gets highest ratings ever for UK's No 1 talk show, with host Jerry Logan.'

Of course, none of this was true, even the name of the host, but hey, 'print the legend', even if you can't spell it right.

There were all sorts of other challenges. Maeve Binchy (delightful Irish novelist) got stuck on the stairs going down to the studio floor, when a very frail 100-year-old interviewee was attempting to come up. So we heard: 'Ladies and Gentlemen, my next guest has sold huge numbers of books and I'm pleased to say that she's a dear friend of mine. Please welcome the delightful Maeve Binchy...'

At this point, nothing happened, no one appeared, sending Terry into paroxysms of laughter. Other presenters might have panicked and blathered on. Terry just laughed at the incongruity of it all. He truly was the Greatest Living Irishman.

The Bee Gees were involved in a different kind of non-appearance. They'd been booked for a show that also had American writer and humorist Garrison Keillor on it. Terry hadn't heard of Keillor but I thought that the two of them would share a certain sort of wit and humour. Keillor is a very dry, part-Midwestern, part-Scandinavian guy with a down-home sensibility. His delivery is careful, measured, but very funny. He presented a long-running radio show called *Prairie Home Companion* every week on American Public Radio from Minneapolis-St Paul. He has invented a place called

How to Produce Comedy Bronze

Lake Woebegon *'where all the women are strong, all the men are good-looking, and all the children are above average.'* It's an imaginary town showing America as it never was, but maybe as it should have been. Lake Woebegon and its creator appealed to Terry. Here was a discovery for viewers and host alike.

Our problem was that Terry liked him so much, he wouldn't finish the interview in time to let the Bee Gees perform their current single. When we signalled frantically to our host that he had to finish the interview, dancing up and down and miming cut-throat signs at him to indicate the *urgency* of the situation, he just shook his head and c arried on. We (and he) just had to apologise to the Brothers Gibb and suggest that they 'Come back on Friday'. It was one of our production myths that if we missed something on one show, it could appear in the next. It never happened. *Our* schedule might have allowed for this, but no one else's ever did.

Terry sometimes unfairly got it in the neck for 'not listening', for 'loving the sound of his own voice', for 'not giving the guests a chance'. He wasn't a forensic interviewer, or a razor-sharp investigative journalist, but he was just what was needed at that time of night: a friendly host with a friendly delivery and a real interest in his guests. He was also a good man in a crisis.

When we went to LA to do a one-off special on the set of *Dynasty*, only to find that they didn't know – or care – we were coming, Terry was at his finest. *Dynasty* was behind and shooting three episodes at once. Their biggest star, Joan Collins, wouldn't speak to us at all because of some contract wrangle involving ITV. At this point, some hosts would have walked out and blamed the producer (some have even been known to punch their producer). Not Tel.

Terry on Tranquillisers

He could sniff a crisis even though we did our best to keep it from him. So he sent his wife – the estimable Lady Helen – off shopping with the executive producer, Frances, and he knuckled down with the rest of us to try and pull some sort of show out of the mess. *He* knew that if *we* knew that *he* was on side, it wouldn't just help us, it would help him. Strings were pulled, phone calls were made to the office of Aaron Spelling – *Dynasty*'s head honcho – and for all I know to his wife Candy Spelling (who was famous for having a room in their house devoted solely to present-wrapping). Sets were borrowed, and spare actors dragged on to a couch opposite Mr Wogan. Large amounts of professional mettle were displayed by the Greatest Living Irishman, and we began to put some something together.

Even then it was not plain-sailing or plane-flying.

The show was scheduled for BBC1 on Christmas Day, and we had three days left. I was given the 'rushes' for the show in a tartan shopping bag on wheels, and took the first flight possible from LA to London, which involved a connecting flight at New York. Like the good producer I wasn't, I kept the shopping trolley of film as my hand luggage. My own stuff was in the hold. Surely nothing else bad could happen on this gig? I was wrong. I arrived in London but my luggage didn't. It had gone to Spain. The tartan wheelie bag was met at the airport and taken to the labs to be processed. I went home for a short sleep and then followed the film to an editing suite where I spent most of Christmas Eve. We finished making the show minutes before the Christmas bells rang out. We were just in time. The show went out on Christmas night.

Sir Robin Day, then a veritable panjandrum of politics, wrote about the show in the *Daily Telegraph*. 'This was the worst hour of television that the BBC has ever broadcast!'

Thanks, Robin.

Big thanks, Terry.

And now I think of it, where's my my luggage?

7

Comic Relief, 1991

'**Y**ou're the only person who got in touch to say, "well done".'

Can that really be true? Richard Curtis said these words – true or flannel – after I complimented him on the first Comic Relief seven-hour TV telethon, *A Night for Comic Relief.* I had been truly impressed as a viewer. It was a huge achievement, not least in persuading the BBC to give up an evening for charity, and 'alternative comedy' charity too. Richard had made the show with just one other person, Gilly Archer, working from a cupboard on the fourth floor of BBC Television Centre. The very least he deserved was a pat on the back.

The second thing Dick said was more of a poser: 'You've been on *Wogan* for years. You must have a really good address book. Could we get you off it to help us do Comic Relief 2?'

Now that's a compliment, but also a challenge, mainly because at this point I hadn't produced *any* TV comedy! Not only that, but if I was known for anything it was a sick sense of humour. Quite early on in my Comic Relief days I was suggesting slogans to help raise money, *none* of which are printable. (Make up your own, find rhymes for slang words for money.) Anyway, I, Richard or both of us talked to Jim Moir, my then boss, and it was agreed that I would be loaned out. In fact, 'loaned out never to return' would be more accurate.

Producing, or more accurately *helping* to produce Comic Relief, is unlike any other job in television. You're asking artists to work for nothing, and that's certainly different. When you ask talented people with families and/or expensive coke habits, to work for nothing, you can't expect *quite* the degree of commitment and reliability you'd get if they were bound by a well-paid contract. The seriousness of the cause helped a lot. The drop-out rate was tiny.

Flexibility is everything. White boards collapse under a punishing assault: scribble, wipe, scribble, change, wipe, scribble, scribble. Running orders are more works of fiction than fact. During the course of pre-production there are just a few events over which you have any control. Around these swirl a shifting cloud of availabilities, casting possibilities, mad suggestions, rumours and hope. Plans look like this (remember it's 1991):

7.00: Opening remarks: Lenny, Jonathan, Griff (JR maybe late coming from Chn4)
7.04: VT menu for the evening
7.05: Why we're doing it; appeal film compilation *(will require editing long into the night in order to appear unsentimental in best traditions of the charity.)*
7.08: Funny bit featuring kids, or kids' presenter or Jim Davidson or Paul Daniels or Phillip Schofield. Maybe competition that can also be played at home to generate income

Comic Relief 1991

7.14: Bananarama and Nannaneenynoona (French, Saunders and Kathy Burke) do the Comic Relief Single: 'Help' *(can only be then cos Bananas have to do Wembley – might have to be VT)*

7.20: UK appeal film – with warm starry woman? Annie Lennox with single mums in Dagenham? Annie would love to, but not available/approaching Alison Moyet – can't, in USA; approach Joan Armatrading – she is unhappy about presenting. Word is that it's worth approaching Goldie Hawn – says 'yes' but will need 4 x first class airfares in order to do it for nothing. 'No' from Sheena Easton. Approaching Dawn French – probably doing too much in the show already. Approaching Nicholas Lyndhurst? Woman better with single mums?? Lyndhurst better for crack abuse doc. Approaching *Blue Peter* presenters, only male presenters available, but one is up on smack charge. Maybe Mel Smith? or Syd Little?

7.30: Sketch show part one TBA (yet to be written, cast, shot, played to audience at someone else's show for laughter, and edited. Should have maximum number of stars in maximum number of sketches)

And that only gets us to 7.30! When we're going to lose half our viewers to *Coronation Street*.

We will need *ten* more of these running orders (similar only better, and not fiction) to get to midnight, plus one for BBC2 to cover the half-hour when we make way for the news on BBC1. It's hard to come up with items, let alone cast them. It's a frantic process, and as the evening gets closer I rent a flat close to the studio in order to get any sleep at all. As well as rewriting the pesky running orders, films need editing and re-editing, usually by a kind man called Ed who is prepared to stay until two or three in the morning for no paid overtime. The 'charity films', as they're known, are made in Bristol by a whole different team so this is just the comedy stuff. Then the editorial departments of the BBC's charity arm (who are more used to the Week's Good Cause and the slightly gentler *Children in Need*) request a meeting at 9.30 a.m. the following morning...they are worried about sponsors etc. etc. Sleep is at a premium.

We're not immune from insult either. We send a reasonable/ not-brilliant-but-not-a-stinker-by-any-manner-of-means sketch to Pete Townshend of the Who. 'It won't take long, we'll look after you, you'll be in very good company and it's for a very good cause.'

We got the following reply.

'No. If all your sketches are this bad, I don't think you deserve to raise any money at all, Pete.'

Yeah, thanks a lot! Love your work too – hope you don't die before you get old. He didn't.

The show gradually comes together with the help of large numbers of very generous artists and equally generous sponsors, film-makers, charity workers, comedians and editors and tired producers from all over the world. It is an extraordinary thing.

Just one example.

Anthony Minghella, the man who directed and wrote *The Talented Mr Ripley* and *Cold Mountain*, gave his time and his crew for free to make a beautiful film on the subject of disability. It was a simple but moving idea. In a beautifully lit studio, a line of people in wheelchairs manoeuvre towards a brick wall which they dismantle one brick at a time. It was brilliantly done, and made out of real understanding.

Comic Relief 1991

Artists

Quite soon we set up a unit to cover a) those who wanted to do stuff but hadn't yet been used, b) those who were definitely unavailable, c) those who were willing but had a problem with flights, children, cosmetic surgery, d) those who were already doing a lot and shouldn't be asked to do anything else, e) those who simply wouldn't do charity stuff even if they got their ear bent by Richard Curtis. Artists Central was the name of the unit, but even then people slipped through the net.

On the night itself, I was manning the artists' reception desk in Television Centre, the show was going well and lots of money was coming in. If there *was* a problem, it was that we had too much material! So we were cutting things just to get to the ten o'clock news on time. The phone rang. It was Ronnie Barker, a man we'd been begging to appear since we began pre-production five months ago, but who had consistently turned us down.

'Hello, this is Ronnie B. here. It seems to be going very well. I just wondered if you'd like me to pop in to TVC and do something?'

There's nothing we'd like more, Ronnie, *really*! Why didn't you reply to any of our earlier requests? We could have pre-recorded you and made you look wonderful!

I thanked him politely, and said maybe next time. Assuming any of the production team survived the night!

The Night

Here I must introduce the director – a remarkable man called Michael Hurll. He directed and produced *Top of the Pops* in its heyday. He created Noel Edmonds' *Late Late Breakfast Show* (someone had to).

How to Produce Comedy Bronze

So. It's the day of the show. Every red nose has been sold, every T-shirt has been bought, thousands of people have worked charity miracles the length and breadth of the land. Chests have been shaved, faces have been painted, baths have been filled with beans, (baked not green) marathons have been run, supermarket trollies have raced one another across Dorset. All done to help people in Africa and the UK – children in Sudan, old people in Hull, the disabled in Cardiff. The show on TV will be a way of saying 'thank you' to all the people who took part.

Hurll is masterminding the operation from the gallery of TC1, the main studio at Television Centre. It's the afternoon. Individual items are being rehearsed and gradually the whole shambolic thing begins to take shape. Out of the primeval sludge a recognisable structure emerges. Nobody has any idea how this happens but it does.

There are two main centres of power. One is Michael Hurll in the gallery with access to all the pre-recorded bits and pieces that we're going to play in. Not *quite* all. Even on the day there are items still being edited: regional reports about how many people have dressed up as biscuits or swum 200 lengths in the local pool dressed as Ancient Britons.

The other focus of power is Richard Curtis on the studio floor with the presenters, writing and rewriting the script for them. He refuses to let go of the script until it's honed to within an inch of its life. The honing leads to a certain friction. Michael in the gallery keeps seeing chunks of script finalised, then altered, then fiddled with, then dumped – and all of this takes time away from his chance to rehearse studio events and musical numbers. Michael was known for his charm, but also for his belief that things should be done with as much precision and energy as possible. He was famous for coming onto the studio floor of his own shows each morning and having a shout. He didn't really mind who was the target, and everyone knew this was merely Michael's way of saying, 'I'm here, let's get started', so they didn't take too much offence or, come to that, too much notice. It was Michael's way. We at Comic Relief didn't know this, when suddenly at 4.15 in the afternoon he throws his much-changed script onto the floor and yells into the studio tannoy: 'Now LISTEN! It's 4.15 in the afternoon and we're on air at seven o'clock to do a seven-hour live show! We're currently on page 19 of a 97-page script! If you lot [meaning Richard and the presenters] don't get your act together NOW and stop changing things, we're just going to fall off air! GET IT SORTED, this is live TV!'

I was sitting in the gallery next to Michael and turning white. I was imagining all the harm that would be done by us falling off air, all the money that wouldn't be raised.

He switched off the tannoy and turned to me, saying in the calmest voice imaginable, 'Don't worry, it'll be fine. I'm just trying to make them get on with it.'

My blood pressure reduced to just a few hundred points above normal. 'Michael, you're enjoying this.'

* ★ *

We kick off with a good first hour or so. We start with material aimed at children and families that gets a bit more adult as the clock ticks on. For me, one of the highlights is the great Ken Dodd. He's fairly fresh from a skirmish with the Inland Revenue but is well up for doing material about it. He is famous for simply going on and on for as long as he can, he has agreed to do eight minutes of material and only eight minutes but sails passed that with jocular abandon. I think he simply has no sense of time and he's enjoying himself and the audience are enjoying him so why stop? We have arranged to give one of our main hosts a hook to drag him off. That doesn't really work so in the end, after about 12 minutes, Lenny Henry and Jonathan Ross simply pick him up and take him offstage. A legend at work. A sad loss.

We have a number of other demented ideas. Wouldn't it be great if we could get onto all four TV channels (it was only four in those days), *live* at the *same* time, just before the 10 p.m. break for news on BBC and ITV! We can easily get onto BBC2 with a bit of continuity collusion. ITV won't play ball, but Channel 4 will. They have *Whose Line is it Anyway?* It's on air at ten, so we ask its host Clive Anderson to interrupt his Scottish holiday, come down to the BBC, and stand by in a tiny continuity studio to do a hand-over link to Channel 4. We'll be on three out of four channels and that'll be – well – amazing, not to say power-crazed! Yes?

Er…no, because Channel 4 works by computer. They line up all the shows and all the ads on the computer in advance with our gap built in at say 9.58.52. However, as we get near 9.58.52 (say at 9.56.30), we realise that we're going to run over, not a *lot* but a bit, because of things like laughter and applause and items going over their predicted length. We ring C4 and ask if they can take Clive at, let's say 9.59.40. They can't. 'Computer say no', even before that was a catchphrase. The computer is loaded and uninterruptable unless the monarch dies, or there's a successful house purchase on *Location, Location, Location,* or World War Three breaks out. You know? In the heat of live TV that's exactly what this feels like! It *is* World War Three to us – we need to raise the extra money for Africa and projects in the UK that this Channel 4 reminder will help make more possible! This is important! Please! NO. Sorry. Channel and computer cannot be interrupted as they go about their business. Our attempt at charitable hands across the airwaves has fallen flat, and Clive Anderson has come a long way south for nothing.

He is let out of his tiny cell of a studio and the bad news is broken to him.

> **LESSON: Never try arguing with a programmed computer, you will simply come off angry, or worse. (See, 2001: *A Space Odyssey.*)**

A better piece of cross-channel invasion happened later. Lenny Henry took a live camera with him out of our studio and interrupted the thoughtful late night discussion hosted by Clive James that was taking place in another studio, on another channel. Clive knew what we were about and had agreed to do his show live (it was usually recorded), but his guests had absolutely no idea. The reaction at their high-brow discussion being crashed into by Lenny Henry was well worth the effort. Factor in the novelty, and the channel-changing that must have gone on, and the jape was counted as a triumph.

Later in the evening, our viewers were treated to something that can only happen (or in this case not happen) on live TV. Paul Daniels had decided that his contribution to our charitable festivities would be a live magic trick featuring our three main presenters and some milk. As far as I recall, and I only do so with a cold sweat, our presenters were put in a line to look like a cow. In rehearsal, they had been reluctant to do this, and slightly disdainful of Mr Daniel's artistry. But I persuaded them it could be fun…honest.

At one end of the cow, Paul would seem to feed in some grass, and at the other after a vigorous milking routine, he would generate liquid lactose. This was done with a pre-filled paper cone that would seem to squeeze milk into a pail and

Mr Daniels would utter his inimitable catchphrase 'It's magic'. Except that it wasn't, he didn't and only the tiniest amount of milk emerged. Oh dear. There, on live television, before an audience of millions, NOTHING HAD HAPPENED. Least of all magic!

I think we then cut to something tragic and sombre from Africa where real cows would be a good idea.

Recriminations happened simultaneously, both from Mr D who thought that our presenters had set out to make him look an idiot, and from our presenters, who thought that Mr D hadn't explained it correctly and they'd been made to look like idiots by him and by me.

But it wasn't long before they found it had become one of the most memorable things in the whole seven-hour comedy fest. Thank God.

I seem only to have mentioned the things that went wrong. Most items went wonderfully right, so apologies to everyone who succeeded and gave their services for nothing. Also, thanks to the BBC for letting us break vast numbers of rules and edicts. The ones they knew about and the ones they didn't.

That night we raised £20 million. Over the years, Comic Relief has raised £1,047,083,706. Cheers! Deep breath! HUGE cheers! Stagger back in amazement! *Humongous* cheers! Just stupendous, and THANK YOU EVERYONE who has ever done anything for the charity. All this because Mr Curtis had the brave thought, 'Look at all the money Bob Geldof and the music industry managed to drum up, couldn't the comedy business get together and do the same?'

Yes, they could. Thank you, Richard Curtis and all who gave, just thank you.

8

Notes for Aspiring Producer_s

Now that I've reached the time when I became immersed in the world of comedy and producing, I think that it's about time that this book had a go at living up to its title, so here goes.

Advice for the Aspiring

1) Aspire a lot.
   The second you stop aspiring is the time to give up.
2) Watch and listen to a lot of comedy – if only to make you think 'I can do better than that.'
   This is exactly what John Sullivan did when he was a scene shifter at the BBC Studios. He was one of the chaps who took the scenery in and out. He watched the recording of comedy shows whose scenery he was about to move and eventually approached the producer of one, and handed him a script he'd written. It proved that he could do better. Sullivan was the man behind *Only Fools and Horses*.

3) Find out what makes you laugh.

As a kid, I religiously listened to *I'm Sorry, I'll Read That Again* and to the wonderfully surreal *Round the Horne*. The first was a group of young performers that included John Cleese and Tim Brooke-Taylor doing sketches and the other was a show written by Barry Took and Marty Feldman starring the king of straight men, Kenneth Horne, surrounded by a gang of bizarre characters, a number of which were played by Kenneth Williams. Both shows were made by funny people who didn't believe in boundaries. I knew that these shows were funnier than – say – *The Clitheroe Kid* or *The Navy Lark* which were on at around the same time and – to my junior ears – felt as though they were *straining* to be funny.

4) Pull the wings off butterflies (not literally, *please*).

If you can, fathom why and how things work. It's a good skill to have. To do this get hold of some scripts. Quite a few are published, and if not then contact the writer or producer of the shows you like, to see if they have a spare copy (this might throw up all sorts of copyright problems so engage a good lawyer before you write). Look at how ideas and jokes are 'seeded' and how they pay off later. At its simplest, if Vicar Geraldine Grainger didn't see her future husband Harry kissing his sister, then all the comedy of mistaken intention wouldn't work in the climactic scene of the proposal episode.

Look at how characters are introduced, what quirks they have and then how they're woven into a show.

Look at *Fawlty Towers* and see how quietly each episode begins compared to how it builds and finishes. Notice how apparently small scraps of information are planted so that something funny and unexpected can happen later as a result. Sybil rings from the hospital to remind Basil to perform various small tasks in the kitchen whilst he is in the process of hanging a moose's head on the wall. So the head is left on the counter for a minute or two – the counter behind which Manuel is invisibly crouched, dusting. A guest arrives, and everything is set up for the gag of a mysteriously talking moose. Joyous.

5) Get hitched to some talent – literally, if you must.

Go to the Edinburgh Festival, go to comedy clubs and theatres. Watch supposedly funny people working. See how audiences like them (or not.) Are they going down a storm (even between punchlines) or dying on their arses? If you find someone who makes you laugh and hasn't already got a BAFTA, have a chat with them. It will either be the start of your happy comedy career or you'll get done for stalking (which could be an idea for a comedy series...maybe not). Either way a relationship has started up. If you know who you find funny and why, then it's more likely that you'll be able to see that quality in others. It's well known that Joanna Lumley was cast in *Ab Fab* because we'd seen her being really good in a relatively bad stage show. It just so happened that she was displaying all the right qualities for our script. Later in your career as a producer you'll start to use casting directors, but you really *ought* to know who they're talking about. 'Charlie Chaplin?? *Charlie*...mm...what's he done? Can you show me his photograph in *Spotlight*? Can you get him in?'

6) Find a wealthy and benevolent relative.

You will need them. Persuade the relative to start a production company, then a dedicated comedy TV channel. Then persuade them to put on your show. Failing all that, go down the usual route: have a good idea, develop it, send it to a broadcaster...wait...wait some more...

prepare for sorrow…sorrow arrives. I sometimes imagine conversations between channel controllers and comedy commissioners (no, NOT commissionaires, they're men in funny uniforms outside hotels):

COMMISSIONER: Jon's brought us a comedy.

CONTROLLER: Grunt.

COMMISSIONER: It's written by John Cleese and Woody Allen.

CONTROLLER: *(alarmed)* Expensive.

COMMISSIONER: It stars Tom Hanks, Whoopi Goldberg and Dawn French…

CONTROLLER: Is it funny?

COMMISSIONER: They gave it a standing ovation at a try out at the London Palladium.

CONTROLLER: More of an ITV thing?

COMMISSIONER: It ticks all the boxes!

CONTROLLER: Splendid! So we definitely won't be doing that then…

7) Be clear who owns what.

The usual assumption is that the writer and his or her agent owns everything to do with the future of a project after it's been broadcast. However, the company that made the programme owns the programme, but NOT the script. In other words, it's Jennifer's decision as the writer whether to write episodes of *Absolutely Fabulous*, but it's up to the BBC to decide when to broadcast the episodes and to whom they sell the shows.

8) Respect the talent.

Some producers (Harvey Weinstein) bully the talent in order to make shows and to make themselves feel good. DON'T DO THIS. Respect what the talent does, and know that without them you're not very important. Be an enabler, not a bully. If you think you can do better than the talent then either you're in the wrong job or you're just plain wrong.

9) Tell people what you're doing.

People won't see what you're making if you don't tell them. It used to be said that if you wanted your show to be a secret, the wisest course of action was to tell the BBC Press Office. Thankfully those days are behind us, and there are now some very good people who understand that you can't just tell the newspapers, you also have to tell Facebook and the Twittersphere, and all the other online platforms that have been invented since I started this sentence.

10) Come in on budget.

To tell the truth I've never really known how to do this. I *do* know that it's a good idea to surround yourself with people who do. I always saw it as a mark of distinction to be able to say, 'There you are, I told you we hadn't got enough money.'

As I'm sure you understand, this is not a great way to carry on because it leads to a bad case of not being employed (unless you're very good at shifting the blame). I've always thought that what you're *supposed* to do is decide the amount of money each department needs – cast, lights, design, music etc. – and then make it *their* responsibility to operate within their budget.

This rarely works, especially if the heads of department can claim DFI ('different fucking information') that is – we were told one thing and then the director/writer changed it or LFI, ('late fucking information') we had to build a replica of the Taj Mahal five minutes before the scene had to be shot.

Most times they *can* claim one of these things.

This does bring up the question of what to pay people. I've always thought that it's bad manners not to pay people what they ask, but this could be why I never bring shows in on budget. If you're happy to be difficult as a producer, then negotiate like a mad thing, but be prepared to lose the people you want and a degree of self-respect.

As time goes by you will get to know the other producers and companies who last paid the very expensive artist who wants much more than you're offering. Or at least, according to the managers and agents you're haggling with. Call these other producers and tactfully find out who's telling inflationary porkies. When you call the talent's bluff, the agent will say: 'Oh, did I say that they paid him a thousand a day? I think my secretary handed me the wrong contract.' (Sound of banging and crying on the other end of the phone. This is not the secretary, it's the agent beating his or her head against the desk.)

The current argument, if I understand it correctly, that all talent should be paid the same as the Archbishop of Canterbury and each other seems to me to miss the point. Some people are just better at what they do, and bring in more people to see your show. If I had persuaded Mel Brooks to appear as a regular on *Little Britain* I would have expected a lot more people to watch it, and would therefore have given in to his agent's excessive demands. He would have been paid more than the 49p a day that we paid everyone else on that show.

P.S. We never approached Mel Brooks for *Little Britain*. He's Jewish and could never become Archbishop of Canterbury. Get real.

11) Believe.

Notes for Aspiring Producers

As a producer, the most important thing about a comedy script is that you believe it. The people, the place, the plot.

You have to believe that these characters are real and that the characters would do these things in this situation. That a man like Basil Fawlty would react the way he does when his dreams of a culinary evening are thwarted by his car. That Edina Monsoon and Patsy Stone might actually wake up on a rubbish barge going down the Thames after a tough night on the town. That Rik and Ade would set fire to the funfair gondola they find themselves in, stranded high above Hammersmith. You have to believe that the characters believe in their world.

It won't be exactly like our world, but for them, it's real. Comedy has to come out of this reality. No reality, no comedy. I would happily jump into a five-foot-deep puddle while dressed as a vicar just to prove that point.

12) Have a go.

It's not easy to get things on TV, but it's easier now than it's ever been to *make* things (cheap equipment; YouTube; fewer union restrictions). Give it a go and don't be afraid to write to people whose work you like or admire, to get their opinion.

'NO!' I hear colleagues cry, 'DON'T!! I haven't got time for all that stuff people are going to send!'

Remember the producer who took out a full page in *Variety* that just said in very large letters: 'NO! I WON'T READ YOUR FUCKING SPEC SCRIPT, SO DON'T SEND IT.'

Let me rephrase my advice. Don't write to people until you're absolutely sure that what you're sending them is the very best it can ever be. Lock the idea or script in a drawer, take it out after three months and see if it's still as good as you thought it was. It won't be. Adjust accordingly, then lock it away for another three months. If you *still* like it after a further three months, then possibly try to get someone interested.

OK everybody? This advice delays the amount of stuff you'll all get sent by at least six months.

13) Ratings.

Take no notice. Yes, they tell you if your show connected with viewers, and yes, they tell you if you're likely to get recommissioned or ever work again. But ratings won't tell you that the scheduler placed your first episode opposite a drama series that had already built a big audience and was revealing that night 'who did it'. Ratings also won't tell you if it was the first nice evening since 2010, and people went out for a stroll. They also won't tell you that the trail that the broadcaster made for your show really was as bad as you thought.

The consolidated ratings are the ones to wait for. These add in the number of people who have watched your show within seven days on some sort of catch-up service. Careful though, nobody will catch up on something that they haven't heard about from someone they trust who watched it when it first went out!

Life is short, so maybe your show just stinks!

You should be the only person who *really* knows if your show is genuinely any good. Go with that. Also, the figures for the second episode of a comedy always dip after the first. Viewers forget they watched the first episode, and the series is probably not being trailed so much. If the show is going to work, then after the first two or three episodes, audience figures should slowly build.

Notes for Aspiring Producers

They might not, but hey, get over it. It's only a comedy.

FINALLY: DON'T blame me when you don't win a BAFTA at your first attempt having followed these rules. DO feel free to thank me enthusiastically by name when you finally do win. Just as the music comes in to play you off.

9

What's so Funny About That?

Just before I plunge on again with my life among the clowns, I thought I might pause just a bit longer for reflection on the arcane subject of what makes people laugh.

A few weeks ago, I was invited to a large-ish birthday party for someone who was having a large-ish birthday. At the end of it, I was chatting to a kindly erudite man I hadn't seen for a while but used to know quite well. He once wrote for a national broadsheet. So he's probably not an idiot. Probably.

'Do you know, Jon, nothing makes me laugh any more…'

He paused, and he could see that I was a bit thrown.

'Except maybe slapstick. I was watching *Blazing Saddles* by myself the other night. Not funny any more. Quite witty, made me smile. Odd bits of slapstick. Only things that made me laugh.'

In defence of *Blazing Saddles* – one of the great, ground-breaking comedies – I mentioned a few sections that still get a guffaw out of me. The old guy who sees the black sheriff arriving through his telescope, and tries to tell the townsfolk but is continually drowned out by the town hall bell.

'Not saying it's not funny. Just didn't make me laugh.'

He wandered off slowly into the night.

It set me thinking yet again. So what is 'funny'?

Of course, there's no universal answer. One man's hilarious Charlie Chaplin skit leaves the next chap wondering why the sad, shoe-eating loner ever made it out of the asylum.

Another man at this same birthday party told me that the funniest moment *ever* in *The Vicar of Dibley,* was the exchange between Geraldine and the Verger that went, according to him, (and he could barely tell me for laughing):

GERALDINE: What's brown and sticky?

ALICE: I don't know, what's brown and sticky?

GERALDINE: A stick.

This joke, and the autopsy of the joke as Geraldine tries to explain it to Alice, was, for this man (an eminent barrister) the very Empire State of funny.

I remember seeing an interview with the wonderful James Stewart who was talking about making movies.

'It's really about "moments", that's what people remember when they come out of a movie. They remember that moment when you looked at her that way or the way you walked down that main street.'

In the land of comedy, that's what slapstick is. The moment when Jennifer falls out of the car drunk (actually, it's the moment when she falls onto a crash mat just out of shot). The moment when Dawn French as the vicar comes downstairs having had sex upstairs. Her hair is now stiff and erect (I shall say no more). The moment when Patsy falls into a grave, carefully dug and lined with foam mats, so she doesn't break any bones. Our moments are well prepared. They are the moments that stand the test of time, and all the reruns, and quite often they *are* slapstick.

Back to Mr Not-Very-*Blazing Saddles*. Of course, one of the reasons he didn't laugh was that he watched the movie alone. There is something communal about laughter. We encourage each other. We're glad that other people find this thing as funny as we do. And we laugh because we're happy to be in a group of people who are clearly happy.

Equally, we don't like being the person outside a room where a lot of people are laughing and having a great time but we're excluded. This explains why people are upset by 'canned laughter'. It's usually not canned, it's real. People in the studio are actually lit up and delighted by what they're watching. But that won't stop outbursts like this from someone outside the room: 'And another thing that annoys me about these so-called comedies is the inane braying of a clearly canned audience that these producer-johnnies think we need, to tell us when they're funny. We're not stupid, you know,' writes Mr S(notty) Gitt of Havering to the *Daily Mail*.

The problem is that Mr S G of Havering is sitting outside the group of laughers and he feels excluded. He longs to be in their midst. If we – the producers – play the actual laughter too loudly, then the audience at home will feel left out. But play it gently, at the right level, and Mr S G will feel part of the joy, and, hopefully, titter himself. If he ever does.

So, what's funny? (At least to a majority, not sitting alone, and in the right sort of mood.)

I think it's something to do with *serious intent*.

The best shows I've worked on have a serious idea at heart and the audience recognise this and go along with it. At the heart of *The Vicar of Dibley* is the serious idea that women can make really good vicars, so what's all the fuss about?

At the end of every episode, we hoped that every parish in the land would want Geraldine Grainger as their vicar, and some even wrote to Dawn asking her to come and be just that. At the heart of *Absolutely Fabulous* was a real anger felt by Jennifer about the shallow world of fashion and PR. (The fact that the people who worked in fashion and PR thought that the whole series was a love letter to their industry tells us all we need to know. Some even said that *they* were the model for Edina. Really? Did they treat their daughters disgracefully and run their businesses so badly that they were a laughing stock?)

At the heart of *W1A* is a love letter to the BBC (and other institutions) and an earnest request that they don't tie themselves up too earnestly in jargon and navel-gazing and managerial gobbledegook, and that they allow good people the freedom to *get on and make good things*.

I get sent a lot of scripts. Many of them are aiming SO hard at 'funny' and very often the problem is that 'funny' is *all* they're aiming at. The writer watches comedy on TV, when they can find it, and thinks that it consists of people who say funny things, getting themselves in and out of funny situations. Then they look at where they live or work and think, 'This is a helluva sight funnier than all that stuff on telly. I'll write this!'

That leaves out the most important ingredient:

'WHY ARE YOU WRITING IT?'

'Well – um – to make people laugh and to make me rich.'

First of all, forget the rich bit. Do you know what the BBC's and even ITV's writing rates are? (Netflix – different story, maybe.)

Second, I think that unless you're hugely talented and unless you have something to say and a reason for saying it, it won't be funny and an audience will see through you. You've got to know and they've got to know why you're doing it and they've got to agree that the reason is a good one

When the man who now runs the *New York Times*, Mark Thompson, was running BBC2, he commissioned a comedy that he was offered at a party. This *doesn't usually happen*. Usually, the experts in a particular genre crave an audience with the controller, and they are graciously allowed to bring their carefully considered and sometimes even 'piloted' offerings to a big office at Broadcasting House.

I suppose you can't stop controllers being assailed at parties, though they are usually made of sterner stuff. Mark commissioned the show in question from a small Scottish comedienne, who had had an idea that she was going to write and star in it herself. She sold it to Mark on the basis that she had discovered the secret that makes US comedies 'much better than our own' (yawn). This revelation was, according to her, that 'US shows weren't about anything.' Oh, I see. That was why *Seinfeld* was so good, and why Larry David employed all those writers. REALLY??? So that they could write shows that 'weren't about anything'?? I seem to remember that every episode of *Curb Your Enthusiasm* is about the huge consequences of a small selfish action. When Larry refuses to take his shoes off at a dinner party given by someone who is overly precious about their white carpet, the result is that he alone can walk out after smashing a huge glass ornament into razor-sharp pieces all over the floor. The comedy may not appear to be 'about' anything, but it is rooted in a profound understanding of human vanity, tunnel vision, paranoia, self-delusion. One person's obsessive pride in their interior décor bumps into another's obstinacy and clumsiness. Larry's self-absorption is so total, that he makes things fall apart. The décor zealots are immobilised by their own ridiculous demands. But it's not 'demonstrated'. There aren't footnotes at the bottom of the screen, for heaven's sake. This is the art that *conceals* art, but it sure ain't an *absence* of ideas or substance.

The Scottish comedienne's show was not a huge hit and was not the easiest show to rehearse when, from time to time the titular star was late for her own rehearsals.

True – this is a trait she shares with others. But that's for another chapter.

• •

LESSON: *Always* **wear shoes, and know what your show is ABOUT, so we do too.**

• •

Finally I would say that comedy is about surprise; not what you thought would happen, not where you were sure the comedy or characters would go – but where you're suddenly *surprised* to find them. Laughter is a registering of shock, a release.

So – what's so funny?…BOO!!!!

10

Two Big Women in my Life

B ack to my life. It's Boxing Day 2017. Last night a show called *300 Years of French and Saunders* went out on BBC1 to a large number of viewers and some nice comments in the press. So now might be a good time to talk about the mechanics of how shows get made, and my life with the two ladies without whom I wouldn't have a career.

Mechanics first.

Back in April I got a call from the girls' agent. She is a remarkable woman called Maureen Vincent who's looked after Dawn and Jen throughout most of their professional lives. She looks after lots of other people as well but no one, I suspect, who takes up so much of her time. This is partly because neither D nor J live in London. Dawn occupies a gorgeous house on the edge of a cliff in Cornwall, and Jen lives on a farm in Dartmoor with lots of horses. She once explained her non-appearance at a rehearsal with the extraordinary, 'Oh sorry, I completely forgot that the farrier was coming over!'

Anyway, back to Maureen, stalwart champion of these two

funny women almost since they left the Central School of Speech and Drama and set off towards the strip club in Soho where their careers began. The very first call I got from Maureen was asking me to see them perform at the New End Theatre, Hampstead. The New End had previously been a mortuary. They did a number of sketches, some funny, some less so, involving teachers and American tourists. They performed to a less than packed, but remarkably tolerant audience.

I had already come across Dawn and Jen when they were part of a pilot show I worked on at Granada. A show that remains rightly unbroadcast. Not banned (this time), just unbroadcast. It was hosted by the late Derek Jameson, hard-nosed ex-editor of the *Express* – newshound and actually not a bad guy. We tried to construct a show that might be a bit *That Was the Week That Was* (30 years after), a bit satirical and a bit young, a bit tough but still acceptable to advertisers. Those behind it hoped that the show would prove how ITV could move in on what was principally BBC terrain.

It didn't work on any level.

The show was trying to be all things to all viewers. Derek was there to be man of the people and deliver the odd scoop. Dawn and Jen and Alexei Sayle (brilliant old communist and comedian) were there to be edgy and different. But. Granada were nervous about the project, so we involved some slightly less edgy, more 'comfortable' comedians from BBC radio's *Week Ending*. These guys were doing mainstream material in case the 'alternative comedians' went too edgy and off-piste. It was as though TW3 had been hosted by Jacob Rees-Mogg and Russell Brand. The show was a mess and never made it to air. I recall that one of the writers, Neil Shand, ex-script editor for David Frost, walked out because Alexei wouldn't do a joke that Neil had written about gay sailors on the Royal Yacht *Britannia*. Shand expected that others would follow him out of the door – but they didn't. This may have been the moment when old comedy gave way to new.

So I first worked with Dawn French and Jennifer Saunders over the dead body of a cancelled show in Manchester.

Back to the mechanics of making a Christmas special. In April, Maureen rang me to say that 2017 was the 30th anniversary of Dawn and Jennifer's first TV series. A series that had begun with then head of entertainment and variety, Jim Moir, saying to his future stars, 'I'm putting my dick on the table for you girls!' (This was not an early Kevin Spacey/Harvey Weinstein moment. Far from it. Merely an exhortation to excellence and a measure of Jim's faith in his new protégés.)

Maureen's 2017 suggestion was that the BBC, a rather different place from the one in which Mr Moir's member had been proffered, should be celebrating her clients in some appropriate fashion, perhaps with a parade of their triumphs over the years and a smidgeon of new material. An admirable idea, especially as we then learned that her esteemed clients didn't have much availability to write or prepare an entirely new show.

Back in the Jim Moir BBC, this call from an agent might have resulted in a nice lunch to discuss the proposal before moving it forward to a relatively informal process called 'offers'. The head of a department would meet with the controller of BBC1 or 2 and the HOD would 'offer' the controller a range of show ideas. The HOD was a trusted soul in those far-off days, and would usually get instant approval for the shows offered, so that productions could get underway quickly. Possibly after another lunch. Rarely were there any disagreements or deviations from the established routine.

There *was* one famous exception, so legend has it. The case of Syd Little and Eddie Large. For those who have forgotten, they were the poor man's Morecambe and Wise. They did sketches, 'front cloth' material, and not hugely accurate impressions. This was their bill of fare and it was liked but perhaps not loved by those who liked but didn't necessarily love – well – sketches, 'front cloth' material, and not hugely accurate impressions. They regularly appeared in 'offers' as a returning item on the menu. The controller of BBC1 to whom they were being offered on this occasion, was Jonathan Powell, an estimable chap who had produced the excellent TV version of *Tinker, Tailor, Soldier, Spy* starring Alec Guinness. He said, 'Oh Jim, let's have no more Little and Large, *please*. Honestly, they've had their day. They're just not great and they don't rate.'

In other words – not enough people watched them.

'They are much-loved stars in the show business firmament,' retorted Jim, 'and you've still got one series on the shelf unshown.'

'Fine, OK, we'll show the one we've got, but no more after that.'

Jim Moir did what he always did when the time came to part with artists. He took them and their agent to the Savoy (or was it the Ritz?) for lunch.

'Now, lads, you've had a good innings but all good things must come to an end and I'm afraid this is it. I've fought hard for your cause but sadly the channel has decided against another series. I'm sorry but there it is. Let's drink to better days!'

Time passed and eventually, probably in the summer, the final series of Syd and Eddie is taken down from the shelf, and broadcast. For the first time, it's scheduled much earlier, at 5.15 p.m. on Saturday afternoons. And it does *really* well because kids love it! It's a hit! So, at the next 'offers' meeting, Jonathan Powell said to Jim, 'We *must* have another series from Little and Large, they're doing great business for us. *Well done.* Did you get new writers, Jim?'

Cut to the Savoy (or the Ritz), where a new lunch had been hastily arranged.

'Boys, we'd love to have you back. Let's get the diaries out and work out when you can fit us in.'

'That's great, Jim,' said the guys.

'Yes, really great, Jim,' said their manager. 'But the fees have gone up I'm afraid, because the show's been such a hit.'

'Really? Have they?' said Jim nervously. 'By much?'

'One hundred per cent.'

Legend has it they were paid a *very substantial amount* for their next series.

Nowadays, things are different, not least because whatever the papers may tell you, the Savoy is well out of the BBC bounds – and the proliferation of channels means that success can lead to offers from many sources. There is also a huge difference in the way in which shows get made. So that even in the case of a show celebrating French and Saunders, which perhaps looks like a 'no-brainer', I have to go to the head of the department, which is now independent and able to offer shows to any number of channels, who has to go to the BBC commissioning head of comedy, who eventually meets with the channel controller who says 'yes' or 'no'. In this process, the supplier (me) never directly meets the buyer (the channel). The buyer never gets a chance to look the supplier in the eye and say, 'It had better be bloody funny' and the supplier never has a chance to say to the buyer, 'It *will* be, but please broadcast it on a day when and at a *time* when it is likely to do well.'

Even having secured an agreement from the channel, we then have to discuss money. Comedy, even though it is much loved and desired by the viewer after a hard day at work, is not a priority for the BBC. They are good at it and always have been, but it's *not* a priority. The main priorities are drama and news. They get bigger audiences, drama is much more saleable overseas than comedy, and it is much more expensive.

There is a much longer moan about finance elsewhere in this book. Warning signs will indicate it, so you can avoid having to read it.

Let's get back to basics. The production of a one-off special celebrating the joy brought to a grateful nation by French and Saunders.

The order of events for a producer/executive producer goes like this:

A) Establish when the girls are available to make the show. Are there a couple of weeks when Dawn isn't writing a book, acting for Sky in *Delicious*, or judging *Australia's Got Talent?* Will that coincide with Jennifer not doing any major animation voiceovers, guest appearances, or important meetings with farriers?

B) Not always a necessity, but if possible find a writing room and rehearsal room midway between their two houses, so they have equal inconvenience/convenience in terms of travel.

C) Book a studio that knows how to look after major artists and understands the demands of making shows with a live audience. This is not quite as easy as it sounds, because of the small number of studios left in London that aren't already booked by Simon Cowell, *Strictly Come Dancing* or (in the case of what used to be BBC Studios at Televison Centre) filled with ITV Daytime shows like *Loose Women* and *This Morning*.

Note to self: find empty shed in London, buy lights, a few old cameras and seats, then wait for bookings and money to roll in.

D) Talk to the ladies about what the material they want to do might be, and when in the next nine months they might be able to get together to write it. See above for availability and travel problems.

E) Find a producer. We did in the form of the excellent James Farrell. Find a director, who was in this case Ed Bye, and also find someone who has watched everything F&S have ever made, or someone who may be willing to do so. May I take a moment to pay tribute to the lady that we eventually found, and who was happy to undertake this Herculean labour? Her name was Jackie Ramsamy and over the months that we spent making the show, she became a rock. Especially whilst we were editing. Thus: 'Jackie, it's us in the edit here. Is there a moment in any of the series where the girls are dressed as pirates?'

'Series two, episode four, 12 minutes into the show'

She was brilliant, and must know more about the shows than anyone who'd actually been involved in them, including Dawn and Jennifer.

F) Find a designer. If possible, a designer who knows that in the end, very little of what we *ask* for will actually be *used*, and who also appreciates that the girls may suddenly need – say – a hotel foyer built from scratch in the last two days before shooting. He or she should also register no obvious concern when green needs to become pink. The more robust designers will take this quietly in their stride, the more sensitive will scream a little.

G) Be careful when one half of a double act rings you and says: 'I haven't spoken to Dawn/Jennifer/Stephen/Hugh/Vic/Bob/Rik/Ade about this *yet*, but I was *thinking* that it might be good to do a thing where there's a choir dressed as medieval monks *and* we're in some sort of musical *Name of the Rose* thing *and* there's a big fire.'

React in an apparently interested way and suggest a few improvements but under no circumstances do anything about it. The words – 'Oh yeah, hi, Jon, I've spoken to Ade/Dawn/Hugh etc., and we think we probably don't need that medieval musical thing' – are sure to follow. Then – 'It might not work unless we can persuade say Jeremy Irons or Sean Connery or Liam Neeson or someone to be in it. Could you just check those guys out?'

Check them, but with the fervent hope in your heart that they're busy on something huge and impossible to get out of, with a cast-iron contract.

H) Guests. In the case of the F&S show, I thought it might be fun to get a sprinkle of starry names to say how much Dawn and Jen's work had meant to them over the years. This turned out not to be such a great idea. Sickly. Yucky. Honestly.

A better idea turned out to be getting the likes of Joanna Lumley and Lulu (they have no 'likes' – I KNOW) to say what a terrible time they'd had working with the girls. In the case of Lulu this was probably true. In an early *Reservoir Dogs* parody, she'd been tied to a chair and threatened with sub-machine gunfire if she didn't stop singing 'Shout'. When she refused, Dawn and Jen mowed her down, which involved a large number of explosive caps being attached to her body. Perfectly safe, she was assured, as long as she didn't *flinch*, which would bring the cap on her lower arm into contact with her upper arm. Well, she flinched (who can blame her?) and the cap excavated a small hole in that bonny Scottish limb. It was at this moment that we found out two things: first, that Lulu was a real trooper for not screaming with pain until after the director had shouted 'Cut', and second, that the BBC Studios' first-aid team goes home at six o'clock. It was now 8.50.

A producer's job description should now include driving injured Scottish songbirds to Charing Cross Hospital at night, while persuading them that *really* they don't want to sue the show they've just made a guest appearance on, because the show has *no* money...*and* neither do they want to sue the BBC *as a whole* for the inevitable cost of plastic surgery. It should also include sitting with said pop star in A&E (as I did) surrounded by ill people who are not quite sure whether the woman over there is the chanteuse who sang 'Boom Bang-a-Bang' in the Eurovision Song Contest, or whether she is a symptom of their condition?

A guest that we have been pursuing for more than 300 years is Madonna. She has occasionally teased us with what seemed like a 'maybe', but the truth is: there is no good reason other than bankruptcy why she should ever say 'yes'.

One problem is 'getting to her'. At various times, we thought that we had a line through to her manager, her business manager, her tour manager, her yoga teacher, her personal shopper, and the man who does her lawn. But no, nothing. Nada. Zip. Rien. A 'piss off' would have been progress.

As this year was possibly the last chance for all of us, I wrote the following letter to someone who we'd been told was close to Ms Ciccone. I knew it was like writing to Santa but hey. Here's part of the letter.

How to Produce Comedy Bronze

Dear Friend of Madonna,

(general fluff about D and J and then)

For Christmas on our main channel in the UK, BBC1,
Dawn and Jennifer are doing a show currently called
300 Years of French and Saunders *and I'm writing to*
ask if by any chance Madonna could be persuaded
to appear in the show. The girls are, needless to say,
huge fans, and would not be making fun of Madonna
in any way. [Obviously they would, but hey, let's
get her in the building first.] *I know this is a big ask,*
and – if it would help – I can send examples of their
work with Dusty Springfield, Kylie Minogue, Cher, and
Elton John. I also know that an agreement to appear
is only likely if Madonna happens to be in the UK
[producer's insurance], *although flights and hotels*
could be provided. Madonna has frequently featured
in the show as someone the girls would dearly love to
have as a guest.

If this is impossible, can I float one other idea,
namely that Madonna record a small message saying
that she has no intention ever of appearing with
them and perhaps asking that they never trouble her
again or mention her in their act. This might then be
played into the show. Fees for this can be discussed if
required.

I should have saved the BBC the cost of a stamp (or
whatever it is that you stick on transatlantic emails). No
reply.

Still, her silence is preferable to events surrounding our
approach to Bette Midler.

Her manager said: 'Yes, of course Bette would love to
do the show whilst she's in London.'

Two Big Women in my Life

Hoorah, no airfare for the BBC to pay. Someone else has already done that. File under 'too good to be true'.

A special sketch was written. It featured the girls as two gay male hairdressers whose dreams come true when they're called on to fix the hair of a screen goddess. We thought that Ms Midler might recognise the type, because she started her career at the Continental Baths in New York where 'straight' was an extinct species.

A couple of days before we were due to record the sketch, D and J were summoned to a glossy London hotel for a chat.

According to later reports, the meeting went like this.

'You', the Divine Ms M. says, looking at Jennifer, 'You're funny. I know you from that show on Comedy Central.'

She is referring to *Ab Fab*.

'You', she looks at Dawn, 'You. I don't know *you*.'

Not a great start.

'So, what is it you want me to do?' Bette asks.

The by now slightly unnerved double act explain the hairdresser idea, and that Ms Midler will surely recognise the type. *Au contraire.*

'I don't know these sort of people. Do me a bit,' is her response.

So now Dawn and Jennifer have to audition the sketch. This is not something that they had expected, because doesn't the best comedy come from collaboration, and Ms M. might have some of her own ideas?

The meeting softens a little after D and J have performed, and no one says 'no', and times and places are discussed.

The next morning, however, I get a call from Bette Midler's manager.

'Hi, so what's the latest Bette could be with you tomorrow morning?'

I explain that we have quite a lot to do on the 'pre-record' day before our audience show, and that obviously we'll give the sketch as long as we can, but the set has to be turned into something else in the afternoon, so maybe if Bette could be with us for noon or 12.30?

I'm in a good mood. The sun is shining. We've got a big star in the bag.

The manager says: 'I'm sorry that's too early. Bette won't be able to do the show.'

Now picture Icarus falling out of a clear blue sky.

Maybe wires had been crossed earlier when the manager was so confident. Maybe she had over-estimated Ms Midler's love of *Ab Fab* or maybe she thought it was a talk show. Maybe – as Alan Bennett once almost wrote – '*yes* means *no* (so much at least Freud has taught us)'.

Anyhow, it didn't happen.

In the 2017 Christmas special, the girls wanted to have a go at *Poldark,* playing the busybody extras we've often seen in previous shows. So, we asked (nicely) the production company who make *Poldark* to lend us the set and some of the actors. We wouldn't be too horrid about their show. Really, we wouldn't. In the past, we haven't asked those from whom the piss is about to be taken if they *mind*, but this time we knew that *Poldark* was in production in the West Country. They were very happy and cooperative but Mr Poldark himself wasn't available. Despite my grovelling letters, in which I pointed out that since Dawn French had married Richard Armitage on screen in the *Vicar of Dibley* (are you keeping up?) Geraldine Granger was therefore *married* to Thorin Oakenshield! (Yes?) And Thorin Oakenshield was Mr Poldark's sworn leader in *The Hobbit* movies! A-ha, I thought, game, set and match.

Two Big Women in my Life

'Sorry he's just not available that weekend.'

Oh well, we tried.

Delmelza and George Warleggan turned up and did splendidly. Good for them. Thank you.

I) (Yes we're back on the alphabetical listing after a long diversion.) Timings. No matter how often I work with Dawn and Jennifer, I always forget that their work *expands* in front of a camera and an audience. It never shrinks, because the audience laughter and the girls' ability to improvise always adds time. When I first worked with them and the hugely talented director, Bob Spiers, I saw that he never shouted 'Cut' when we'd captured what was on the page. He always left a second or ten, just to see what might happen next. Sometimes not much, but on other occasions...well, the funniest material was often nowhere to be seen in the script.

For instance, in an early series, there's a sketch where the girls are playing the owners of Prickly Pear farm, supposedly a facility which hires out animals to film and TV productions. Dawn's character says that she can recognise an animal by its faeces, even though this is clearly a lie. Now Dawn knows that the faeces we've placed all over the farmyard are made of chocolate spread, so, at the end of the take – still in character – she uses her trowel to pick some up and taste it. Hilarious, wrong, and I did get letters about setting a bad example to children, BUT, it's in character and very funny, so it stayed. This is why the estimated timings that it is the script supervisor's job to give you at the start of the week, have always expanded considerably by the end of the week. Especially in the studio. With an audience.

J) Sort out warm-up. 'Warm up' is usually when a comedian (not in the show) comes on before the recording and attempts to get the audience in the right mood. It's usually pretty ghastly, so since the second show I produced with French and Saunders, I do it myself.

It is, curiously, much easier to go out in front of the audience with a few bad gags than it is to pace up and down behind the monitors wondering why it's all taking so long and going so badly. Saves money too.

K) Record the show. YOU MUST NOT FORGET TO DO THIS.

Having gone through steps (a) to (j), you should be able to record the show. You play-in the material you've already pre-recorded, and set Dawn and Jen free with the audience to work their magic. Oh, and always remember to book a room for the cast and crew (and their 300 friends) so they can have a drink and a quick congratulate after the show.

THEN – take everything into the edit. This used to mean a subterranean room under Television Centre where you'd sit with one of the few men who knew how to operate the vast editing machines of another age. *Very* early on in my career, this man would know how to throw iron filings onto two-inch tape in order to bring up a magnetic image of what was recorded there. The machines in those days couldn't fast forward in vision. If the image conjured up with iron filings was of something small surrounded by something big, then it was probably Ronnie Corbett doing a monologue. Anything else was probably Ronnie Barker.

We now take the show up four flights of stairs to an airless room in Soho, where there is a new man (Homo microsoftus) who knows how to operate a much more sophisticated but smaller machine from a computer keyboard. No longer two-inch tape, but a file in the memory of a computer. Our editor is called Jake, and for two weeks he has to sit patiently while the director, the producer and Jon Plowman argue about the running order. It's one of the rituals associated with sketch shows that you always keep fiddling with the sequence of your material. Is it funnier if we start with some old sketches then go to new ones, or vice versa? Is it better to put all the famous movie parodies early so people feel a warm glow, or later, so they look like the top of the bill? Isn't there a better clip from the old sketch or a better angle in the new one?

There is no perfect answer. So, you just keep fiddling and looking and *feeling* – does it *feel* right, is it funnier this way or that way? Just *occasionally* we ask the editor what *he* thinks. (Steady.) When we've assembled some sort of show, we ask Dawn and Jennifer what *they* think. Then a new cog in the machine, a commissioning editor, gives *their* opinion, and of course they have more power, so sometimes we take their opinion on board. But only sometimes.

In case it's enlightening, I just came across my notes from an edit session for *300 years of French and Saunders*. I promise that unless you have an intimate knowledge of the girls' output (or my psychology) it probably won't mean a thing, but this *really* is what an executive producer does.

1) Cut out Bond and Christmas Special and Sausages, move to '300 years' quicker
2) Cut 'Alien' white room, cut Blobby. Light change quicker
3) Tighten off 'coffee' then Short sketch leading to 2 and move. Go off GG1 to Wagon wheel to GG2? or Move.
4) Cut 'Piano'
5) J&L In – 08.55 Out – 09.06. Trim Passport
6) Save the dance and trousers for Tonioli. Go from LGBT to 'You a lesbo, miss?'
7) Cut dialogue re biscuit wrappers

8) Cut the coach and cigs
9) Cut down 'Poldark' titles
10) Cut first AbFab
11) Cut Irish dancing
12) Prickly Pear earlier?
13) Cut off *Titanic* lifebelt (actually that's what they did in 1912)
14) Lose Rhianna?

And that's an abbreviated version.

In any other world, this would be nonsense. Come to think of it, it's not far off being nonsense in ours.

Eventually, there is grading. This is where you fiddle with the colour and the tone and quality of the picture. You highlight that small prop in the corner or make things that shouldn't be in shot, like boom microphones, disappear.

Grading, which fiddles with the picture, is followed by the sound dub, where you fiddle with (guess what?) the sound. Should we have church bells in this sweet village scene? Should we go for audible dialogue just for a change, and maybe that traffic is rather loud?

Then the most unromantic part of the process. After weeks and months making the show as good as it can possibly be, there are no fanfares or red carpets. Someone just presses 'Send' and the file goes over to transmission.

TV producers live in a permanent state of anti-climax.

Ten TV Comedies that I wish I'd Made
These are all way better than Comedy Bronze

The Larry Sanders Show: Having spent a good bit of my career in talk shows this seems like a very accurate documentary.

30 Rock: Sorry if this is reading like a list of shows about shows but Tina Fey created something special here and her cast ran with it.

Sergeant Bilko: the Phil Silvers Show: OK, it's old and has some slightly less funny episodes but Silvers was wonderful and the writing was always sharp in this classic story of a smart guy trying to beat the system.

Till Death Us Do Part: I'm lucky enough to be of the generation that saw this first time round. It was truthful in a way that shows rarely were in later days. It exposed prejudice and ignorance in a way that comedy should. Broadcasters who worry that this will be taken the wrong way are right to worry but wrong to censor.

Fawlty Towers: We should all just watch in awe and learn what we can.

Blackadder: A brilliant starting premise to set each series in a different period. A terrific cast playing character types that translate from period to period. I know that writing it was an uphill struggle for all concerned but it was so worth the pain!

Brass: A vastly underrated ITV show by John Stevenson and Julian Roach. A parody of a gritty family saga set 'up north' with Timothy West, Barbara Ewing and Caroline Blakiston.

Perhaps inspired by Susan Harris's excellent *Soap* but wholly its own thing and very funny – even when it came back.

Will and Grace: Congratulations to the network people who saw that the main characters in the pilot script should be ditched because Will and Grace, who were side characters, were the funny ones worth pursuing. Then congrats for inventing Jack and Karen to fill the gap. Bigger congrats to the team who kept up the standard and to the people who realised that Trump was a good reason, if they needed one, for reviving it

Steptoe and Son: Once more we see that 'it's the writers, stoopid'. Galton and Simpson created two characters that we should loathe and despise but we don't. Their father-and-son relationship is funny and sad, but above all truthful.

Father Ted: A comically surreal situation that shouldn't've worked because it goes in and out of reality with abandon and without caring. Then again that's the very thing that makes it work. It tis, it tis, it tis, so it is.

If I'm allowed another two that are current then *This Country* and *Witless* prove that there's still great life left in the form!

My five biggest mistakes as a producer

1) I could have been Jon Stewart's life-long creative partner! No, really. (Stewart is a brilliant US comedian and satirist – visit YouTube). He agreed to do a show with us called *Where's Elvis, This Week?* (It was 1996, Bill Clinton was running for president the second time and Jon was going through a bad patch.) And *he* thought we'd have a big writing team for him. And *I* thought he'd do it all himself so we didn't have any except him. Thankfully he didn't walk out. I lie awake at night imagining that we'd looked after him so well that he asked me to produce *The Daily Show*. Wrongly, I inflicted our British 'Take the rough with the smooth' philosophy on him, and he wandered sadly back to satire and stardom leaving me scrabbling for crumbs.

2) I could have been Sasha Baron Cohen's best mate and well-paid producer. He walked into my office before anyone knew who he was and told me to give him a series. Stupidly I said no, and told him to prove himself with a sketch on a late-night show on BBC2. His offering involved filming himself as a prototype Ali G character whose comedy turn involved persuading upper-class girls to say 'c*nt' to camera outside a rather up-market party! We fell out.

3) Never employ researchers who enjoy practical jokes. I was once wound-up good and proper by getting home one evening to a message on my answering machine apparently from a Frenchwoman who maintained that I had run over her beloved cat, '*ma chere fou-fou, elle est morte, je suis desol*é.' I completely believed that my driving home from a recent holiday was responsible for this intense outburst of grief. Only when I was interrogated by other researchers about what had happened on my week away did I begin

101

to stop feeling guilty and start to smell a rat rather than a dead cat. The lady behind the rat now sometimes hosts *Woman's Hour*. I shall spare her blushes further but I will say that it wasn't Dame Jenni Murray.

4) Beware actors who say yes to projects too quickly, except Joanna Lumley. I was once involved with the pilot of a show about marriage counsellors. It was pretty good and we found a leading lady of some stature to agree to be in it. She was an actress known for comedy and warmth but I suspect that she got a better offer just after ours and so set about making sure that our show didn't get anywhere. She announced within hours of starting rehearsals that she would be giving the character a Geordie accent! She could not be dissuaded. She wasn't from the north-east or known for her accents. Neither was the person she was playing – she was homely and home counties. Our leading lady knew that a sure way of screwing up the project was to have viewers up and down the land saying, 'What's she doing? We don't watch her for her voices, we like her for who she is.' It was as if Penelope Keith suddenly decided to play Welsh!

5) Avoid pianos. When I was working on *Wogan*, we had as a guest American singer and songwriter Rupert Holmes. He was the man who wrote a song called 'Escape' that has the line about getting caught in the rain with a piña colada. It was often played on Terry's radio show. Mr Wogan thought it would be a good idea if someone brought on two piña coladas before Rupert sang the number. I was that person. I then tripped and managed to pour not one but two coconut-based drinks into the heart of a very expensive Bechstein grand piano. Terry's comment on live TV was, 'That *was* my producer. It's always good to see someone's last day in television,' as I exited stage left.

11

Working with the Girl$_s$

Dawn was the larger of the two
but so was Jennifer.

So we've covered the mechanics of how their shows are made but here are a few random thoughts about what they do and how they do it.

Looking at the archive, you quickly see that Jennifer can disappear behind wigs, make up and frocks and be a comic character or whoever she wants to be. Dawn can also do that and is slightly fonder of a gag than her partner. Jennifer is more likely to improvise and kick an idea around to see where it goes. Dawn would like it sorted a bit more, although on an evening when Jennifer was flat on her back in pain but an audience was already coming in to Television Centre to see a recording, it was Dawn who flew by the seat of her pants.

She did a wonderful sketch about a woman alone doing the washing up whilst listening on headphones to the Eurythmics.

How to Produce Comedy Bronze

We immediately see how difficult it is to sing along to Annie Lennox who takes her tunes all over the place where few can follow. (Try it.) She also did another sketch about a woman prevaricating about going out. That's it. Just should she or shouldn't she and if so wearing what and looking like whom? Just Dawn alone. The whole evening was a tad 'needs must' but none the worse for that. Both Dawn and I insisted that Jennifer should say a few words from her bed on speakerphone in order to convince both the audience and us that she wasn't skiving.

Jennifer, of course, when upright can fly solo just as well. She can disappear into the character of a gin-soaked Raj dowager with such seriousness that your heart and liver go out to her. Together, they can play a pretty wide range of emotions: lonely schoolgirls, one of whom is about to go off to spend Christmas with her dad and one of her stepmums whilst the other faces Christmas alone in the school, left behind by her parents who are Jordanian royalty. Heart-breaking but perceptive. Yet, lest I sink into the dangerous but contemporary trap of prizing tears over laughter, let us not forget that they could make a studio audience roar to the point where I have had to ask the sound crew to lower the levels of the audience mikes so that spoken lines could be heard at home.

At other times they were in make-up chairs at 5 a.m. so that they could have prosthetics applied and emerge as the fat men or women – same make-up, different wigs – or as Bros by 10 a.m. Once they were in these masks, it wasn't just harder to tell them apart but also harder to talk to them as anyone but the characters. After they'd done their stuff as these characters their faces needed an hour at least to 'rest' before the next characters' make-up could be applied. We always double-checked that there really was nothing else for the fat men or ladies to do before letting them get changed back. If something was forgotten you had to wait another five hours to 'pick it up'.

Much of each series was filmed on location. The first series I did with them was based around a mental hospital in Eastbourne and one of the later ones was based just south of Dartmoor. Today, filming has to be confined within the M25 so that no one has to be paid 'overnight rates'. The money a film crew spends is obviously phenomenal, back when we were first making French and Saunders it was about £15K a day, including hotels to keep a crew on the road. These days it's double that even within the M25 and no accommodation.

There was one memorable day when we were in Devon when things got rather extended. In the morning we were in Paignton, shooting part of a parody of those great California dreamers, the Mamas and the Papas. We had lunch in a seafront place, but whilst we were eating, the camera car was broken into and the Mamas and the Papas footage and cameras were nicked. The police were amused and the insurance company informed, but the sketch had to be reshot and the rest of the day 'achieved', i.e., filmed as per schedule. This included some *Thelma and Louise* stuff where Dartmoor doubled for Arizona and a Pretty Polly stockings ad parody for which a relatively complicated set had been erected on the stage of the Torquay Theatre. This was available to us for one day only. It was a device that would allow one of Dawn's legs to rotate completely around the clock. It was then realised that one of her three shoes (one for the false leg that had been built) had been left back at the hotel on Dartmoor. I drove back at some speed in the dark, for it was now night, and got it. The day was achieved but it ended late. Just how late we found out later that week when the electricians put in a chit for a 23-hour working day!

The *Thelma and Louise* parody ended with the two girls

driving off a cliff. We selected our cliff on an obscure country road on Dartmoor and brought the crew and our effects people to the site to check it a couple of days before shooting. We booked our stuntmen and we booked an expensive helicopter, rented by the hour from Plymouth, to appear as they go over the edge. So far so good, yes? No. The first thing was that in the days between the recce and the shoot it had rained. Not a lot, but a bit. So that the first reaction from the effects team responsible for getting the car over the cliff-edge was, 'You didn't tell us it was going to be muddy, that changes everything.'

'We didn't know that it was going to be muddy but it does tend to happen after it's been raining!'

'Yeah, but it'll make it a bit more difficult.'

'Well, do your best because the helicopter is booked to be here in an hour.'

For some reason, the effects guys had devised a system of what seemed like rubber bands set up in a way that was a bit like a catapult. They would be in an out-of-shot Land Rover driving away from the edge and that would wind things up to the point where the stunt car would go, by sheer force of physics, the other way and then over the cliff. (Don't ask because I didn't understand either.) The mud might make it difficult for the effects guys to go fast enough in their direction to get our main car moving...why hadn't this occurred to them before now? (Rhetorical: might as well ask why a £1,200 per hour helicopter can't be stopped?)

So, we shot the girls and got their dialogue in the car. We shot the helicopter coming up into vision above the car windscreen. We sent the Land Rover off in one direction and watched expectantly. Our suicide car went a few yards towards the edge and stopped dead, close but not enough. There were probably 50 guys on Dartmoor that day with film equipment and cars and rubber bands and helicopters trying to make a car go over a cliff with two mannequins in it. It didn't happen.

Plan B happened a few days later when we'd found a deep old quarry with an edge and our car and a few strong guys. The camera was at the bottom of the quarry but far enough from the car's proposed trajectory to be out of harm's way. The strong guys went behind the car out of shot, they pushed, car descended, job done.

I am reminded of similar larks when we were filming a parody of *Misery* for a later series.

You may recall that there is a car accident, in a forest, in a snowstorm. We have our car, a different one from the quarry, we have our forest and we have our snow machine. We have also paid not quite as much as we ought for a stunt driver. Here's the job. There is a one-wheel ramp hidden on the forest floor, which he will have to drive up at speed to turn the car over. That's what he needs to do, but he either won't or can't. We do four or five takes. With stunt guys, it's always their call when you do the take. Film/tape/computer chips will not go through the camera until the stuntman is ready and happy. It's his neck on the line so it's his call, not the director's or mine or anybody else's. He says, 'go', he powers towards the ramp but then almost visibly his nerve fails yet again and he slows down slightly. Onscreen it will look like he drove over a bump with no problem. Not quite what we wanted. So after take five we stop and resort to our old Plan B friend: brute force. The camera, quite a long way from the car and on the end of a long lens, is pointed at the car. Behind the car are some well-built guys. On the word 'Action' they push the car over towards the camera. 'And cut', job done.

> **LESSON: Forget technology, forget effects, but always remember a few good men. And never try to book cheap stuntmen, you will get what you paid for.**

The way that Dawn and Jen work is still mostly a mystery to me. I know that they have an idea, kick it around between them, and the one who likes it most writes it, but is that all? Bob Spiers, director, and I were the new team for series three of F&S and when we went to meet them for the first time it was in a small toilet-sized office in Hammersmith. There were lots of Post-it notes on the wall but no fully written scripts on the desk, if there was a desk. It was a short visit in which we found out a few things but not many. They wanted to do some film parodies, not the kind in which there are a series of gags at the movie's expense, but the sort where we make a sequence from the film but with them in it. It's how the film would have been if the director had been mad enough to cast Dawn and Jennifer in the leads. At first it was a tricky distinction to get your head round, but it's why we always had the VHS (those days) of whichever movie so we could shoot it as it had originally been shot, same lighting, costumes, make-up, close-ups and wide shots, just slightly cheaper and with different dialogue and actors.

Sometimes we also needed the VHS so that the girls could check accent and performance, something at which Jen, in particular, excelled. Curiously, we never got sued for plagiarism, indeed some of the original directors got word back to us to say how much they liked what we did. The nearest we came to trouble was when we were doing *Batman*. It was our art department ringing the makers wanting to know if by any chance we could borrow the designs for the Batmobile.

'No, you can take a running bat-jump or we'll bat-sue your ass.'

We did what we could to avoid this attack by giving the car and the costume a slightly different but legally noticeable twist. This is why Batman and Robin both have round not pointy ears. In case you cared.

As far as locations went, the disused Eastbourne mental hospital where we were based for series three stood in for *The Exorcist*, *Dangerous Liaisons*, and the Mother Superior's cell in *The Sound of Music*. In later series, we roamed further afield. There was a day when we filmed sequences for *Baywatch* in the morning on the beach at Burnham-on-Sea and then *Braveheart* in the Quantock hills above in the afternoon. Bikinis and floats made way for woad, kilts and dirks over lunch. Happy days!

They could dance pretty well too.

They were and are bloody funny!

12

Mel and
Griff

Just to be clear, Mel was the chubby one and Griff is the thin(ish) Welsh one.

When Mel and Griff asked me to work with them, the industry was changing. Not just the comedy industry but television as a whole. Before the mid-eighties, if you made a show, you made it for the channel that was going to broadcast it, and for the comedy department of that channel. The arrival of Channel 4 (who didn't make programmes, only 'published' independently made programmes) changed all that and the BBC, whom governments in power have always hated, came under more and more pressure to let producers make shows with independent companies. Stars, agencies and producers all started to form their own 'indies', in the sure knowledge that where there's laughs, there's brass. They realised that if you controlled the development of your shows *away from* the channel, you would have more control over content, and you could pay closer attention to how they were made, how much they cost and where they were sold. Today that motivation is still an important part of the very large entity that is the 'UK creative industries'.

Among those early arrivals at this well of finance, control and prosperity were the cast of *Not the Nine O'Clock News*.

NOTE: *Not the Nine O'Clock News* was broadcast on BBC2 from 1979 to 1982. It was a heady mix of satirical sketches on current stories and news items, as well as parody songs, like 'Kinder lingers'...sing it quickly and you'll see what they were getting at. I was nothing to do with any of it. Sadly.

Rowan Atkinson, Pamela Stephenson, Mel Smith, Griff Rhys Jones and producer John Lloyd could see that they'd made far more money out of the theatre tour, and the books and records that were published in their name, than they ever did from the TV show itself. The broadcast TV show was, of course, wholly owned by the BBC.

Rowan went off with Mr Bean to see a chap called Peter Bennett Jones, who founded Tiger Television. John Lloyd went off to do a brilliant assortment of shows including *Spitting Image* and *QI*. Mel and Griff, on the other hand, had already realised there was money to be made from radio ads. They'd set up the Not Any Old Radio Commercials company, and had a part share in ad agency Smith, Jones, Brown and Cassie. Now, they added a TV production company called Talkback to their empire. Talkback took over what had been *Alas Smith and Jones* at the BBC, and they began to make plain *Smith and Jones* for the BBC's fledgling independent department.

Mel and Griff

The business/creative end of the company was looked after by a chap who had been the pianist for Cambridge Footlights but later, after he sold Talkback for a little over £60 million to Pearson, a man who went on to run both BBC1 and ITV (not at the same time, obviously). This was Peter Fincham. Piano-player turned gamekeeper turned estate owner. He was a clever businessman.

Peter asked me to work with the infant company after their first couple of seasons. The set-up there was pretty familiar, except that it was based in a smart town house on Percy Street, just off the Tottenham Court Road. We were in the land of dodgy cut-price stereo shops and very smart restaurants. This was expensive latte-land just before it took over the planet. Talkback felt less inhibited than Television Centre and it seemed that everything was geared to making the show. It was reasonably calm, except for the occasional thump of a typewriter being thrown from the top windows onto the road outside, and the feral howl of Griff that followed, inveighing against…well…pretty much everything, but bad writing in particular.

Before I go on to insult him any more, I would just like to say how much I *like* Griff. Really. Energetic, original, clever, funny. OK?

This was how the comic partnership worked. Griff would rage and storm through the building. He was *convinced* that if enough scripts were produced, eventually he would be rewarded with the perfect sketch containing the perfect lines. It was a quest! An obsession! Day and night he searched and searched. Wild-eyed with frustration, he had to keep looking (and blaming the huge numbers of writers on the show for not producing the goods).

'Why, why, why do I have to rewrite everything *myself*? Aren't we paying these guys enough? *Why* haven't we got any good quickies? I don't think Fincham [Griff and Mel's agent as well as the MD] knows what the hell he's doing! And where's Melvin Kenneth Smith?'

This was a daily litany, which I learned to take with the same amount of salt that everyone else did. Though every so often it would change.

GRIFF: You see! Look at this! This is what we need! Funny stuff. We need to get these two writers in and get them writing more for us!

ME: But that's from Guy (Jenkin) and Andy (Hamilton) and they're under contract to Hat Trick to write a film…

GRIFF: They should be writing a film for us! This is where Fincham falls down. See if they'll write some more quickies for us! Why do I have to write everything myself?

Melvin Kenneth Smith, meanwhile, to the irritation of his partner, took a much more phlegmatic approach to the whole process. He never let problems such as scripts, budgets and deadlines interfere with his daily perusal of the *Sporting Life*, the racing pages of the broadsheets, phone calls to his bookie, amiable exchanges about his next film, his last film and how bad everyone else's films were. Sketches, their rehearsal and shooting, were secondary to the results of the 3.15 at Aintree.

An odd thing about Griff was this. He stormed and raged all the way through to the first day of filming. It may well have been what the series needed. But then he completely changed and became Griff Rhys Jones, actor. He was now content to do what all actors do on sets: sit in their trailers doing crosswords and reading huge novels – *Anna Karenina*,

Mel and Griff

Patrick O'Brian – books like that. Engaged in pursuits that help them pass the time while director and lighting director and the rest of the team were frantically trying to get everything ready for the actors. And of course, they would go over their lines.

This was another source of frustration for Griff. Mel had a near enough photographic memory. You would show Mel a page of material that we were about to film and his reaction was usually something like, 'Yep [reading], yep [reading], OK, look [reading], yep, got it. Shall we do it?'

This annoyed Griff no end.

'He makes no contribution to the writing, takes one look at it, and *knows* it! It's outrageous, and it's not fair!'

It wasn't.

Mel was a really good actor. Not that Griff wasn't. He was terrific – meticulous and precise. Mel was spontaneous – he could create a character in seconds, and it was always good, honest and truthful. His ability to find a performance that wasn't just off the shelf, but that you'd never quite seen before, was a joy to watch. A windscreen cleaner at a traffic light, a Vogue'ing Madonna, a police inspector not realising that the phone needs answering, a tetchy polar explorer annoyed at the late return of his colleague. All of them quickly but perfectly drawn. Griff's ability was just as great, if a tiny bit less spontaneous. Equally beautiful characters emerged but took five seconds longer. Who cares, it was all gold in front of the camera.

Over the years, Griff mellowed hugely and calmed down a great deal. He's now a very affable chap. Griff's problem was being a perfectionist in a very imperfect medium. What's funny to person A, is dull to person B. A drab line delivered with a marginally different inflection suddenly brings the house down. Tough to be a perfectionist in a world like this.

How to Produce Comedy Bronze

The pressure of sketch shows weighed heavily on him: the long process of finding the funny stuff and losing the rest. He had been a radio producer so he knew how hard it was.

Over the series of *Smith and Jones* that I produced, we worked with 42 writers, though of course, several only contributed a couple of nice jokes. We were blessed with two very good script editors in Chris Langham and Jim Pullin. They went through every sketch that was submitted and either tossed it in the bin or breathed a sigh of relief and set about making it as good as possible. They found great new writers, then bled them of every gag they had.

Jim and Griff found Graham Linehan and Arthur Mathews, who later wrote the brilliant *Father Ted*. The sketch they first sent us involved Hitler addressing a huge crowd. Archive footage, obviously. Then cut to two people in the crowd: crusties selling the *Socialist Worker*. They're arguing with Adolf and trying to get the crowd around them to buy the papers and join them. It did what comedy is supposed to do. It surprised you and pleased you. Jonathan Coy was hilarious as an SS officer saying to the crusties, 'Hey guys, quiet down. Give Adolf a chance, he's doing his best,' in a wonderfully middle-class and reasonable way. When we asked Graham and Arthur to come into the office, they turned out to be unassuming Irish guys. Both of them had been rock journalists on *Hot Press* in Dublin, but comedy was where they belonged. They gave the nation *Father Ted* and later *Black Books*. Graham wrote and directed *The IT Crowd*. They knew where the funny stuff was buried.

In that Hitler sketch, they showed what an odd beast the sketch is. It has to tell a story. It has to contain a big surprise (crusties at Nuremberg). It has to have immediately recognisable characters because you're only going to meet them for a few minutes. It has to have funny dialogue, and it has to have a neat conclusion. Not necessarily a punchline, but the last seconds should get to a laugh that's good enough to cut away from. It's a very tricky thing to find and write, but even more difficult is the 'quickie'. This is the well observed joke/sketch that's over before you know it.

> **CUT TO**
> *Swimming pool changing room. The small disinfecting footbath area you walk through on the way to the pool.*
> **Griff walks across behind it.**
> **Mel (who looks ridiculous in swimming trunks) walks into the footbath and disappears below the surface, then re-emerges shaken. The bath is unexpectedly very deep.**
> **CUT**

The quickie was the most valuable thing on our show, because it allowed us to have a high gag rate and to move swiftly along to the next item. One of the reasons shows like this aren't made now is because of the need for quickies. First, they're hard to write and you get through them at very high speed. Also they are expensive. Every one needs the same costume, make-up, lighting, music, location, and directing effort as a ten-minute scene in a sitcom. Sometimes more.

> **CUT TO**
> **Mel and Griff are skinheads on a train demanding money with menaces from a passenger.**

> **Within two or three lines they turn out to be ticket collectors.**
> **PASSENGER: I need a return to Penge, please.**
> **CUT**

For this you need a film crew and a train, or something that looks like it and bounces around like it. You need to light it and shoot it and then put in some background that seems to be moving as the train goes through the countryside. You need costumes. It lasts onscreen for just over ten seconds.

No wonder sketch shows are out of fashion.

The most memorable sequence in the shows was often the head-to-head. The duologues were mostly written by Griff when I was producing them, but had previously been written by Clive Anderson, among others. Mel and Griff played two dim characters verbally trying to understand the confusing world around them. The idea came from a series of ads (I think) but were a set piece throughout their TV careers. Here were two stupid people, but one was just a bit more stupid than the other. Topics they discussed ranged from sperm banks through to divorce to pop music and the monarchy. Griff's character was usually the more stupid of the two, but not always, and this was part of the reason they survived. The audience could be wrong-footed by an unexpected insight from one or other and never knew exactly which way the wind would blow.

The set-up for the head-to-head was always very carefully organised: the black screen behind, the relative height of Mel and Griff's chairs, and the width of the table between them. The whole thing was filmed in one shot. Not necessarily one take, 'corpsing' and forgetting lines saw to that, but certainly one shot. There was a time when the demand from companies eager to use the head-to-head format for advertising purposes was so great that a replica of the TV set-up was built in the basement of 33 Percy Street. The famous duologues could be knocked out by the yard without the need for those tiresome calculations that the set-up demanded. It made sense to have it handy.

M: That's money for old rope that is.
G: What's that then?
M: Two blokes talking to each other and getting paid for it.

Looking back, I see that the difference between Mel and Griff and Dawn and Jennifer was one of attitude. Indeed, Griff once said to me, 'How come those two girls are just allowed to be silly on TV?'

I've already described Griff's meticulous approach to the pursuit of the perfect gag in a perfectly judged sketch. Dawn and Jennifer didn't work like that. They tried an idea out and tried to make each other laugh. If they succeeded, then one of them went away and wrote it up and then they kicked it around some more, making a sketch as good as possible before we had to record it. It's not that one method is better than the other, just different (and one maybe slightly less ulcer-inducing).

Now to matters much more important than comedy.

I have to thank Griff for indirectly saving me a lot of money dealing with damp in our kitchen. He used to present a show which asked the public to choose a derelict building somewhere in the British Isles to be saved and restored. On this show he had two young experts, eminently charming, a man called Ptolemy and a woman named Marianne. I met Marianne at a party of Griff's and she was very worried that the impressionist show *Dead Ringers*, of which I was the exec producer, might take the piss out of her. Seeing an opportunity I seized it. Enjoying the moment, I told her that I would call them off if she would come round to our house and give us some advice about damp proofing. She said this wasn't really 'her thing' but she knew a guy whose thing it was. A little while later, a distinguished-looking cove came round and advised on a cheaper and better way forward for our kitchen walls, thereby saving us a lot of money. It turned out that, at the time, he was restoring a Hawksmoor church in east London. She'd put us in touch with the very best in the country. I felt that I had abused my position so, can I take this opportunity to say thanks to Griff and to Marianne, and to apologise and to confess?

Mel was a great guy, a very good actor and a mate. He died too young, and he died without fully achieving the career he really wanted as a film director (though *The Tall Guy* is a good and funny movie). 'Smudger' was a man whose fondness for a good cigar, a large drink, a day at the races (when he wasn't banned from the course) and some even less healthy vices made him a great lover of life. He had a verve that I have seen in very few others. He had a tremendous natural talent. He was genuinely gifted. He was highly intelligent. He embraced every part of life and in the end it overwhelmed him.

So, what did I do on the show? I did what producers do: I tried to keep as many people happy as possible. I tried to make sure that the ship ran smoothly and that the caterers produced food that was at least edible. And some of the time I was an arbitrator between the two stars: 'No, Griff,

Mel and Griff

what Mel meant was…No, Mel, Griff wasn't talking about you when he said…'

I was also there to go to weekly meetings with the accountant and the production manager, an ex-film guy called Clive.

'Well Jon,' he would say, 'here's where we are.' And I would be handed a weekly budget statement that didn't mean a huge amount to me. All these columns, all these figures, so many noughts, so many crosses. But I could pretend.

PRODUCTION MANAGER: As you can see, we're on the edge of over…

I could see both the edge and over it.

PRODUCTION MANAGER: So next week you have to decide between the brass band sketch which will also involve three tuba players, a red London bus full of extras and Mel as a lollipop lady, or the missionary set-up including the church interior, Mel and Griff being carried on litters plus two giraffes and a tiger. Are the animals real or extras in suits? We can't afford both sketches. Which one shall we drop? You decide.

We probably did both in the end. I'm not sure how but somehow. I was learning.

13

Murder Most Sordid

Peter Fincham had an idea. He probably had lots of ideas, who knows, but this one was about Dawn French. He thought that since I was working for him and had been working with her, I might be well placed to ask if she'd like to work for Talkback on a solo project. I did and she was.

We decided to make six individual stories, in each of which she would play the lead. Something more should tie them together, and this, we decided, should be murder. Dawn might commit it, or be the victim of it, or investigate it. Solving a murder mystery was the trickiest of the three. Morse had two hours, we only had 30 minutes.

I wrote to a long list of writers and asked them to pitch ideas. Surprisingly, only a few said, 'Go away' (or worse equivalents). We chose more than the six we needed (something is always going to go wrong with a couple) and the writers went off to their respective desks, quills, typewriters and word processors of sundry manufacture to create magic.

How to Produce Comedy Bronze

Rather like *Inside No. 9* years later, the anthology format attracts good actors because they know they'll be tied up (only *sometimes* literally) for a week at most. Jim Carter, Minnie Driver, Hugh Laurie, Jane Asher, Tim Spall, Sarah Lancashire, Ray Winstone and Amanda Donohoe all got involved early on. The writers included Ian Hislop and Nick Newman, Anthony Horowitz and Steven Moffat, all of whom had either achieved greatness or went on to have greatness thrown at them. Three of our directors were Bob Spiers, Coky Giedroyc, and Edgar Wright (producer, writer and director of the great *Baby Driver*). Oh, and we also had Dawn French as a police officer, a cookery writer, a Brazilian housekeeper, a kids' TV presenter, her own doppelganger, a quantum physicist and a round-the-world yachtswoman.

It was big fun. And educational! I learned halfway through the first series that I was being too generous! I was offering the artists too much money! I like actors, as you may have realised by now, so I don't see why they shouldn't be paid reasonably on the rare occasions when they get work. My associate Sophie Clarke-Jervoise (later head of BBC Comedy and then Tiger Aspect TV) was worried about the budget, so I did what any sensible person would do, I told her to do the negotiating herself.

> **LESSON: It's rare to hear the words 'producer' and 'generous' in the same sentence. You're more likely to hear the words 'producer' and 'mean bastard', or 'producer' and 'penny-pinching pig-weasel' or 'producer', 'stuff it' and 'up his jaxie' in the same sentence.**

Murder Most Sordid

Agreeing deals is always tricky on an anthology series like *Murder Most Horrid*. As I learned when an actress who shall remain nameless (no, honestly, it wouldn't be fair) came to me and said she'd discovered that the actor she was playing opposite was being paid more than she was. (This is a current hot topic rearing its head 20 years too soon.) What should she do? Sack her agent? Leave the set? Listen to my explanation? (Come *on*, even *I* wouldn't have been convinced by that.)

She had said 'yes' to the job (and the money) very early on, when we were just *starting* to cast the episode she was in, and she'd accepted our modest first offer. We then had great trouble finding someone to play opposite her. When we finally found someone reasonably well known with a pulse and his own set of teeth, we were so relieved that we gave in to his agent's demands for a fee that would have made a professional footballer jealous. So I said to the actress, 'Well the thing is that *you* get killed on day three of a six-day shoot whereas *he* doesn't get arrested until day six. Also, your agent is a pushover, and the actor you're playing opposite is a lot less famous than you, but he and his agent are both money-grabbing greedy gutter rats.'

What I *actually* said was, 'You're so good that we had to spend a long time looking for someone good enough to play opposite you. Sadly we need him for a teensie bit longer than we need you. Oh, and by the way, I love what you're doing with the part, and I've *always* loved your work!'

She replied, 'Thanks and I sort of understand, but I wonder whether, because my fee is so low, I might keep my costume?'

'Let me talk to the costume designer and see if that's OK,' I said, seeing a way out of the conversation.

I talked to the costume designer and she was happy. Well, she was happy until just after the actress had said her goodbyes. Suddenly I had a rather desperate costume designer running towards me.

'Jon, she's gone to the costume racks and taken *everything in her size*! She must've thought we'd finished. Most of the frocks weren't even for this episode, let alone her character. She's not the only size [I remain discreet] on this shoot! So we need to get them back, *now*!'

'Hello.' (I'm on the phone to her home) 'Good, you got home all right, and thanks *so* much for your work with us, which the editor tells me is looking *very* good. There's just one small problem. Those things from the wardrobe department, not all of them were for your character, so there's a car on its way to pick them up. If that's OK.'

The driver got them back to us whether it was OK or not. I still wonder. Was it a mistake, or revenge for being, in her opinion, underpaid?

I think I would work with *her* again but not with the clearly overpaid actor. After all, he must have told her what he was getting for the job! No help at all. And such bad form!

> **LESSON: Be careful what you agree to, even if you're in a tight spot. Exercise the same care that you would when offering a locust just the tiniest nibble from a lettuce leaf.**

I learned another lesson on the series, and that is – always check the shot. Surely that's the director's job or the cameraman's job, you cry. Yes, thank you, I agree. But as the producer, you are definitely the one left carrying the can.

There was a large reception scene in one episode, set around a small outdoor swimming pool. Several extras were milling about with drinks in their hands and the main action took place between two characters in the foreground. These are the people we were meant to be watching. Good. But then I went to the edit.

I don't often go to early edits, because the editor and the director should get on with it until they've made a first cut, so I was just passing by. I watched a section of the party scene and then asked them to 'freeze' one of the wide shots. There in the corner of the party, was a HUGE 10K light which none of us had noticed before. This is a light on a stand. Think of the sort of thing you might see on the edge of the stage at a rock concert – a swaggering, pumped up, pleased-with-itself, un-ignorable light. There it was in the middle of the shot. One of those things that *somehow* you don't spot, and then can't take your eyes off. It was there for all the actors to see, but *they* wouldn't have known how wide the shot was. The cameraman clearly either missed it, or thought it was 'set decoration'. The director was clearly watching the actors. But there it was! We got rid of it with some expensive bit of magic in the edit, but it just shows that even with 27 eyes on something it can go wrong. (Er – yes: 27.We had a one-eyed props man.)

It happens. The estimable director John Henderson tells me that he was directing a film in which a naked actor, Nigel Planer, had to run across a shot. Everyone is concentrating so hard on Nigel and his bits that they miss the presence of a sound man fully clothed – holding a boom microphone – crouched in the corner of the frame. In this case, it took an eagle-eyed viewer to write in when the film was broadcast. Clearly Nigel held no charms for this member of the public.

LESSON: Check what's in the frame. It may surprise you. See stories about plastic water bottles on shelves in period dramas, iPhones on escritoires in *Pride and Prejudice* etc.

We all of us screw up from time to time.

I should also say that Dawn and the various writers did very good work on the series. It is perhaps one of the problems with this sort of show that its main performers are slightly taken for granted. Reece Shearsmith and Steve Pemberton in their series, and Dawn in this deliver a huge range of characters and performances over a series without anyone batting an eyelid. One character over six weeks of a sitcom must be slightly easier than waking up every Monday morning and realising that a new character must be created this week and then another next.

14

Travels with
Ab Fab

'Don't worry I'll put some jokes in later'
– J. Saunders

So in order to write this chapter I've spoken to Jennifer and she said that she can't remember anything. Joanna said that if I mention her at all in connection with the show then she'll 'send the boys round'. Julia Sawalha was sweetness itself but said that she's been going through a lot of therapy in order to forget. Jane Horrocks said that she will sue if I associate her with the show in any way. June Whitfield said, 'Yes dear, I was in it. What was it again?'

So, I'm on my own here. I remember that it was a mixture of huge fun, chaos and nightmare. OK, it was fun more than nightmare. By a short head.

Somewhere early in 1991 I got a phone call from Jen's agent, Maureen Vincent, saying, 'Now, Jon, you know Jennifer better than some, and this is just to give you a heads-up.

Apparently, Jennifer is writing a sitcom. Now you know and I know that this may never happen, but I just thought I should let you know.'

I'm very glad that she did.

It was written in pencil in an exercise book and it was based on two characters who had been in a sketch from the previous series of *French and Saunders*. The sketch was called 'Modern Mother and Daughter'. Jen played Adrianna, a bohemian woman with a shop, who was about to party hard downstairs. She wants her straight-laced daughter, busy working at her desk, to join in the fun. Saffron, the daughter, is studying hard upstairs. Adrianna wants her to put her books away. And not go away to university. Especially to study physics.

ADRIANNA: Where is it you're going?
SAFFRON: Aberdeen.
MOTHER: Aber-bloody-deen! I don't know anybody in
            Aber-bloody-deen, darling. What am I going
            to do?

It's all about Adrianna and it will always be all about Adrianna, even when she changes her name to Edina.

The script has been written partly because Jennifer is feeling a bit neglected. Dawn and Lenny want to adopt a child and we have a French and Saunders on the slate when a little girl comes along who is just the right size. So the series is put on hold and Jennifer thinks, 'I'll have a go at a sitcom.' She is a little wary of it, hence the exercise book and pencil. We get it typed up and it is presumed that I will produce at least the pilot because of my history with *French and Saunders*. So that's another fine mess I've got myself into.

When I read it, I can see that it has a lot of energy and good character gags, but the landscape is unfamiliar to me

– it's about fashion and PR, a world I don't know anything about (it's often been said that I have the dress sense of a colourblind pig farmer). I'm concerned that it may just appeal to an audience who are 'in the know'. Are these designers real, or has Jen made them up? Who is Bubble and who is Patsy? Is this based in any kind of reality or is it a comic creation? Are we OK that Princess Anne is coming to a fashion show? Will we need a lookalike? Are we laughing at or with the characters?

Everyone agrees that a pilot might be useful (a 'pilot' is a kind of try-out as well as a fish, and a man at the front of a plane). Some of my questions are answered by a chat with Jen, but not all. I'm sure I'll find out more as we go along. At least I now know that Christian Lacroix is a real designer. I also know that his creations are expensive, so let's hope for a big budget or some cheap imitations. Ring costume designer.

So on to auditions and casting. Jennifer is obviously playing Edina and Bob Spiers is directing. He is keen that we see Julia Sawalha for Saffy, because he has worked with her on 23 episodes of *Press Gang*, a teenage drama written by Stephen Moffat for ITV. We see her, and quite a few other girls, for the part and the only problem with Julia is that she is a tad older than the schoolgirl Jen has written. But she can act the part very well, so we offer it.

Patsy is more of a challenge. Jennifer has based her partly on a character from a TV film by Les Blair about advertising, but the actress who played that part isn't quite right. We offer it to another well-known comic actress who sits on it for quite a while and then says, 'No, I'm really sorry, but I feel I've played this part before.'

When? WHERE?? Did anybody see her do it?

There's nothing unusual about this, but it is frustrating.

At the time, there is a play running in the West End (but not for long) called *Vanilla,* directed by Harold Pinter. It stars Sian Phillips, Charlotte Cornwall and Joanna Lumley. By chance I've seen it and so has Ruby Wax (friend and confidant of Ms Saunders), so we send Jennifer along to the show because Ms Lumley is proving that she can play high comedy very well. Her character is something like Imelda Marcos, and (in a play that doesn't quite work) she's giving it everything she's got. The play has come off by the time we're in a position to offer Joanna the part, when – as previously noted – she's babysitting Terry Wogan's chat show. We get the script down to her at the Television Theatre in Shepherd's Bush and 24 hours later she has said 'Yes.' Thank God! We've found Patsy and she proves, as the world now knows, to be beyond great (or indeed – absolutely fabulous…). Her background as a sixties fashion model is also very useful in developing the character. Joanna has been there, done that and worn the frocks. Also, as she demonstrated to the audience during the studio warm-ups later in the run, she went to the Lucie Clayton Modelling School and knows how to get in and out of a Mini in the shortest of skirts without showing anything unnecessary. A useful skill. She knows first-hand the world of *Absolutely Fabulous.* Speaking to her recently about her first impressions of the script she said, 'I just thought – bloody hell this is funny, I'd better do it. Also, the first episode was about fashion shows and models and I knew about that. It was "full on" in a way that most comedies at the time weren't. These characters had no redeeming features and that seemed so good and daring, and they were talking about things like "having tits down to their knees". Goodness. I couldn't resist. I didn't know that comedy could go this far, but I thought – well, if they will, so will I.'

Bubble is no relation of socialite Bubbles Rothermere. She is part-PA and part-ungrateful child. As first written she was a Sloane, a not-very-bright girl who probably lived in a basement flat just off the King's Road two doors down from Fergie and knew people. Bubble has a fantastic address book and that's why Edina wants her. We'd seen a few girls who could play that but who didn't have the requisite madness. We were still seeing people for Saffy when Jane Horrocks walked in. We all agreed that Jane was a bit too old to be Jen's daughter and, frankly, a bit too northern. She was, and is, an actress of considerable range, with a mighty singing voice hardly used in *Ab Fab*, so Jen then asked her if she'd have a look at Bubble.

'What voice do you want it in cos I might not be very good at Sloaney?'

'Try it in your own voice.'

She did, and Bubble now came from Rochdale, but curiously that was perfect. Later she told me that she based Bubble on her six-year-old niece. We were lucky to get her because *Little Voice* was a big hit at the time.

LESSON: Now, I know that writers of books like this always say: 'It was at that moment that we knew we had our Lady Bracknell!' without mentioning all the other people who came in and could, very possibly, have played the parts. So let me say at this point 'Thank you' to anyone who came in to see us for this (or any other show) and didn't get a part. You should have and you will. Keep at it!

With the show cast, Jennifer turned her attention to what it might look like. She knew more than many of us about the kind of houses that Edina might live in. So she went shopping with the set designer, a gentle chap called Bryan Ellis. He was close to retirement, but the challenge of this show brought him back to life. Suddenly he was able to work from the catalogues of designers whom he *knew* about, but never in his wildest dreams thought would be needed for a sitcom. He was born again. No more three-piece suites and Magnet kitchens, we were in the world of one-off wrought-iron beds and kilims from Turkey, isolation tanks and panic rooms.

Jennifer also spent a lot of time with the wardrobe department. They would always get things for Edina that were several sizes too small, so that Jen looked as fat as possible. Sarah, our wardrobe lady, told horrific stories of going into Harvey Nichols with Jennifer and making her try on gorgeous designer clothes that just didn't fit. As time went on, shop assistants got the joke, but in the early days there was quite a lot of, 'Madam looks great but we do have other sizes that might flatter her shape rather more.' Imagine their anguish when Jen insisted on an 8 rather than a 14 (I'm just guessing here) and had to breathe in a lot.

We began rehearsing the pilot and then the first series. It was an interesting process, and showed how things would be for the next few years. We had a script that was – essentially – a skeleton. Flesh and muscle were added as we went. Sometimes Ruby Wax would watch a full rehearsal and then take Jennifer off for lunch and suggest sharper exit lines or entrances or whole scenes. Jen would scribble these down and then come back and say: 'I'm going to rewrite a few sections I've been talking about with Ruby, so maybe we should finish for today and there'll be a new script tomorrow.'

Actually, this *didn't* happen on the pilot, but once we had a series, it happened more and more. Scripts at the beginning of a production week became more and more skeletal, and had to put on greater and greater amounts of weight during rehearsals. I can only recommend this way of working as a means of increasing sluggish blood-pressure levels.

I'm looking at a script dated 31 May 1994.

The front page says: 'Series 3, Episode 1, Door Handle by Jennifer Saunders' then in slightly smaller type, '1st Draft – No jokes at all yet.'

She was right, and that's how it always was until rehearsals got Jen's comedy brain working.

Back to the pilot. Rehearsals went pretty well as people found their characters. Joanna got over her fear that Jennifer hated her (no, really) which early on prompted her to call her agent to see if she could get out of the show. Thankfully, her agent told her to stick it out. If Jennifer didn't talk to Joanna to begin with, it was simply because Jen was a bit shy. Yes – Edina Monsoon – shy! Over time they became the closest of friends. At the start, Jennifer's idea was that *Ab Fab* would be Edina's story and Patsy wouldn't always be in the show. The moment we went in front of an audience all that changed. The audience *loved* Ms Lumley being louche. She *had* to be a main building block of the show if it was to go to series.

On the afternoon of the pilot recording I was in the gallery of the studio. The rehearsal had played well with the crew and a few invited guests, but when I approached the then head of comedy, Robin Nash, his view was different.

ME: Well what did you think, Robin?
ROBIN: I've never found women being drunk very funny.
ME: Ah. There goes the series.

Thank God, the audience in the evening had a different view! They laughed long and loud. If we had a problem, it was that the show ran too long. It should have been 28/29 minutes but it actually ran 36 with laughs. Something had to go. Fortunately, Nickolas Grace, playing a neurotic designer at the fashion show Eddy has organised, had a long monologue that could be cut without damaging the main plot, so that was where the axe fell.

> **LESSON: Never be a guest star on a pilot show when your main contribution is in any way extraneous to the plot. The production team will have timed the show without laughter, so if the audience get hysterical, your guest star credit may be destined forever to look odd. Sorry Nick!**

Now all we had to do was persuade the ribald, round and rigorous Jim Moir (he of the famous willy-waving) that we should make a series of the show.

A person who helped us hugely with this was Jim Moir's PA. She had heard that our show was very funny, so when a copy went up to Jim's office she got hold of it first and invited a few friends round one lunchtime to watch. Jim came in while this screening was underway and saw a group of ladies having a very good laugh. The show had reached its target audience early, and Jim virtually nodded the show through there and then, telling the controller of BBC2 he had a new hit on the way.

I hope his PA got the small brown envelope of used fivers we left on her desk?

We were also helped by the way in which French and Saunders had come to work at the BBC. They had arrived via the variety artistes' entrance, not the one reserved for comedy. This meant they were treated in the same way as, say, Morecambe and Wise, so they had two days in the studio for each show rather than just the one that comedies normally had to manage with. I don't know how this stroke of luck came about, but it meant that we had one day to pre-record difficult stunts with Eddy and Patsy and one day to record the show with an audience. So in later episodes, Lady Penelope had the time to get her strings in a twitch without anybody seeing how long and complicated a process this was, and Jennifer had the time to wear ludicrous collagen lips in a dream sequence. Ah the luxury!

So Jen set off to write the series. As with most TV shows, we did the filming before we went into the studio. This was made up of all the exterior sequences that would be 'played in' to the studio audience on the night of the otherwise 'live' recording. Jennifer wrote the scenes we had to film first, and it wasn't until after we'd shot these that she wrote all the scenes for the studio (the bulk of any show). I think she has a thing in her brain which says, 'If I kick it around as much as possible in my head before I write it down, then there's a chance it will get good. As soon as I write it down it's dead, and I can't change it, so I won't write it down till the last possible moment.'

If this wasn't the case, then it's difficult to account for certain behaviours. For instance, Jennifer sidling up to me halfway through making the first series to ask if she can just have a *quick* look at what we'd filmed for episode six, because she can't exactly remember and she needs to fit the filming into what she's now writing for the episode. In other words, she needs to retro-fit the filming into the script. This is not how it's usually done. Usually, all the episodes are written ahead of time. We let Jen do it her way, because for her it works even if it does for no one else. And this is very important. Of course, it's tricky for the rest of the production team, who have to get a complex event ready to record. There are deadlines to meet and sets to build, cast to book and costumes to sort. There are also actors who want to know when they can start learning lines. I'd say they mostly had to do this the night before the show. Her method works but it's nerve-wrenching for everyone else!

The person I felt sorriest for was Joanna. Early on, Jennifer treated her as if she were Dawn French. With Dawn, Jen would throw her a line and if it was different from what was scripted, then Dawn could go with it and bounce something back. Joanna wasn't used to this way of doing things. She wanted a script and then, once she knew it, she could loosen up – but not before. Sorry, Jo.

★ ★ ★

During series one we adopted a good idea of Jennifer's. Why didn't we reduce the filming for each episode and use the money thereby saved to finance one foreign trip per series? So in series one we went to France, in series two we went to Morocco and in series three we went to New York, where in fact we shot inserts for two episodes. Good idea, especially given the international flavour of the business that Patsy and Edina were in: 'Fash trash rags and fash PR'.

The French episode was the story of Patsy, Edina and later Bubble going to the south of France where they mistake a tiny workman's cottage for the chateau that they thought they'd booked. No one speaks French so they can't understand the old man who keeps turning up to try to put them right. Fiction and fact weren't so far removed because *our* French wasn't that fluent. For instance, I couldn't easily explain to the owner of a vineyard where we filmed that these two loud Englishwomen wanted to taste wines and would be acting drunkenly in his 'cave' during their 'degustation'. We were not laughing at him or his wine but at these ladies. So *I* played the wine-maker myself, and the look of frustration on my face is no part of my performance. It's just worry that we were on take 12, using real wine, which made these 'ladies' unable to finish a take without collapsing in helpless laughter.

Despite this, we were more adventurous on the Morocco trip in our next series. There was a sequence where Eddy, Patsy and Saffy had to walk across the very crowded Jemaa el-Fnaa. This is a famously beautiful square in the centre of Marrakesh. By the end of their crossing, Saffy has disappeared because Patsy has sold her into the slave trade. The square is fairly notorious and women are advised not to cross alone. We had three large bodyguards with them at all times but this did not stop a great deal of propositioning, touching and pinching. Jennifer wrote the scene, so only had herself to blame, but Joanna and Julia had to put up with a lot. The crew were fine because we were filming the whole sequence from the safety of a hotel balcony three floors up on one side of the square.

Even more dangers awaited us on series three in New York. (My blood runs cold as I remember this.) (Thank you for the sympathy.)

By this time in the narrative Patsy has taken a job with a magazine in NYC but is alone and lost. Eddy misses her and so flies across the Atlantic for a reunion. They meet on top of the Carnegie Hall tower in midtown Manhattan. Eddy comes up over the edge of the tower in a helicopter. Patsy is drinking from a bottle of vodka alone on the roof. So far so tricky, especially given that one of our stars, also our writer, is scared of heights and we are 60 storeys above a city of 1.5 million people in a helicopter. Something that is now illegal.

It could have been worse and nearly was. As we were setting up to do the sequence, we got word that reporters and a photographer from the *News of the World* were at the same heliport as Jennifer, downtown. They were planning to hire another helicopter to chase ours across the skies of New York in order to get a shot of Joanna on the roof of the Carnegie Tower. This would endanger lives, make Jennifer even more nervous, and screw up our shot. It showed no respect for life, limb or comedy, and all for the sake of a photograph! I left the set-up and went downtown immediately to reason with them. Needless to say, I failed.

'We just want a set-up shot, mate. That's what we've been sent 3000 miles to get. That's what the London desk want.'

I explained that whilst I do not wish to stand in the way of their artistic and pictorial endeavours, frankly I'd be happier if they could take a helicopter to JFK and catch a flight home. Maybe I suggested this a tad un-politely.

They rejected my suggestion. The only way out of this ghastly dilemma was to give them what they wanted, a picture of Joanna Lumley with a bottle in her hand on top of a skyscraper with the Manhattan skyline behind her. A simple enough request you might think, just one 'click' and they've gone. Except that photographs on set are valuable currency that every newspaper wants. Properly handled, this picture could have appeared in many papers. Once just *one* of them prints it before the others, then none of the others want to know. The *News of the World* were aware that the BBC had said 'No photos while filming' and yet they'd decided to ignore that request. However, nothing was worth endangering Jennifer, Joanna and the lives of 1.5 million people for. Reluctantly we gave them what they wanted, we saved Mr Murdoch the cost of the helicopter, and the picture appeared the following Sunday in a *quarter*-page spread on page *17*. Bastards! Still – the *News of the World* is now dead and buried. There is some justice.

The *Radio Times* for 7–13 November 1992 has a picture of Joanna and Jennifer on the cover and the subheading '*It's Lumley and Saunders keeping up with the trendies. Absolutely Fab! New comedy for autumn on BBC2.*' On the programme page it says that this is 'the first of a new comedy series set in the trendy world of media'. It is. The show is watched on that far-off November Thursday by 7.7 million people. This is a *very good figure*. A new series starting on BBC2 now would rejoice at a million and a bit. The audience now is dissipated over far more channels and choices.

The reaction to *Ab Fab* is good: 'Funniest sitcom of the year' says one critic, 'works magnificently', 'Joanna is a revelation', 'vicious, bitchy and brilliant'. There is one exception, *The Times*, whose critic says that the show is 'Out of date and a little old-fashioned'. Oh, and George Melly (of all people!) on a TV show called *Did You See?* tells viewers that it wasn't funny because 'alcoholism, particularly among women is a serious business and not really to be laughed at.'

The rest of the press clearly disagree and we notice headlines like 'PM says economy is *Ab Fab*' or 'Stars come out for *Ab Fab* time at new club', that sort of thing. When our lines and title begin to be used in stories that are nothing to do with us, we know we've entered the consciousness of the nation.

Papers begin to invent more possible models for the characters. Patsy is based, according to a double-page spread in the *Daily Mail*, on Janet Street-Porter! Can I just say on behalf of Jennifer *and* Janet Street-Porter that the idea is ludicrous? I don't think that Janet ever really modelled or did a fashion shoot in her life. Yet it is in this way that we know before the end of the first series that we are a hit, bordering on a National Institution. A second series is quickly commissioned. The mere announcement of this gets us a front-page picture in the *Independent*.

So why does it work? Well, if you've been following me you'll already know the answer: character and surprise.

The character bit is obvious. Patsy and Eddy are like very few comedy characters we've ever met, and the same goes for Saffy, Bubble and Mother. They're unfamiliar, but strongly delineated. We know how Patsy will react in any given situation and that Edina will follow her. We know that there's a tiny bit of Eddy that feels just a smidgeon of responsibility for her daughter and her business. Just a smidgeon. We know that Bubble will always fail to grasp anything asked of her, the very opposite of a good PA. Saffy, the most straight of all the characters, is the polar opposite of her mother and her mother's best friend, which is why Patsy would love to stub cigarettes out in her hair. Bubble is a dysfunctional child, but Mother is also a child. Sharper and more wily, she is a kleptomaniac, and tactlessly critical of her daughter.

And it's endlessly surprising.

It's surprising that Edina falls drunkenly out of a car and then drunkenly down into the basement of her own house.

It's surprising that after all her incompetence and betrayals, she can still get hold of 'names, names, names' for her fashion show and not be lynched.

It's surprising that Harvey Nichols will still let them in, that Eddy can persuade both ex-husbands to pay her alimony and that a blind woman gets her own back for being mocked, by feeling Eddy and pronouncing her fat!

Reversing expectations is often the key to the greatest surprises. When Patsy is trying to bring back coke into the UK (no surprise), we're delighted (and Patsy is horrified) when the substance she's hiding turns out to be just talcum powder. Her dealer conned her! That springs a great surprise.

LESSON: If you're writing a comedy, make the characters consistent, make the situation one we've not seen before, and the surprises HUGE. P.S. you'll need good actors.

An extra surprise for *us* was that, after a couple of series, the show was sold to America, initially to Comedy Central. The Americans took us to their hearts, certainly on the East Coast and the West Coast, maybe less so in 'the flyover states'. In New York, they proudly published glossaries explaining things like Stolly and Bolly and Harvey Nicks but also things like: 'Shandy: a benign combination of lager and ginger ale popular with those new to drinking' and 'Lulu: singer, plays herself, known to US audiences for 1967 film *To Sir with Love*. Has continued to have career in the UK ever since'. Best of all 'Buggery bollocks: abusive term, usually connected to self-flagellation.' Nearly

Ab Fab has something in common with sharp, quick-witted American comedies, Jennifer had always been a big fan of *The Lucy Show,* and there is something of Lucy in Edina. It's perhaps a bit of a stretch to imagine Lucy telling her daughter that Vivian will be allowed into America because she hasn't got a drug conviction, and Vivian replying, 'It's not a conviction. Just a firm belief.' (Patsy's response.) It's quick and sharp but probably not something that Ms Ball would ever have allowed. 'Fabulous' is not a lifestyle choice, it's a way of life.

This next section might involve dropping a few names,

forgive me. I haven't exactly been a shy retiring no-namer up to now but I'm going to get worse.

When series three was launched in the USA we were flown out (not at the BBC's expense) by Concorde to New York, because the New York Senate had decided to pass a bill. The bill stated that there would be an *Absolutely Fabulous* week in the city to coincide with what Jennifer called 'LBGBLT week'.

We didn't really have to sing for our supper. Jen and Joanna had to judge a Patsy and Edina drag look-a-likey competition at a gay club in the Meatpacking District, but that was about it. Before this, there was a big reception at the New York Senate House. We slightly misjudged this. It was an event with a serious side. A number of people who had done very good and important work for the gay community (doctors, nurses, writers) were also in attendance (Aids was still rampaging through the community). Jo and Jen came not *quite* in fancy dress, but nearly – clothes that hinted at Pats and Ed. Thankfully, nobody minded. It was a celebration of all things LGBT, after all. Michael C Hall was there from *Six Feet Under* and *Dexter*, Olympia Dukakis from *Tales of the City*, and Peter Paige from the US *Queer as Folk*. Rufus Wainwright and Whoopi Goldberg were there too.

Whoopi was due to present Jen and Jo with their award for services to the LGBT community at the top of the bill. Prior to the presentation, a much-praised lesbian received her award from the Senate and after thanking everybody said, 'Can I just take this opportunity to say how much I've always really fancied Jennifer Saunders who is here tonight!' Cheers and applause.

For Jen, this was a nightmare: being praised in public was one thing, but being flirted with! She's a shy person, and at this moment she wasn't just shy but also *confused* and *embarrassed* and didn't know how to react.

Whoopi stood up. She said, 'Damn you, woman, I was going to use that line!'

This, of course, helped to defuse the moment, but there was still some embarrassment. Maybe because Jen still had a stars and stripes scarf tied raffishly around her Stetson.

Later that evening after some alcohol had been consumed (you may find that hard to believe) we were in a limo on our way to the gay meatpacking disco. As we neared the club, the car was surrounded in the nearest thing to Beatlemania I have ever experienced. There were queens dressed as Patsy and Edina all round the car and all around the block. There were even a few dressed as Marilyn and Cher, some confusion, surely. As the ladies and I got out of the car we were mobbed and had to fight our way into the club helped only by two or three queens dressed as security guards (or hey! It's just occurred to me – maybe they *were* security guards.) We were led to a roped-off VIP area above the general mayhem and introduced to Debbie Harry and her group who were there just because they wanted to be.

Jennifer and Joanna then began judging. Some of the guys had made a huge effort, some slightly less so. They paraded up and down a catwalk and some looked like hookers on the prowl (indeed they may have been) whilst others looked like home counties ladies in twinset and pearls. They gave a special award to the guy who'd come as Saffy to help his obviously low self-esteem. Overall our girls were *maybe* a little too British in their comments – 'Well done for trying so hard' rather than 'WOW you've gone to so much trouble!' – but, as Joanna said, it was all '*pour encourager les autres*'. Speeches and thanks were made and then we were introduced to Cyndi Lauper, who was also entertaining the guys that night. She didn't know whether it was Tuesday or Christmas, and certainly didn't know what *Ab Fab* was.

In any event, I think that I was back in my hotel room by about 2 a.m., very little harm done. The girls came back a *tiny* bit later.

Having conquered a bit of America, the show now went skiing in Val d'Isere, for a two-parter called *The Last Shout*. We arrived late in the season which meant that there was a shortage of snow. So, crew and cast had to lug cameras, lights, costumes, boxes of lipstick, crates of Bolly, snow-proof wigs and themselves ever higher into the thinning Alpine air.

The second part of this special was the rather chaotic filming of Saffy's near-wedding to Paolo (Tom Hollander). It was shambolic because you need a lot of coverage to film weddings, and here we had the added problem that Jennifer hadn't quite finished the script. Shooting took place in the Scottish Presbyterian church in Pont Street, London. It was typical of the day that the vicar was played by the *actual* vicar of the church, because we hadn't had time to find a fake one.

We also went to New York *again*, to film an episode at New York Fashion Week where Edina is reunited with her son Serge, who, to Eddy's joy, turns out to be gay. He works in the Strand bookshop and she eventually finds him after a long safari past miles and miles of shelves. We filmed up and down them and in and out of them, and the Strand couldn't have been nicer. They even let the production team (me) have a sneak peek at their Shakespeare first folio and allowed us to buy books at staff discount. Thanks, chaps. Sometimes filming has its perks.

Obviously, our main home for the show was Studio 8 at BBC Television Centre, Wood Lane. We had a loyal camera crew some of whom worked well past their BBC retirement age just to be with us. But as the millennium approached, Jennifer grew slightly less in love with the show and began to feel that maybe, enough was enough. She wrote a new show called *Mirrorball*. I say a new show, although it had exactly the same cast as the old one. They were just playing slightly different people. Vivienne and Jackie are fading actresses played by Jo and Jen; Julia now plays Jen's younger sister – a much more successful actress; Jane plays an Icelandic lady with the wonderful name of Yitta Hilberstam; and June is an ageing character actress – Dora Vermouth. The show had some very good jokes: auditions for *Angela's Ashes*, the musical; Jennifer walking over a row of cars in Covent Garden. It was fun *but…* It's difficult to convince the audience about a new set of relationships *with the same cast*. We made the pilot, it was watched by a good-sized audience and then Jen went away to write the series. A few weeks later I got a phone call from her,

'Hello, it's going OK, but I'm finding it quite hard to write without Eddy and Patsy popping into my head. I thought you should know.'

'Well, if that's really a problem why don't we do another series of *Ab Fab* instead. It's the same cast, so they'll all be available. No one's going to object to another series of *Ab Fab*, I'm sure.'

'Let me think about it, but it might be a good idea. As long as you're sure nobody will mind.'

They didn't.

We carried on.

Every so often there was talk of a movie…

★ ★ ★

Somewhere in the middle of all this nonsense – I think in 2007 but I could be way out – I was invited to attend the Royal Television Society Awards. Ceremonies such as this sound terribly glamorous but by and large they're not. They're just a tiny bit tough. We were invited to quite a few with Ab Fab.

How to Produce Comedy Bronze

'How can he be so ungrateful?' you cry, 'sitting there with a glass of champagne in one hand and a forkful of steak in the other and surrounded by people we've only dreamed of meeting, and he says "tough"! I'm reading no further.'

Well yes, I understand. But consider the badly concealed rivalries, the frustration at seeing rewards for the second rate, the risks of bumping into the person who's never replied to one of your proposals, the chance of being insulted by some drunk who thinks that he could do your job *so* much better, the chic guests gradually turning into a tipsy rabble and the sheer LENGTH of the whole thing... 'tough' is putting it kindly.

So to the RTS. I had been told that Jennifer Saunders was going to get a lifetime award for services to comedy, so I was not surprised to find myself with her and her husband Ade. Over there were June Whitfield, splendid Maureen Vincent, my esteemed friend and producer Jo Sargent and entirely delightful Paul Mayhew-Archer, co-writer of *The Vicar of Dibley*. So far so good. Friendly, and just as it should be. And yes – my partner Francis was there, good. But oh, here's a nice surprise – my great friend and hugely esteemed designer Lez Brotherston, who does theatre and dance rather than TV. He knows Jennifer, of course: he's designed a stage show for her and Dawn. But what on earth is my friend Michelle Paradise doing here – an exotic and very tall American model who doesn't know Jennifer at all? Francis tells me he recruited her at the last minute because a friend of Jennifer's dropped out.

Mmm. OK. So. I went along with it for most of the evening until the RTS Judges Award for Outstanding Contribution to Television was due to be announced and it was Jennifer who got up to give it, not get it. The recipient was *me*. It had all been done behind my back. Francis handed me a sheet of paper as I got up to accept. It was the bones of a speech and came in hugely handy because my brain was completely befuddled.

LESSON: Award ceremonies aren't all they're cracked up to be; sitting at a table with a bunch of chums makes them much more bearable; getting an award is very nice indeed – thank you very much; getting an award is oddly disrespectful to a lot of talented people elsewhere in the business; and there's usually a vegetarian option if you don't eat steak.

15

A Little Bit of Stephen and Hugh

Given that one of them is now very definitely a national institution ('Oh pish-tush, Jon, and fiddle-de-de,' he says), and that the other is the highest paid actor on TV in the world ('Not true any more, Jon, I'm afraid I'm definitely on my way out'), it's quite hard to remember when they were just plain Fry and Laurie. Not that either of them are *plain*. No, plain is certainly not the word.

In a way, they weren't so different back then in the early nineties. I'd worked with both of them at the very beginning of their careers so I knew what they were like, except that now they were more so. Stephen was still horribly bright and would swoop down on the tiniest errors in my use of English, though he still couldn't sing and movement was never his strongest suit. Hugh could sing well and play the piano and the guitar *really* well, but he still had the confidence of a baby hamster being interviewed by Jeremy Paxman.

My abiding memory of rehearsals is Hugh saying, 'This isn't

very good is it? We're going to die a sad horrible death in this sketch, aren't we? I just suck in it, don't I?'

After which his partner would begin by reassuring him, 'No, Hugh, you'll be fine in this. It's not the greatest sketch ever written but it's damn close.' And then, when Hugh would not be heartened, the tone would change. 'No, you're absolutely right, Hugh. There'll probably be some loud booing followed by the sound of seats flapping up, as most of the audience leave. More blood will be spilt than there was that November day in Dallas.'

Both of these approaches were forms of encouragement for 'm'colleague, Hugh' who would get on with it but was always a slightly nervous performer. At Cambridge, Hugh was captain of *Goldie* (this is a boat, not a *Blue Peter* dog), which has a race against *Isis* (the Oxford boat) just before the Boat Race proper every year. He told us that he still had dreams, even then – *years* later – about *just* losing to Oxford by a very short distance. He still woke up from time to time in a cold sweat. I hope he's over all that now.

★ ★ ★

Ab Fab had brought a bit of fame to its producer and director, enough at least to mean that some nice things came our way.

Bob and I worked on the fourth series of *A Bit of Fry and Laurie*. Hugh and Stephen had come up with a different style for the show for this series. Instead of several sketches strung together, they wanted to try a format that had more in common with variety shows. Acting as hosts, they would introduce two guests who were going to be their principal supporting artists (or fodder) for the evening. Sketches would follow. Some of these were fake vox-pops with all the characters played by Stephen or Hugh, male and female, some were longer sketches that might feature the week's guests. At the end of the show, the guests would gather round Hugh's piano and a bar where Stephen would make disgusting cocktails. All four would then raise a glass of whatever hideous concoction Stephen had made for them.

This made for a slightly friendlier, warmer show than before. It did mean, however, that they had to write it *as a show*. Indeed, it's the only sketch show I've ever worked on where the whole thing was written from start to finish, more like a sitcom. They knew from the get-go the order in which the material would run, unlike most sketch shows where the sequence is worked out later in the edit, with or without the artist's input.

Watching the shows again recently I was struck by how hard-hitting they were. There is a parody of *It's a Wonderful Life*, the Frank Capra film where an angel stops James Stewart committing suicide by showing him how much sadder the world would have been if he had never lived. Stephen plays the angel and Hugh plays Rupert Murdoch. In this version, Murdoch is shown how much *better* the world would have been had he never been born. The angel gets so depressed that finally *he* jumps in the river instead of Murdoch.

The show itself begins with Hugh lamenting the dark state of a world where, 'The air in our cities is unbreathable, and politicians are so feeble-minded and gutless that you can't even hate them…'

…thereby bringing his previously bright and optimistic comedy partner to the same gloomy point of view. In another sketch, a woman arrives home to find that her husband has stabbed both her parents to death. They quickly come to the view that the low standard of the local social services is to blame. They should have stopped him doing this, it was clearly a tragedy waiting to happen. Another exchange reveals that the show will be abiding by the 'comedy charter' and that 'charter marks' will be awarded for good material and gags delivered with the right timing. Not too fast and not too slow. The disdain with which Stephen utters the words 'charter marks' indicates his contempt for the state of the whole of Britain today

Even the songs in the show, written and sung by Hugh, have a dark, dystopian tone. One – a love song – is written in the character of Steffi Graf's stalker, and another is a Dylan-esque number that promises an answer to the world's ills, and contains this chorus. 'All we gotta do is…' followed by incomprehensible muttering and perplexed expressions. There is no answer.

The shows may have had a bleak edge, but they're bloody funny. Their stars have never stopped entertaining us, here and in the US, ever since. Maybe they were going through a bleak phase because they'd just finished being *Jeeves and Wooster* – two of the brightest creatures who ever walked or drank tea. Maybe they were both terminally depressed and I just didn't notice. Or perhaps comedy is always a bleak business skewering our fate as helpless slaves in a cosmic dictatorship of meaningless chaos.

Yup. That'll be it.

16

Bottoms and Arm$_S$

We were in Nacogdoches, Texas back in 1978 when Rik Mayall broke my arm.

'Who's "we"? Explain yourself. And don't expect pity.'

'We' were The Oxford and Cambridge Shakespeare Company and we were touring America with a production of Mr Shakespeare's *A Comedy of Errors*. Keener fans of the late Mr Mayall will know that he was not an Oxbridge chap; he was here in Texas by talent alone. The theatre company, OCSC for short, had been the idea of some people like Jonathan Miller and John Madden (*Shakespeare in Love* director) back in the late sixties and early seventies. Its aim was to tour American universities with productions of Shakespeare performed by the cream of the crop of Oxbridge actors. The tours were organised and enabled by a US theatre and music promoter.

We flew to New York and did our first performance in Berkeley, California, covering the intervening 4,139 kilometres on a specially hired Greyhound bus. The promoter had realised that he could save $63 by not flying us directly to San

Francisco. The vast road trip gave us a chance to get to know America and each other on a diet of drugs and hamburgers.

A Comedy of Errors requires two sets of identical twins, one pair posh, the other less so. We had decided not just to recruit actors from the two universities that chase each other in boats up and down the Thames, but also to expand our intake via the National Student Drama Festival in York. It was here that we met and cast Rik. He was brilliant on first meeting, a combination of nervous energy and ferocious comic ability, a must-have even then. Onstage, he fascinated both the eye and the mind, and invented comic business as though he'd been doing it for years. You can imagine. Playing Dromio of Syracuse, the sparky and bewildered twin brother of the identical Dromio of Ephesus, Rik stole the play. He not only won over the crowds but he gave us a hint of what was coming in *The Young Ones*, *Kevin Turvey* and later, *Bottom*.

He was also irritatingly good-looking. God, I hate talented, good-looking people. How dare they?

Back to my fracture.

Nacogdoches is not necessarily a must-see town nor is it a sparkling centre of Western civilisation as it's not so very far from the East Texas border with Louisiana. It romances you with that heady mixture of Way Out West, Way Out East and Way Down South. It has a sister city called Nachitoches (no, really) and is the biggest blueberry producer in Texas. It was the first place where oil was struck in the state. It also has the Stephen F. Austin State University and our intrepid promoter must have spotted a theatre there. So it came to pass that in 1978 a bunch of university 'mummers' unpacked their skips and hat boxes in Nacogdoches. It was also the place where I was leaving the tour because I had a job to get back to in the UK, at the Arts Council (astonishing).

In honour of my farewell, a party was held after the

show in the motel where we were staying. This motel had a swimming pool and Mr Mayall and a few others decided it would be a good idea to throw me, fully clothed, into this pool to celebrate my departure. Meanwhile I had decided that it might be amusing to shave off half the beard that I was sporting in honour of the half of the tour they all had left to do.

As Rik and friends picked me up to swing me into the pool I was, to be honest, against the idea. So mid-swing, I managed to get my left hand free and put it down on the ground. My body continued on its swing out to the pool, with the result that my arm snapped with one bit of it pointing north and the other bit towards Mexico. Agony. AGONY. All awareness of comedy gone. No sense of humour anywhere to be found. My admiration for Rik, now questionable.

I could just hear the following dialogue over my screams, and suddenly realised that a) I was not under the NHS out there (what's that all about?) and b) the merry band of players had scarpered…with a few honourable exceptions who were now getting me some medical help from the motel staff.

'Sir, sir, would you like an ambulance to be called?'

'Yes, I bloody would!'

'Would you like an anaesthetist?'

'Yes of course I damn well would, I'm in agony.'

Note the British phlegm and good cheer in the face of adversity. The ambulance arrived pretty smartly.

'Sir, sir, which hospital would you like us to take you to?'

'I don't care. The nearest might be a good idea cos I've broken my bloody arm!'

We get to the nearest medical facility, the excitingly named Nacogdoches Bone Clinic, and the first question I'm asked when I'm stretchered off the ambulance is: 'Excuse me sir, but was this a shaving accident?'

'What do you think?' I scream.

The staff were now asking my entourage for credit cards.

The kind friend who was with me throughout this whole fracture debacle was one of the producers of OCSC and the man who later persuaded Richard Curtis to write *The Vicar of Dibley*. His name was Peter Bennett-Jones and he tells me that my screams could still be heard as they were setting my arm, despite the fact that by this point I had definitely been 'put under'. Years later, he received a letter telling him that he was banned forever from the Nacogdoches Bone Clinic because of insurance irregularities when we settled the bill. My name, thankfully, was unknown to the NBC to which I hope never to return, insurance, or no insurance.

Time passed. Rik became 'known'. He began to work with his Manchester University friend Ade Edmondson in a show called *Death on the Toilet*, a quintessential Edinburgh Fringe title. Ade was every bit as funny and inventive as Rik. If onstage Ade played the anarchist to Rik's idiot, offstage he was more often a steadying influence. For which he never gets the recognition he deserves.

Rik created Kevin Turvey on the train up from London to Manchester where he was making an early appearance in a show for Granada. Turvey is based on childhood friends from his time growing up in Redditch. He caught the gentle, steady tedium of their outlook.

Rik then moved from being 'known' to being famous as a mainstay of the sensational *Young Ones*. This was the first show to really tap into the energy of the 'alternative comedy' world in a way that spoke to millions. After that show, his agent Aude Powell (whom you rang on a London number, which then put you through to her Northumberland castle) was the first person I ever heard – when discussing Rik's movie fees – to use the phrase: 'Darling, I know it's hard to believe, but we're talking telephone numbers!'

Bottoms and Arms

When Rik and Ade worked together on television the telephone numbers shortened a bit. This was largely because they enjoyed what they did, and quite quickly found that the big money came from taking their bottoms and, later, *Bottom* on tour.

By the time I worked with them, they had already done two series of *Bottom*. Maybe they fancied a fresh face making decisions (I've always been known for my fresh face). Maybe they just wanted Bob Spiers to direct. Whereas Mrs Edmondson/Saunders wasn't the speediest at script delivery, her husband and Rik worked more quickly. The series' scripts were complete before rehearsals began so we only had to deal with rehearsal alterations and adjustments. Our principal task was to work out how to do the stunts, pratfalls and certifiably dangerous routines they wanted to perform in front of the studio audience. How do you set fire to Rik's genitals and keep them burning for quite a long period, without any harm coming to his chances of work as a porn star? How do you smash actors repeatedly with fists and doors and other household objects and not cause catastrophic injury? How do you set a Ferris wheel gondola ablaze, supposedly hundreds of feet in the air, and then let Rik's weight problem cause a dangerous hole in the thing before one side of it collapses?

The answer is you pre-record the stuff that might be tricky, and play it into the studio audience on the night. The other answer is a band of brilliant special effects guys and an elaborate series of ropes that let you safely drop half a gondola. A good sound team helps when you need to make things sound more painful than they actually are. The Ferris wheel episode, which is one of my favourites, was mostly done in a gondola set about three feet off the ground. Like some of the best episodes in the series it was just the two of them for half an hour. No other cast, just Rik and Ade and the

Hand of God. In other episodes, it might be a riot happening just out of sight a few floors down from their window.

And do you know? It never *never* occurred to me to have my revenge for the broken arm. It never *once* occurred to me to make them sit in a real gondola, 400 feet above some concrete, and ask the set builders to construct the floor out of balsa wood. Never. Now you see what a nice, forgiving person I am? Really.

Mmm.

As people, Rik and Ade were rather different. Ade understood the practicalities, and knew that comedy was a serious business in which you have to *plan* if you want to set your farts on fire, or hit someone three times with a broom handle and not end up in outpatients. Rik knew this too, but was always a slightly more wayward character – less inclined to plan, and more inclined to think it would work out on the night.

The most surprising thing about him was how nervous he got before recording. He always said, 'If you need to give me any notes before the show, give them to Ade. I'll be in my dressing room throwing up' And he was

Yet the moment he was out in front of the crowd, he was the most confident, self-assured, funny guy you could wish for.

As a final thought can I record that when, a few years before *Bottom*, I was in hospital with a broken leg, one of my first visitors was Rik.

'I never had a chance to say sorry about your arm, so I thought I'd make up for it by coming to see you legless.'

Thanks, Rik. On behalf of everyone for everything…except my broken arm.

17

The Vicar

The news can inspire comedy. Shows that seem aware of what's happening outside the comedy bubble feel as though they have more going for them than just their gags.

Gags? What are gags?

In 1994, it looked increasingly likely that – finally – women would be accepted as priests by the Church of England, and during 2006 – only 12 years later – more women than men were ordained as vicars. *What brought about this change?* Essentially, one woman who ran a small Oxfordshire parish and who, against all the odds and despite a few very stupid parishioners, rose to become a religious icon with 'a bob cut and a huge bosom'. In that respect she was much like Mother Teresa, or Joan of Arc, or Madonna. That woman was Geraldine Grainger, Vicar of Dibley.

It all began when Richard Curtis, a sort of saint himself, let it be known that he was going to write a comedy series about a female vicar. He put his marker down early, because others were very likely having the same thought, and he wanted to make sure that rival dog-collared ladies bit the dust. His first idea was to write two or three scripts, then let other people take over the characters. He would be like a US showrunner, keeping a benign eye on proceedings while a writing team did the donkey work. In the end, he found that he couldn't let Geraldine and the Parish Council go, and she wouldn't let him go either, despite finding a brilliant co-writer in the glorious form of Paul Mayhew-Archer.

Richard is extraordinary. He is originally Australian but doesn't let that stand in his way. His charm is legendary. It enables him to lure the brightest and the best to appear on Comic Relief and to be in his movies and TV series. His seduction of talent rarely fails, because people feel that it would be morally wrong to turn him down. Of course (it has to be said) they would also be passing up the chance of a lifetime.

I have known Richard since he asked me to take a look at a show he was working on with a rubber-faced comedian called Rowan Atkinson. They were appearing at the Edinburgh Festival and I was acting in a student show there. I'm not sure I was of any use to either of them. I suggested one or two entrances and exits – quicker and neater than the ones they were doing. The show grew and grew. Eventually Richard gathered a crowd of friends to help present it for just one afternoon at the Mayfair Theatre in London, so that it could be seen by a London theatre producer called Michael Codron and his investors.

(This is a lesson in how showbiz works, at least when people are starting off. A show has to be re-mounted, so that 'the money' can see it before investing. *Obviously*, the money travelling any distance to see the show is out of the question. The comedy mountain comes to Mohammad.)

Anyways, back to Dibley. Richard had just had an enormous success with *Four Weddings and a Funeral*, so the whole of

The Vicar

British Equity was on its knees before him when it came to casting *The New Vicar*, as the first script was called.

We spent a long time meeting actors. We met the great and the good (and the less great and the not so good) for what was always going to be an ensemble comedy. Everyone on the Parish Council had to be a character in their own right and the laughs would be pretty evenly distributed. First, however, we had to find Geraldine, the vicar herself.

The part was not created for Dawn, and whenever there were hiccups during rehearsal, Richard would delight in reminding Dawn that he 'had a list' and 'other actresses could always be brought in'. We never met any of the ladies on the list, because Dawn always seemed an obvious first choice. If Richard had reservations, it was only that Dawn and Jennifer had a reputation for improvising, so he was worried that she might play around with the script. But no. She was as good as gold. Honest. If *Dawn* had reservations, it was about how funny she could be, surrounded by the strange and wonderful characters orbiting the vicar. She wanted Geraldine to be as funny as possible and she and Richard had long discussions about the problems of putting a wholly good character at the heart of a comedy. There were many creative solutions: for instance, the pictures of Mel Gibson, Robson Green, Sean Bean and Robbie Williams next to the picture of Jesus above her desk. These conversations with Richard and their meetings with the wonderful Rev Joy Carroll (who was our technical advisor) assuaged some of Dawn's worries that vicars can't have fun. When Dawn saw the number of 'empties' at Joy's house, she suddenly felt much better about the whole idea.

In the end the answer was, as it often is, sex and chocolate.

Casting the other parts in the show was by turns obvious and difficult. The late Roger Lloyd Pack was an early shoo-in as the farmer Owen Newitt: never happier than when thrusting his hand up a cow's backside or discussing intimate relations with other livestock and the legality thereof. Liz Smith was an obvious gift as Letitia Cropley, the woman whose carrot, Marmite, pickle and banana cakes were always more of a threat than a treat. Finding Jim Trott was harder. Not everyone found a way of saying 'Yes, yes, yes, no' in a way that made sense. Trevor Peacock is a fine character actor and star of the National Theatre. He 'got it' straight away, bringing the character to life effortlessly. In fact, Trevor established Jim so well in the first series, that later his character was given other foibles and much stranger and broader quirks. In one episode he tells us – with absolute sincerity – about his marriage to a Bangkok ladyboy during the war. Yet this man can rarely have left the village. On one occasion we also meet his wife. She says 'No, no, no, yes'.

Good acting always encourages good new ideas from the writers.

John Bluthal was a character comedian who had worked a lot with Spike Milligan. He was also the only member of our cast who had been in *A Hard Day's Night*. There was always something surreal about him – and consequently about Frank Pickle, the pedantic parish council secretary. In one episode he unexpectedly 'came out' on a local radio broadcast, telling of his long-time passion for a farmhand called Justin. The expectation of how bad he might be as a broadcaster meant that none of his fellow parish councillors had listened to what was actually a very touching confession.

Finding actors to play David and Hugo Horton was hard (David was the local squire and Hugo his son). Richard C was pretty set on James Fleet for Hugo: James had done great work in *Four Weddings*. He seemed a bit older than the Hugo some of us had imagined, but Richard was right: funnier to have someone of 35 with the outlook of a 13-year-old and James is very funny.

Casting David proved much tougher. English leading men are an odd bunch. Some are very grand and would never countenance playing opposite someone as funny as Dawn. Others might come in to see us, but quickly showed how hard it is to play comedy lines well. Richard's text couldn't be played knowingly – there was no room for camp parody – but if played with no comic brio at all, the lines could fall flat and seem dull. We met actors of great heft and standing. We saw actors who wouldn't normally come to auditions, and some who wouldn't normally 'stoop' to television comedy. We saw actors who had worked with Olivier in his pomp, and one who'd worked with Woody Allen in his prime, but only a very few really 'got' David Horton. Early on, Gary Waldhorn was suggested to us. He's an actor who instinctively knows his way round a TV comedy and could see at once that to make the character a success, he had to bring out David's pompous and possibly unlovable side. The antagonism between David and Geraldine gives way, after the first few episodes, to tolerance and eventually to real affection. Gary earned it all. It has to be noted that David must have fathered his son well below the age of consent. James Fleet is just seven years younger than Gary Waldhorn. Ah the magic of television.

A word about auditions.

I think that every young actor should be allowed to sit at the back during some proper auditions. They would see that success does not just depend on how good an actor you are. It's as much a question of whether you're the right height, the right look, the right age, the right sex, have the right accent and so on. It's only partly to do with pure talent. You *are* what the director or the writer had in mind, or you're not. Of course, there's always the chance that everyone involved except the performer is a complete arsehole, in which case the young actor sitting at the back will also learn *never* to work with these people.

He – the young actor – Bill, Charlie, Gaston – would also see how complicated a process meeting up with actors can be. Firstly, the well-known actor's agent will say, when you enquire about their client, that it has to be 'an offer'. In other words, the actor won't meet the director or the writer or the producer unless he or she is offered the part ahead of a meeting. Then, if they're not offered the part, the agent will sometimes come back after a period of radio silence and say, 'my client *will* meet, but *won't* read,' or the producer will say 'Look, Frank, we *love* Pamela; David, the director, *loves* Pamela; and we all *love* the work she did in that *brilliant* show at the National, is there *any* chance of a meet, maybe? I *so* know they'd *really* get on and the part was virtually written with her in mind.' Of course it wasn't, but the actress that it *was* written for refused to even look at it, because six months earlier she'd accused the writer of stalking her for three years and demanding a blowjob at the National Theatre Stage Door.

Then the producer will say to the agent: 'It's not so much that *we* want to meet *her* but that we feel that *she* should meet *us*, because she really needs to make sure we're all up to it!'

This is horse dung, by the way.

So the actress arrives and even though she's read the script and is available at the right time, 'she won't read'. In a few cases this may be because she can't read: a mixture of dyslexia and vanity and not wanting to blow it. Most often it's part of a game in which both sides know the rules:

The Vicar

ACTRESS: It's a very funny part and thank you so much for thinking of me.'

DIRECTOR: I know your agent said that we shouldn't ask you to read, but it would be wonderful if we could hear you do just a *tiny* bit...

ACTRESS: Oh I think that's just Frank, my agent, being silly, I'd love to read for you. Where shall we start?

FRANK: Not all agents are called Frank.

Back to Dibley.

We didn't see many actresses for Alice (the verger). Alice is – well – in a world of her own. And engagingly 'different'. And naïve. And irritating. And there didn't seem to be many people who could make this both funny and endearing. Emma Chambers was a young actor whom I'd seen give a very good performance in a production of Pinero's *Trelawny of the Wells*. She was truthful and very funny. She auditioned alone and then with Dawn. They fitted together like – well – like fish and chips but without the greasy paper. They were hot, crisp and ready to take home. We couldn't have asked for better. Emma let Alice be in a world of her own when she had to be, and at other times Alice was curiously shrewd.

Emma won a British Comedy Award for her performance, and rightly so. Her loss recently is a very sad one. She was a very clever and capable comic actress who could hold her own with Dawn and later with Julia Roberts in *Notting Hill*. She was very bright and good to have around. Her laugh alone could light up a rehearsal room and so could she. Alice may never have been the brightest, but Emma certainly was.

I've just been looking at a few early Dibley scripts, and I'm reminded that the 'jokes' between Alice and Geraldine which became such a feature of the show, were never there in the rehearsal scripts. They arrived partly because Alice was bliss, and partly because of Richard and Paul's desire to give the audience as many treats as possible, even after the credits rolled. We recorded two or three jokes at each session, and were often held up by Dawn or Emma collapsing in laughter. NO – stop – no – the characters can't find this funny! Stop!! Please! STOP LAUGHING!

Thank you, Emma.

★ ★ ★

The next thing the production team had to do was find a village! Dibley was loosely based on a village in Oxfordshire where Richard C used to live, so it was in Oxfordshire where we first started to rootle around. For those who wonder whether a career in rootling around (or 'location management' as it is properly known) is for them, know that it's sometimes tricky. Locations are now often found online via prettyvillagesforfilming.com (or something) so they get snapped up. The rest are hiding down such small country lanes that the sheer size of several equipment lorries plus three huge catering vans plus mobile dressing rooms, stand for ever between them and the chance of big or small screen exposure. Not to mention the actors and directors who refuse to work anywhere further from their agents and Soho House than junction 14 of the M25. The village we eventually found was almost too picturesque – and this also meant that it had already featured in a number of ads, and several Midsomer murders had taken place in the surrounding fields.

So the village was tired of film folk and their noisy, filthy ways. They wanted no more Porsches, Pontiac Trans Ams and Honey Wagons arriving before sunrise to clog up the common and then disappearing back to Charlotte Street on the words 'That's a wrap, everybody'. Not to mention the legions of first, second and third assistants asking villagers

The Vicar

to turn down Steve Wright every afternoon, or to 'Switch off your engine for a moment or two, luv, if you would – just while we get this shot of 30 overpaid townie standby artists dressed as Morris men eating straw, and a brand of crisps too expensive for the likes of you, for the 15th time in the last thirty minutes. Thanks a lot. We know your kids have been waiting at the school gate for an hour. We'll try not to hold you up for too much longer.'

The good people of Turville wanted no more of this, especially in the name of comedy. These funny people might well want to use and probably *desecrate* their lovely parish church. Strong powers of persuasion were needed and a village meeting was called in the church itself. The executive producer and the location manager and the production manager and the producer (me), all had to address it. We promised, on our lives, that we would neither disturb nor desecrate. We promised that we would employ runners specifically to pick up litter and that we would minimise the number of people involved (we didn't mention animals). Finally, and this may have turned the tables in our favour, we mentioned that a small amount of compensation would be offered to those who lived near the church and a smaller amount to those who didn't, particularly if they let us park in the road outside their house. This swung it. Only one resident held out, and to this day there is NO PARKING anywhere near his abode. Don't even *think* about it.

'Don't worry,' we were told, 'he's like this about everything. Even Inspector Morse.'

We'd won the day, but as usual it's the stars that *really* win the day. If 'that Dawn French sits on my sofa while she's waiting for them to finish putting up the Village Fete for that there Kylie Minogue' then happiness is theirs and the posh cars are forgiven.

How to Produce Comedy Bronze

The beginning of episode one of *The Vicar of Dibley* is a model: a brilliant set-up for the series.

The 'set-up' is how you establish the main characters, the location in which the story takes place, and the world into which you're about to drop the bombshell of the main character. At the very start of episode one, we are in Dibley Parish Church. An oldish woman is at the organ and there is a congregation of four people: a man reading something dull from the Old Testament, a younger man and a single old man by himself. The vicar is clearly very old and is 'helped' by a young female verger. She is timid. After getting the prayers in a muddle the vicar sits down and quietly dies without anyone noticing.

The next scene takes place in the church hall, where the man who was reading the lesson (David Horton) is now briskly chairing the Parish Council, while the younger man (Hugo), his son, is speaking up for the stupid verger. The council leader is barely tolerating his council members: a pedantic minute taker, a woman with odd menu ideas, and another man who keeps saying, 'Yes, yes, yes, yes, no'. A farmer arrives late and tells us of his gastric problems. The main subject under discussion is the arrival of the new vicar. Presumably a man.

We cut to the manor house where a reception committee for the new vicar has started to assemble. We learn more about David, traditionalist and snob, and Hugo, who seems agreeable – though several apples short of a functioning orchard. The squire wants the new vicar on his side and the verger fired. We now have a second opportunity to meet the strange cook, the pedant and the man who says 'Yes, yes, yes, no' as well as the stupid verger. It is raining outside and David is patronising. We are now ten minutes into the show. The place and the ensemble have been established.

170

The Vicar

Only now are we introduced to our star. A figure appears – dripping wet and much wrapped up against the elements. Coats and scarves are removed. David turns to welcome the new vicar – and it's a woman! The stone is dropped into the pool and the ripples fan out across seven series. David is wrong-footed and the others are charmed. Perfect. Establish your world, then bring on the disruptor.

As Geraldine arrived ten minutes in, the audience fell about, and the set-up was concluded, Richard said to me, 'Well, I think we got away with it.'

I think we did.

We carried on with only the odd hiccup. We filmed the studio elements of the show on a new sound stage at Shepperton. We were assured that it was soundproof, although since we recorded in front of an audience on a *Sunday*, surely this wouldn't be a problem. Except for *Judge Dredd*!

Ah, *Judge Dredd*. Not being a Hollywood anorak, you may not remember the Sylvester Stallone vehicle of that name, in which Sly plays a stern and forceful member of the legal profession. It was being filmed on the next stage to ours and – guess what? – they'd picked Sunday evening as their day for pyrotechnics and large noisy explosions. Negotiations followed, and surprisingly we won, persuading them that *surely* the Lord's day shouldn't be interrupted by big bangs of any kind. I suspect that sense was seen because the negotiations were conducted technician to technician. Our sound guys talked to their special effects guys. Had the producers tried to resolve it, we might still be shouting at each other to this day. When in doubt, keep out.

At the end of the first series of *Dibley*, Geraldine decides that she should have a church service for the animals – 'including llamas and stick insects'. This proves to be a very popular idea in Dibley, and also went down well in Turville (the real Dibley) and surrounding areas. Local stables provided horses that galloped enthusiastically towards the church and obligingly nodded in agreement when Geraldine delivered the sermon. All the Turville locals came with their pets – smaller ones inside the church, larger ones outside. The range of fauna was immense: dogs, sheep, cows, horses, parrots, mice, weasels, rabbits and Hugo's stuffed owl. We really didn't know until the day who and what would turn up. The episode is very neatly written by Paul and Richard, and my favourite moment is Geraldine's astonishment at seeing how successful her idea has been. She leaves the vicarage expecting a *very* low turn-out, but is met by a truly impressive stream of people and animals.

Farmers helped us with livestock, and we learned a good deal about DEFRA regulations concerning cattle, and whether they can share a space with other species. They can't. This rather scuppered our plan to get the largest variety of big animals in a group near the church. But with a deal of careful editing and the closure of the one main road through the village, we achieved the desired effect. The production office received a lot of correspondence from parishes up and down the land that planned to have similar services.

They didn't know what they were taking on.

So the first series ended with a good few extra hands clearing shit of various kinds out of the church and contriving not to park cars or animals outside the one 'house of hate'. It should also be recorded that Dibley/Turville is the only location I've ever worked in that gave a party for the cast and crew at the end of the series. Not just because they were pleased to see the back of us, but oddly, because they were genuinely sad to see us go.

We came back a lot. We came for an Easter special in which it seemed appropriate that one of the characters should die in order to rise again. The chosen parishioner was Letitia Cropley. I think that Liz Smith, who played her, thought she'd been singled-out for punishment. But we were NOT punishing her! WE LOVED HER. And we LOVED her Marmite chocolate cake. Mrs Cropley had to die, I think, because Paul and Richard had run out of bad menu gags and needed a death for Easter and Mrs Cropley to rise again as the Easter bunny.

This episode was the only one directed by the wonderful John Howard Davies, the cheery, gentle, soul who had – as producer – given the world *Monty Python*, *Fawlty Towers*, and *The Goodies*. And of course, at the age of nine, his own performance as *Oliver Twist* in David Lean's amazing film. For us, he pulled off the supreme trick. He persuaded the crew and the cast that making comedy could be fun, and so it was!

We also came back to Turville for a special in which the vicar agrees to share Christmas dinner with three different members of her congregation. Hard to exaggerate just how many sprouts were consumed, but it should be said that Dawn ate most of hers in single takes whereas others of the cast had to eat them in group shots take after take. This episode is another example of Richard and Paul's grasp of how to structure a comedy story. An idea is set up – lots of dinners. Then a tension is created. Geraldine is nervous about the prospect of all this food, but terrified of letting the villagers down. We watch eagerly as her resolution crumbles. How long before she keels over, or – like Mr Creosote – explodes. Expectation encourages laughter.

In another Christmas episode, Geraldine decides that a Nativity play should be staged in the village. Filming in a bare field in *December* at *night*, meant that everyone was about as cold as it was possible to be. How we got through it without flying in *Médecins sans Frontières,* is a mark of the sheer guts and professionalism among both cast and crew. Of course courage spreads by example. *If* Miss Dawn French has to have wires attached to her, in order that a crane should lift her skywards while another set of wires magically opens her wings, and *if* the crane operator and the wireman all need another take, and the director wants several more on top of that, then I *guess* everyone else thinks that it would be a mark of true cowardice if they complained. Thermals were definitely worn that night.

The show lived under a kind of happy spell. The spell that was woven by the villagers themselves. The spell woven by real lady vicars (including my old English teacher) who wrote to tell us about how important Dibley was for them, and for the cause of women priests. The spell of gathering together to do the show, and the enormous fun we had. Even the meal we shared with the cast on the night of each recording at Shepperton studios. Bonding and nourishing. I think that we just couldn't escape the spell, not even if we'd wanted to.

Yet it might all have been so different.

A few months before we began *Dibley* production, Dawn and Jennifer were starring in a play called *Me and Mamie O'Rourke*, written by the woman who wrote *Beaches,* the Bette Midler/Barbara Hershey movie – 'nuff said. I went backstage to see Dawn one night and we'd just embarked on some important gossip, when Twiggy appeared, bringing with her the one and only Dustin Hoffman. Neither were really known to Dawn, but there is a sort of unwritten rule that all celebrities must know all other celebrities, so *of course* they have visiting rights in one another's dressing rooms. Dustin kept pointing at both Dawn and Jennifer – saying 'You, actress', 'You, artist'. It was never quite clear which was better or worse. Dustin gave Dawn tips about how one or two pratfalls might help her performance, and then told us that he hadn't currently got any work lined up, and what was she doing next? We told him about the sitcom we were developing for Dawn, how it took place in a small English village populated by eccentrics, and that it was being written by Paul Mayhew-Archer and Richard *Four Weddings* Curtis.

'I could direct that! I'd love to direct that! I'd be good. I'm free as well. Ring my agent,' said Dustin, maybe a bit too eagerly.

Just think what that would have been like. Think how long it might have taken, just to explain the gags to him. So much more 'method' and New York. Imagine if you will *Tootsie* meets *Marathon Man* meets Dibley Parish Council.

LESSON: There are times when a producer's job is to look a gift horse in the mouth. And then punch it.

18

Running a Comedy Department

When I became head of broken comedy at the BBC, frankly I had no idea how to run a comedy department. When I stopped being head of comedy entertainment (*I changed it – who wants to run something that's broken*) and became just plain head of comedy a few years later I still had no idea. By the way, being 'head of comedy anything' is really head of making comedy and offering comedy shows to controllers, not deciding which comedies get on TV.

I got the job because I'd been lucky enough to have a couple of hits, *Ab Fab*, and *The Vicar*, and these are so rare that the theory goes, 'Well, he knows how to have a hit so let's stop him doing that and give him a job where he gets to teach other people to have hits.' It doesn't really work because essentially what a producer does is to *enable*. He enables other more talented people to have hits. So if I did anything with my new found headships it was to try to enable others to do stuff, and then sometimes I was also forced to disenable them.

Let's begin with the disenabling. I love Ruby Wax. I had

known her for a number of years, indeed, ever since the ending of her relationship with Mel Smith led her to throw all his clothes out of an upstairs flat onto the road below near where I lived.

She had been making a series of celeb interview shows for the BBC with some success. She came to me after one particular series and said, 'Jon, Jon, for the next series there's a guy I've gotta have working on the team with me because he really understands me [not an easy task] and gets the best out of me. I must have him, the only problem is he has a contract in [another country] so you've got to get him out of it.'

So negotiators were dispatched to see if this were possible. It was, but at a *price*, which included his accommodation at a very good hotel in London. Well done, everyone. He came to work on the new series.

Maybe a month and a half goes past, certainly no more. Ruby returns to my office. Rumblings have already been heard that all is not as well as it might be.

'Jon, Jon, he's got to go, he really is no good for me, we could get someone so much better. You've got to tell him that he's got to go.'

I explain that – as I understand it – employment law doesn't work like this and that we've gone to a lot of trouble to get him here and to get him out of his previous contract so she's got to give him a chance, at least until the end of the series. Reluctantly, she agrees but I get the sense that he may not be right at the heart of Operation Wax from now on.

We get to the end of the series and the question arises of picking up his contract for the next series. Ruby is dead against. It is decided that I have to tell him that he is effectively being sacked. I check with the producer of the series, the urbane Clive Tulloh, and he confirms that the relationship has hit the rocks and that, Ruby being Ruby, these are genuine rocks.

Running a Comedy Department

I've never terminated anyone before, not in this way – not in any way. I am given lessons by human resources: I have to be very clear. I have to offer no hope. I have to tell him the bad news clearly and then send him on to an HR person down the corridor who will reunite him with his family, or give him a comforting pet to hold, or a large Scotch, or whatever it is they do. Watches are synchronised. My secretary, who is a doctor's daughter, is on standby in the outer office.

It does not go well.

He comes into my office.

ME: So here's the thing, we're very appreciative of you getting out of your contract with your previous people and leaving your home and family and coming here, but I'm really sorry to say that it hasn't worked out and so we're not going to pick up your contract which must now come to an end. I'm so sorry. Is that clear? Do you understand?'

I have been told that I have to ask these last two questions.

He looks as if I've just punched him in the stomach, which in a way I have.

HIM: (*quietly*) Oh OK. Yes. Right. Yes, I understand.
ME: So if you'd like to go down the corridor to the HR people they'll be able to tell you how things go from here and how it all works from their end.

He's still looking a bit bemused but I think he's slowly pulling himself together.

HIM: Oh right, OK, I'll do that then. Thanks.

He goes out of the door of my office and into my outer office where my secretary sits.

He pauses in front of her desk for a minute and then his eyes glaze over and his body crumples. He passes out in front of her and if he had been about two inches nearer her desk his head would have hit the edge of it and split open. I might have been facing a manslaughter charge.

Fiona, my secretary, is a forceful woman.

'Right, nobody panic!' she says forcefully, mainly to me because I'm probably looking pale and panicked, 'Jon – go into your office and stay there and shut the door! I'm a doctor's daughter, I know what to do. I'll summon an emergency medical team!'

By the time the emergency medical team arrived, two guys who once did a first-aid course, he had come back to us and was saying that he was fine and he would get on with things and I was opening my office door somewhat relieved. It was apparently only a temporary health 'blip'.

I'm not really privy to what happened after this. I presume that HR did whatever it is that they do but in a slightly gentler way than normal and that he left the employment of the Corporation.

There were those though that said he was still to be seen around the hotel that the BBC had put him up in for some months afterwards and that the bills were still being paid. Is he still there? Any sightings should be reported. I can neither confirm nor deny anything but I can say that I have never sacked anyone else without checking all the exits and the whereabouts of the nearest medical staff, in advance.

Also in the disenabling area there was a sketch show that I inherited called *The Real McCoy*, a multi-racial show that combined Asian and Afro-Caribbean performers. It was good but seemed to be putting a lot of things into a pot without

1970. The Author in the Prefects' Room at school, photographed by my good friend Gordon Stokes. Note the Whitbread poster behind me and the period hair and tie stylings.

1980. Grace Jones and I on location in Liverpool for Granada TV. She's the one on the left and I'm the bottle blonde on the right.

The Original Abba Line-up before those Scanditwats came along and decided on a different line up for Eurovision.

Above: Smith and Jones. Did these guys know how to Vogue?! Answer: no, not really.

Below: Dangerous Liasons. Dawn and Jennifer with their fans in a mental hospital near Eastbourne.

I'm told that this shows three of the bride's family on their way to Prince Harry's wedding but I'm not sure…

Witless Silence; Producer Corpsing.

Beautiful People (and they were): Olivia Colman (*left*), Layton Williams and Luke Ward Wilkinson singing their hearts out in Bushey, Herts.

Matt Lucas and me – *Little Britain*, the better line-up.

Above: I'm not sure that the 'Former Head of' billing does anyone any favours.

Above right: The author in L.A., standing in front of the new Head of Netflix.

Left: 'Precious my precious, it's mine now and I'm keeping it!'

Above: Quite simply three of the funniest women alive.

Below: As you can see we went for a low-key opening.

Quite simply two of the funniest women alive.

quite making the best stew. The controllers wanted to let it go because it had run its course but out of it came something rather good. A bit of enabling.

A little while after it had done its last series, a producer called Anil Gupta stuck his head into my office and said, quite reasonably, 'Why isn't there an Asian sketch show on TV?'

I said I didn't really know. He said that if I would give him a bit of development money he would gather together the talent and put on a night of Asian comedy.

'I'll show you that the talent is out there and you can persuade BBC2 to give us a show.'

I gave him some development dosh and he was true to his word.

Within a few weeks I was invited to a show at the Riverside Studios in Hammersmith. It was called *Peter Sellers is Dead!* a reference to Sellers' dodgy Indian accent on records like 'Goodness Gracious Me' with Sophia Loren. The evening was extraordinary, partly because some good performers were doing good stuff, but more because I had never heard audience laughter like it. It was long and loud but with a sense of discovery and recognition about it. A sense of, 'Yes, that's how it is, but I didn't know that I was allowed to laugh at these things! I didn't know that everybody else shared this view of Indian grandmothers, or useless husbands or that all Asian teenagers were just like my kids!'

This is not some sort of telepathy on my part it was corroborated by people saying this afterwards and some-times during.

Of course, these guys should be given a series of their own. I, a non-Asian bloke from Welwyn Garden City, found all this talk of 'chuddies' and couples who are trying to be 'more English than the English' funny as well. The show wasn't only going to work in areas where they knew what 'Mrs I-can-make-it-at home-for-nothing!' was talking about. It could work everywhere and might even do a bit of good.

To begin with, BBC2 said that they'd run out of money – when haven't they? So Anil and the group wondered whether the show could work on Radio 4, as a stepping-stone. These were the days when radio and TV comedy spoke to each other a bit more and the idea of starting on one and then moving to the other was a regular occurrence. The head of radio comedy at the time was the remarkable Jonathan James-Moore, an ebullient presence, tall and overflowing with red hair both on top and around his face. He was a man who loved comedy and he and I met frequently and swapped people and shows. The idea of a sketch show written from an Asian perspective really appealed to him but being on the radio threw up a slight problem. The team realised that the Peter Sellers title might be taken the wrong way in the home of the *Goons*, the show that made Sellers' name, so they adjusted the title to *Goodness Gracious Me*. The idea of GGM appealed to those who ran Radio 4 and they snapped it up. On TV it was slightly trickier because now Controller Thompson saw it as a 'minorities show' and gave it a minorities budget and slot. It was not until he saw the TV pilot show that he realised that this was a show that had an appeal to all and even had the makings of a hit. The idea that it should have a similar budget to a show like say, *Network East*, a minorities news show of the time which seemed to be made in a shed, went away forever. The size of budget didn't go up that much though and it still rankled with the team throughout its run, even when the money increased, even when they won awards and lots of praise.

The first show got off to a good start because it included a straight 'reversal' sketch that really appealed to all; 'Going for an English'. A group of young people in Mumbai are shown going for a night out and behaving as badly to the English waiters as the British do when they go out for an Indian on a Friday night. Our Asian group order 'the blandest thing on the menu and 24 plates of chips', it was a great recognition sketch and really made it clear that this show was for everyone. So did the Bhangra Muffins and Smeeten Kitten, and the guy who thought everything, even Shakespeare, came from India first, and Mr 'Cheque Please' and even Skipinder the Punjabi Kangaroo.

The show and its performers definitely made an impact on early 2000s Britain. It's just possible that it spread some understanding in a way that was welcome at the time. I'm not sure that that is always true of comedy and I thank them for it. We could do with a bit more of it now.

The only problem I ever had with the show came when, at its height, the show went out on Fridays on BBC2 and then was repeated on Sundays on BBC1. A sketch in which the warring couples who want to be more English than the English go to C of E communion was a tad problematic for some. Of course our couples don't quite understand its significance and they drink large amounts of communion wine and bring out dips for the wafers. On BBC2 there were quite a few calls to the BBC phone log. The controller of BBC1, Peter Salmon, rang me at home to 'wonder' if the sketch might be trimmed, 'given that it will be Sunday night and etc. etc.' I'd never quite been in this position before but I wasn't going to override the producer and the team by immediately going into an edit. It was the weekend, for heaven's sake! I rang the producer, Anil. To his credit, he put up strong arguments against but did agree to trim, not cut, the sketch.

> **LESSON: Controllers and commissioners may
> not be right but they do hold the purse strings!
> Is it ever worth jeopardising the next series?
> Think hard before taking the moral high ground
> then, go for it.**

This next paragraph may feel a bit moany so skip it if you're feeling 'up'. Early on in the life of a Head of Something or Other he or she is given quite a lot of rope, as time goes on you're given less. At the start I put forward various series and hour-long comedy-drama projects that got onscreen starring the likes of Alexei Sayle, Dawn French, Rik Mayall and Stephen Tomkinson. We also made what must have been one of the last pre-watershed sketch shows on BBC1 with Steve Punt and Hugh Dennis. I would say that the demise of both comedy-dramas and pre-watershed comedies after this is not my fault – but…

Television production has got more competitive over the last twenty years or so with the proliferation of the independent companies like Hat Trick and Tiger Aspect and Baby Cow and about 300 others. Broadcasting has got more competitive over the same period with catch-up services and Amazon and Netflix. The audience has become used to higher production standards and the rise of the box-set. British comedy has become a lesser priority for all broadcasters, except those who rely on old episodes of known titles for their very existence: Gold, Dave, Fred, etc. This is a pity and it's self-perpetuating. If a generation of writers see only drama and old comedies why would they want, bother or learn to write new comedies? I'm pretty sure that the number of new scripts sent into the BBC comedy commissioning department has declined. It's not the force in fun that it once was and this is partly because of competition but also because of the number of hours of comedy that have been lost on the main channels because, apparently, on the main channels people don't want to laugh any more. The British have a distinctive sense of humour and that's why it's tricky to export shows, or so BBC Worldwide keep telling me. Is this an excuse for not investing in shows? It isn't a reason not to make 'em.

End of moany bit.

★ ★ ★

Running the broken comedy department at the BBC was fun. It was producers coming in with ideas. It was scripts arriving from established writers and unknowns. It was also about going to lots of meetings. Many of these meetings were well over the edge of dull. I was going to a meeting once, in the company of others, walking down Marylebone High Road and we were going past the Conran shop. One of the people I was with knew that I was dreading this meet and that sometimes I was inclined to 'sound off' in meetings. This was usually when I thought that perhaps we might all be better spending our time making shows or jam. My companion thought that this meet might be worth attending, so she told me that, if I would keep quiet all through the meeting, then she would buy me the orange Roberts radio in the Conran window. If I didn't keep schtum then I would have to buy it for her. It cost quite a lot then and I didn't want to lose. The challenge worked, much to her and my surprise. I said not a word. So a way to make meetings fun is clearly bribery. As I write this I look over at a still functioning orange Roberts radio, my silence has led to years of listening pleasure.

How to Produce Comedy Bronze

One of the few meetings that I enjoyed was called 'Programme Review'. It took place every Wednesday morning around a huge table in a large room in the basement of Television Centre. The idea was that all the heads of this and that would attend and the chair would first get the ratings people to tell us how various things had done over the previous seven days. A couple of shows that we had all been notified of would then be discussed and the producers of those shows would attend and accept praise or more often have to make excuses for their programmes:

'It was the first of the series and I think you'll see that it gets much better as it goes on.'

'We had hoped to get a bit more access than we did. In the end the government went back on the permissions they'd promised and our photocopier broke down.'

'Filming with stars under water is quite tricky.'

'We just ran out of time!'

'We just ran out of money!'

Heads of department would then usually defend their department's output as if their jobs depended on it. Sometimes they did.

'Clarissa hasn't been with the department very long and I think she and the camera just need time to get along better. We have had words.'

This translated to: 'OK, I know. Don't rub it in. Frankly, Clarissa's a pain, I shouldn't have slept with her mother, and she will be leaving ASAP.'

We would then go through the last week's *Radio Times*

and the chairman would ask individuals for their opinions of various shows. This was sometimes just a game to see how well people could cover up that they hadn't seen something:

'I thought that it needed to be a bit more focused.'

'My children watched it and quite frankly they didn't find it funny at all.'

(Not sure that Louis Theroux on axe murderers was quite aimed at them.)

'What was that background music?'

(There wasn't any, but good shot because there usually is.)

My favourite comment came from a man who was head of football at the time, a chap called Brian Barwick. The Sunday evening drama came up for discussion, which he clearly had watched. It was the serial that followed on from the highly acclaimed adaptation of *Pride and Prejudice*.

'Frankly,' said Brian in his thick northern tones, 'Frankly, I think you're going to have real trouble with that *Ivanhoe*.'

How right he was...

I cannot leave this section without paying tribute to my dear friend and lost colleague Geoffrey Perkins. I had been friends with Geoffrey since university, he had a much funnier and cleverer comedy brain than me. He was the guy who brought *Father Ted* to the world, the man without whom the Hitchhikers would not have had a Guide to the Galaxy. Douglas Adams wrote it but Geoffrey produced it for radio. He was the man who helped develop and nurture *Spitting Image* and Harry Enfield, Catherine Tate and *The Fast Show* and he was my great friend. He was very funny himself, and appeared in the BBC2 show *KYTV* as radio anchorman Mike Flex, long before producing all this other great stuff.

He helped start up Hat Trick productions and I was rather surprised when he agreed to be head of comedy at the BBC. I think in the end he was rather oppressed by the role. He felt that the BBC was more about programme prevention than it was about production. He had what Marilyn Monroe called 'the fuzzy end of the lollipop' because he was the guy who had to find the popular mainstream stuff.

'Can you bring me the next *Only Fools*, please?' controllers would cry.

'Can you find me something that will play well with families pre-watershed?'

He wanted to bring strong shows to them but mainstream hits like that don't fall like ripe fruit from the script trees. He commissioned a lot of scripts in the hope that they would develop into successes. So many that Sophie Clarke-Jervoise, who took over his office, remembers opening cupboards to find them crammed with scripts that he'd commissioned from writers but then not had any time to develop into pitch-able shows.

He was not without success, far from it. He was the guy who gave the world *Jonathan Creek* and *The Fast Show* and *My Hero* and *Happiness* and he imported a gentleman called Fred Barron from America to make *My Family* as a multi-episode, multi-writer, long-running sitcom.

He always took things forward gently and persuaded people to his point of view by kindness rather than bullying. I was doing the easy bit, making niche shows for BBC2 whilst he had to bring BBC1 big hits right from the off. This in an organisation that often thought that 'sitcom' was a dirty word. I only became head of comedy because he finally got fed up and left the BBC to go to Tiger Aspect Productions to start *Benidorm*, a show still running ten years later. Then shortly afterwards he died, very much too young, very much too soon...

Thanks, Geoff, we still miss you.

19

Comedy: the Case for the Defence

**'It's hard enough to write good drama,
it's much harder to write good comedy, and it's
hardest of all to write drama with comedy.
Which is what life is.' – Jack Lemmon**

'I only want hits.'

In case you don't recognise the tone, this is an anonymous programme controller of an anonymous channel speaking.

And this is me: 'I'm not sure that you quite get it, do you?'

It's now. Comedy is in a bad way. It's been a frequent visitor to A&E, but now it needs serious treatment. 'I only want hits' is pretty much the whole problem. Hello? That's all that any of us *ever* want, but it's sometimes not possible with episode one or maybe even *series* one. It took *Only Fools and Horses* three series to land, and *The Office* needed a quicker than normal repeat before people realised that it wasn't a documentary.

How to Produce Comedy Bronze

Working on the tried and trusted notion that 'No one ever set out to make a bad comedy', a hit is always the aim. ALWAYS.

Comedy is tricky and, if you're a TV channel, it's supposed to bring you a big audience compared with other shows. But that's not always the case, so what can you do?

The answer now seems to be 'Don't make it'. That's the ITV answer, or more accurately, it's the *ITV1* answer. The head of ITV Kevin Lygo said the chances for a comedy on his main channel were 'Bleak'. So tuck it away on ITV2 and buy in success like *Family Guy*. The Channel 4 answer, with a few notable exceptions like *Father Ted* (we're going back 20 years) and *Peep Show* (started 15 years ago) is to do less of it than your remit might suggest and also to put it mostly on your side channels. Channel 4 rarely do anything as challenging as a pre-watershed or a studio comedy. 'It's not in our remit,' they cry. Maybe not, but hey, who ever laughed at a remit, although it might be fun to try.

Looking at the *Radio Times* archive, you see that in, say, 1993 the staple diet from 8 p.m. to 9 p.m. most weekday evenings on BBC1 was comedy, narrative comedy in two half-hour doses. (*2 Point 4 Children* followed by *Bonjour La Classe* on Mondays, *May to December* followed by *Us Girls* on Wednesdays etc.). I didn't say it was good but it was on.

There is no doubt that over the last 25 years, comedy on BBC1 has been in sharp decline. Most comedy now is on BBC2 and stays there until it 'proves itself'. It's on against the ten o'clock news, a time when the old go to bed and the young go out, but hey. The BBC also has the benefit of BBC Three as a younger test bed and a small budget for comedy on BBC Four. Neither of these channels feel like they have the heft to create another *Only Fools*. Nor should they. Credit where its due: *Witless* and *This Country* and *Detectorists* are really good.

Here it should be noted that the BBC's self-proclaimed

Comedy: the Case for the Defence

responsibility is to Inform, Educate and Entertain. In equal measure? Does a diet of dramas set in hospitals or at crime scenes, endless episodes of *Britain's Best Hidden Motorway Service Stations* and two hours a week of ballroom dancing quite cover this? Might I perhaps, if it's all right with you, be allowed a laugh?

There have been enlightened channel controllers (Lorraine Heggessey at BBC1, Roly Keating at BBC2, Alan Yentob at both channels), who took the comedy bull by its sharp and thorny horns and said, 'Well, if we can't guarantee that *everything* will work, then let's do lots of it in the hope that *some of it* might.' They realised that when the average chap or lady gets home from work, or clambers wearily downstairs from the home office, one of the things that he or she might be looking forward to is a laugh. Or even a smile. And if he or she achieves one or the other, then maybe the licence fee will be thought to be even more worthwhile. Come to think of it, there was talk at one time of comedy being an area of market failure (to put it bluntly – nobody else does it, so the BBC should). This suggests to me that comedy is one of those things that the BBC *must* do.

But it doesn't, partly because it *can't*. If writers don't see pre-watershed comedy on TV, then they don't learn how to write them and they don't get made. Does that mean that the audience doesn't want comedy? Another factor may be the CVs of the various channel controllers. It's been a while since any of the people sitting in the controller's chair had a background that included making things from a script.

In the age of Netflix and Amazon the audience is seen to want drama even though it's much more expensive than comedy (which is drama with added laughs). So I'm clearly a dinosaur.

Comedy writing is a skill granted to a few gifted craftsmen.

If you don't give them places to see it and hear it and so to develop it, then the craft, like the skill of flint arrowhead weaving, will simply die. Perhaps if British TV wants some new comedy, they should put a tiny bit of money aside and let newcomers sit with experienced writers so they can soak up the atmosphere. And then let said newcomers sit at the back of rehearsals and recordings. I know it's been tried before, but it's time to try it again!

If writers need to be developed then what about performers? Actors who don't get the chance to play audience sitcom never have the opportunity to learn the business of landing a good laugh. And never know how good it is. Go into a green room at the end of an audience recording and the energy from the performers is enough to power the national grid on a state occasion. If comedy actors don't have the space to *learn*, then new characters aren't created, catchphrases aren't born, contemporary personalities remain unobserved, and the acting pool from which we cast shows *dries up*.

The other day, Shane Allen, the commissioner for comedy at the BBC sent me a note. It was a timely reminder. He wrote: 'As a genre, comedy just keeps on giving in a way no other genre gets near. Can a drama pack out the O2 for ten nights like Python did? How can it be that *Dad's Army* gets the highest audience of the week on BBC2 when it's nearly 50?'

Life, and I think it's OK to ratchet up the importance of this, life without comedy is so much more dull.

P.S. I should say that comedy – both the BBC Comedy Department now BBC Studios and the thing itself – has been very good to me. So I should probably stop rabbiting on!

If you want to skip the next chapter about money to get to *Little Britain*, feel free. Don't say I didn't warn you.

20

A Short Moan about Dosh

TV channels in the UK pay approximately £250k–£300k per half hour for comedy. Sketch comedy (even though it's an endangered animal), costs a little bit more, but not inordinately so.

You would think, therefore, that an hour-long *drama* would cost twice that, something in the order of £500k–£600k. Comedy and drama both have writers, sets or locations, cameras and a director, a few actors, some lights, an editor and maybe some music, so no real cost differences.

In your dreams!

For some reason, drama costs somewhere between £750,000 and £1million an hour – average. I do not know why.

Of course, drama can be sold to the remotest nations of the world. If a person is murdered and another person, probably a policeman, finds out who did it; or if someone else, probably a doctor, relieves the suffering of patients and also (if possible) finds out that one of his patients has been murdering people;

or if another doctor travels backwards and forwards through time defeating the men, monsters and machines who want to murder people by the planet-load, *then* it is possible to see it in Papua New Guinea as well as Peckham.

Comedy is a harder sell. I am told that we have a different sense of humour from the rest of the world, and that the rest of the world does not want to laugh. Or rather they do, but only at clowns, and farting, and little stick men in cartoons who squeak, and themselves.

So. Drama costs more because it sells? Comedy has to cost less, because, with a few exceptions, it doesn't sell. Surely the better idea is to make something as cheaply as possible and then make more from selling it?

What is drama spending all this extra money on? Are the costs wildly different from the costs of comedy? Do the cameras cost more, or the lights, or the writers? Do the doctors in *Casualty* get paid, not only many times more than their NHS counterparts, but also more than (say) Ricky Gervais, David Jason, Dawn French or Jennifer Saunders? No! They don't. No ifs, butts or stethoscopes. That simply isn't the case.

Look further, though, and you find that drama costs more partly because, in the mists of black and white, comedy was always the poor relation. Comedy used to be done with two or three sets in a studio in front of an audience, having been rehearsed for a few days, done and dusted in one night. There might be, at most, one short scene on film in which Captain Mainwaring and his men bring down an enemy dirigible in a field. So it was quite cheap. That's not how we do it now. Mostly we shoot comedy on film, on location using the same number of lights and costumes and props as a drama, but we make our shows in less time because we have to...because we have less money.

Dramas aspire to look like movies, so they take more time.

A Short Moan about Dosh

They shoot for 12 hours a day, not the 11 hours that we shoot for in comedy. They need an hour more. In comedy we try to do things pretty quickly and efficiently. Performers are more likely to be funny on Take 1 or 2 than on Take 11, by which time they have forgotten what made the scene funny in the first place.

If a drama director needs 50 extras to walk down a street in period costume then he or she will usually get them. On *The League of Gentlemen* recently, we made do with an angry demonstration of 20 – in their own clothes – plus a few people who are hanging around at the back who were free to join in.

So what *really* accounts, for the huge disparity in budgets?

There is of course a certain amount of fashion and snobbery involved. If you make a drama series that attracts column inches in the *Guardian* or *The Times*, then it's just possible that your star will rise and you will get a movie to write or direct, and channel execs will dine off you. And the channel absorbs some of that reflected glory. Which feels nice, and could be worth shelling out for.

Comedy doesn't get Oscars and doesn't often lead to Oscars either. Most comedy is something that channels feel that they *have* to provide. It's not necessarily something that they *want* to provide.

There is also the question of competition. If everything you make is competing for an audience with *Game of Thrones* then it had better look nearly as good. So money in drama seems to be spent on luxury locations, luxury effects. Nobody ever watched a comedy for the battles, costumes, horses, blood, sex and gore. If they did then they will have been sorely disappointed. (Except maybe with *Blackadder Goes Forth* – even there no horses or members of the undead). Nobody ever watched *Game of Thrones* for a good laugh, you just want to find out what happened next and who is left standing.

How to Produce Comedy Bronze

A half-hour of comedy is, I would contest, harder to write than an hour of drama. In comedy, every line has to earn its keep and, if possible, every other line should get a laugh. Characters have to be original, provoke a reaction, make the audience care enough to *smile*. Serious drama often sinks into cliché, with characters who utter banalities necessitated by the plot.

A quick visit to an imaginary episode of *Gogglebox*: 'What did we see *him* in? Oh you know that other thing about a policeman and his missus...see what else is on?'

'Oh look it's *Mrs Brown's Boys*, I like them.'

* ★ *

Final bit of moan. Comedy writers, particularly those who are starting off, should be paid better. Remember all the shows over which writers have slaved for months that don't get made? No money earned. Quite right, you say, they're not good enough. Possibly, but that's how writers learn, by living through those rejections. When they write something that's *good*, it's sometimes because they had quite a few things turned down. So when their moment finally arrives, aren't they owed a little bit more? They may appear to have hit the big time but they haven't exactly hit the jackpot, unless the show's a real smash.

Perhaps that's why some of them (and I can name names) leave comedy for the fertile uplands of *Holby City* or the death plains of Winterfell.

END OF MOAN

21

Little Britain (Pre-Brexit)

O K, back to my history.
'What the hell does an executive producer do?' I hear
you cry. 'I mean – we just about get what a producer does –
but an *executive* producer?'...I'll tell you! Calm down.

Consider my own role on *Little Britain*. I was in my office
at Television Centre (we still had offices then) and the desk
phone rang (we still had desks and phones). Could I come
down to the studio floor to settle an argument on the set of
the hit sketch fest that was *Little Britain*? My heart sank and
my stomach turned over. Would I have to resolve some huge
row that had broken out between Matt and Dave or between
both of them and some part of the production team? Was the
lighting director favouring Lou over Andy? Were the costume
department giving Emily Howard slightly fewer frills than
Florence? Had Maggie vomited once too often over Judy
because of her lesbian plum jelly?

It was something far more serious. I was being asked, as

the executive producer, to adjudicate over the size of the cum stain on Anthony Head's jacket when, as the UK PM, he emerges from a meeting with the US president. Too big, and it might be deemed gross, too small and it might not 'read'. I decided that a spot of mayonnaise approximately three-quarters of an inch or 1.905 centimetres long would tell the tale and not violate the bounds of good taste. Was I right? The great court of history will in time pass its judgement. That is what an executive producer does.

* ★ *

It had all started with *Shooting Stars,* the Vic Reeves, Bob Mortimer quiz show where Matt Lucas was the eccentric scorer and drummer George Dawes. From there, he joined forces with David Walliams to make *Sir Bernard Chumley's Stately Homes.* Do you recall the search among the stately homes of England for the Golden Potato, the finder of which would win a year's supply of Allen's Crisps, 'the cheaper crisp'? Think of Kit Williams burying a Golden Hare to promote his book, a publicity brainwave that sparked a treasure hunt back in 1979. Sir Bernard was the chief hunter joined by Walliams as Anthony Rodgers, odd-job man and murderer. As well as the treasure hunt and making a TV film, their other objective was to avoid arrest.

This series of ten-minute films had appeared on BBC Choice (which later became BBC Three) in 1998, and emerged from the minds of Matt and David, who had met at the National Youth Theatre. Looking at it now the films seem to be good knockabout character work. Maybe a little 'big', that is 'knowing', played with too complicit a nudge in the ribs, but fun.

> **SIDEBAR: Bernard Chumley was directed by
> Edgar Wright (see chapter on *Murder Most
> Horrid*). I remember that when filming his
> episode of *Murder* I had to explain to Edgar that
> it's better not to direct the actors after someone
> has shouted 'action'. Their focus may well be
> elsewhere, and if it's a car chase you may get
> run over. I attribute all his later success to this
> one astonishing apercu. I expect a tribute page
> in his autobiography.**

At the time, *Stately Homes* had a mixed reception, but many things that go on to greatness start by being poo-poo'd. It is their oddness that both alienates some and intrigues others. Proof of this may be found not just in the careers of Matt and Dave, but also in the first series of *French and Saunders*, in the early reception of *Dad's Army* (when it was seen by some as an insult to the real Home Guard), and in the contemporary reviews for *Fawlty Towers*: 'What is John Cleese doing in this lame hotel farce?' wrote *The Times* of London.

In the case of *Sir Bernard*, critic Victor Lewis-Smith suggested that ten minutes' silence on BBC Choice would be a better use of time. Not true. Comedy should sometimes antagonise the audience to begin with. We have to get to know the characters and relax into their world, particularly if it's a show that's trying to be different. It's like a new family moving in next door. Give them time and unless it's, say, Fred and Rosemary West, everything will settle down and be OK. We might even have a laugh together.

After the series it was obvious that these guys had talent. They went on to do *Rock Profiles*, a spoof music chat show, for UK Play and BBCThree. Again they created versions of their targets that involved a degree of exaggeration, but the characters were more closely scripted this time, and proved dead centre for their channel's audience. There was much excited discussion of a future in the mainstream, BBC2 or even BBC1, but as with other shows it was suggested that radio was the next step. Perhaps this sounds as if radio is some sort of dumping ground. Far from it. It's good for TV and it's good for radio. It means that when artists come to TV from a run on Radio 4 they have a certain confidence, they know that people have already laughed at and liked their ideas. Artists also gain some recognition. In this case, it helped that Radio 4 had a late night slot available, which allowed Matt and Dave to try out material that was OK post-watershed on BBC2, but might scorch the ears of Radio 4 listeners earlier in the evening.

Little Britain had a remarkable trajectory in that regard. It went from Radio 4 to BBC Three and was then repeated on BBC2. The second series started on Three and then by-passed BBC2 and got its repeat on BBC1. It had arrived, it was a hit!

Why?

Well, Matt and Dave created characters from worlds that comedy hadn't yet discovered. Vicky Pollard was a chav, but an unusual one. I'd never come across types like Lou and fake handicapped Andy: cruel creations but highly original... or Daffyd, the only gay in the village, keen on Bacardi and Coke, and Myffanwy his entirely accepting friend in an entirely accepting Welsh community...or Marjorie Dawes – cruel and fat – the leader of fat fighters...or Maggie and Judy, whose shocking prejudice had graphic physical results. These characters and Tom Baker's mad narration were showing us something about a bit of Britain that hadn't been pin-pointed on TV before, but it did exist. There was an originality of observation and a willingness to push the envelope, which made audiences sit up and take notice. The boys were doing something different. Something new.

The ability of the show to touch a nerve is evidenced by an audience averaging 9 million on BBC1, and also this story from the *Daily Telegraph*:

The head of a primary school has got so fed up with pupils pretending to be 'the only gay in the village' that she has asked parents to stop them watching Little Britain.

Apart from young boys parading about pretending to be the Matt Lucas character Daffyd, Hildenborough Primary School, near Tonbridge, Kent, has had its fill of girls muttering: 'No but, yeah but no but, yeah…' the catchphrase of the character Vicky Pollard.

Lyn Hargreaves, the headmistress, wrote to parents saying: 'Please can I ask for your help in respecting the 9 p.m. watershed as the discussions heard are not ones we feel should enter our school culture.'

Some parents, however, have not taken kindly to being advised over their children's viewing habits.

Mark Richardson, whose eight-year-old daughter goes to the school, said: 'I thought this was over-stepping the mark. This is something parents should decide.

'The show is so funny and over-the-top about slapstick elements which appeals to children. The more risqué comments go over their heads.

'I watch it with them with the remote in my hand and censor the really saucy bits.'

Mrs Hargreaves said yesterday: 'Our pupils are as young as four. The programme contains adult humour and some of the words are inappropriate for a primary school.'

How to Produce Comedy Bronze

Radio Times estimated that more than 360,000 children aged between four and 15 watched the last series.

It was a breakthrough. A two-person sketch show where we met characters in short bursts throughout the series and looked forward to their catchphrases and how they'd react to new situations and adventures. It felt as though a new 'big' style of comedy had arrived on screen and a new generation with it. Well done them and I hope that Mrs Hargreaves' pupils, now in their late teens, have not suffered too severely and can find something similar to protect their own children from.

22

The Office and Other Things Ricky

Somewhere around the change of millennia, or millenniums, if you'd rather, I was the guy who said 'Yes' to *The Office*. It's a show that has changed lives and comedy and made careers.

It has a Metacritic score in the high nineties which basically means that almost no one has ever found a bad word to say about it.

Versions of the show have been made wherever there are offices and it's made its creators into gazillionaires. I am not responsible for any of the above, nor has it made me so much as 'two bob and a toffee apple' (to quote a well-known agent), but I was the guy who said, 'Yes, OK, we'll give it a go.'

I'd heard about the idea before Stephen Merchant and Ricky Gervais walked through my door, because I think they'd been offering it to everybody.

'We've been told that you'll say "yes" to anything,' said the smaller, wider one of the two.

They had such chutzpah and confidence about their creation, that (in their heads), it had already won BAFTAs and Golden Globes long before it was even commissioned.

The Office was a comedy but also a mockumentary taking the piss out of docusoaps, a genre that had been popular for the previous decade. It was also taking the piss out of work routines and of course, bosses. It had something in common with *People Like Us,* but in its creators' heads it was going somewhere else. They left me the idea (such as it was), though what they really wanted was an unconditional 'yes'. I can't blame them. In fact, we agreed to make a pilot having secured the rights from their agent. Gervais had come from the music industry, and was about to do a show on Channel 4. But he knew that *The Office* was the real deal.

Stephen Merchant had just finished a director's course at the BBC. For his 'end-of-term project', he'd shot a chunk of his mate Ricky's show. Since so few young directors ever want to shoot comedy of any kind, I was already on his side. The scene he'd shot was near the start of the show, where David Brent talks to a visitor about how a friend had invented the forklift truck safety course. The funniest thing about it was Ricky's Pinocchio impression, which follows what is clearly a lie. Here was a clown as well as a writer.

So we made the pilot and took it to Jane Root, then controller of BBC2. The notion goes that the controller looks at a pilot and decides if she/he would like a series. Jane decided not to decide. Perhaps this was because we were already discussing some other shows, including a third series of John Morton's *People Like Us*, but we hadn't quite got to the same stage with them as with this show. She said that *I* should decide and (roll of drums) I chose *The Office*, on the grounds that one was new and some of the other shows were established, and also because I suspected that Ricky Gervais would give me a harder time than anyone else if we didn't make *The Office*. He got his break through my cowardice? Not really. I thought he and Stephen had a bloody good idea.

So why did it work so well? The casting of the people around Ricky had a lot to do with it. Rachel Freck – the casting director – remembers things this way:

'It was weird that neither Stephen nor Ricky knew any actors, except maybe a few that Ricky's girlfriend, Jane, had worked with on *Teachers* for Channel 4. So they sat down and wrote pretty good character descriptions and then they picked people from *Spotlight* [the actors' directory] who they thought looked like the characters. Just by their photographs, not because they'd ever seen them act! [This is by no means the usual way to cast, but hey.] In the end the people we chose didn't look anything like the people in *Spotlight*, but it was a start. Ricky and Stephen had really enjoyed *People Like Us* and its naturalistic style, and that gave me a pointer as well, so we brought in a few people for them to see.

'Nowadays for new shows we see about 50 people per part, but in those days we really didn't see very many at all and we were lucky, because it was a small show at the start and no one, including the writers, wanted stars. Martin Freeman had been in several things – including a show called *Bruiser* – and they liked him, and Mackenzie Crook had done bits and pieces and stand-up. The first time he came in he was so nervous that he couldn't really do it. I persuaded Ricky and Stephen that they hadn't seen him at his best and we got him back. They really went for people who were authentic rather than top-line funny, and that's always good.'

The main actors were sorted, but Rachel told me that another problem arose after that. 'They didn't want any "extras" or "stand-by artists" to populate the rest of the office. They wanted actors who could be directed and play proper office workers.' The difficulty was – how do you persuade professional actors to play non-speaking parts in the background? Rachel rang round some of her acting mates who weren't busy and got them in. She told me that before long these mates were ringing up to say thanks, because the residual payments from the show had just allowed them to convert their lofts, or put down the deposit on a flat.

They found the offices for Wernham Hogg (paper products distributor) in what had been Thames TV in Twickenham, and shooting began. I was nervous of letting things go entirely unsupervised, with an unknown team and director, so I asked Anil Gupta (of *Goodness Gracious Me*) if he would keep an eye on things. He was concerned at the huge number of takes they were doing and how much film stock they were using as a result. The average ratio of film shot, against film used in a final show, was then 7/1, but these guys were shooting nearer 12/1. There was a lot of 'coverage' – essentially the number of shots from each scene that end up being given to the editor to help with cutting. They were doing multiple shots of photocopiers, and coffee machines, and general office background. This can be useful for getting you out of a scene that seems to be going on and on, and it lets you trim dialogue. You just cut away to a shot of the daily grind. It helped Ricky and Stephen achieve the authenticity they were after. And they kept changing the bloody dialogue!

LESSON: Very often, it is a good idea for producers to go into a well-soundproofed toilet and scream 'WE'RE RUNNING OUT OF MONEY! STOP FILMING KETTLES!! I'M GOING TO BE SACKED AND YOU BASTARDS DON'T GIVE

A DAMN.' Then come out of the toilet and say 'This is a mould-breaking series done in a way that has never been done before and your approach is refreshing and radical. Sometimes it is important to have creative contempt for the limitations of budget.'

One of the big reasons that the show worked was the authentic feel of being in a real office. This was perhaps its primary appeal. Huge numbers of people have worked in offices. It also worked because David Brent is an idiot. Most bosses are idiots, or so we all think, but many shows – *W1A, Vicar of Dibley* – have a sensible guy at their heart who is surrounded by idiots. This show had an idiot as its *lead* – surrounded by only slightly lesser idiots (and maybe a few straight guys). It means that the audience all delighted in being able to say: 'My boss is just like David Brent, he's such a tosser!'

LESSON: Try not to wake up in the middle of the night thinking – 'this show is about ME. These unparalleled bastards are writing a show about a hopeless boss. I am *their* boss!!'

If this happens, ask friends to recommend a good therapist or brahmin. Cut down on your red meat. Take a holiday.

The first series went out in August and early September, never a great time for new shows. The audience is either still away on holiday or outside in the garden making one last attempt to turn their mottled pink bodies into bronzed hunks of desirability. The late-summer screening meant that the show didn't get very good audience figures, *but* there was something unusual happening, for those who notice such things. It scored slightly higher figures at the *end* of its run than when it began. When it started, people weren't really sure what it was, documentary or comedy, but by the end they'd cottoned on and word had obviously spread. So BBC2 did a thing they very rarely do, they repeated it within three months of its first transmission. And it nearly doubled its audience. Suddenly it was perceived as a hit.

The Office is a curious show but it's also very brave. It's brave because it makes you cringe so much that you nearly switch off. When Brent interviews a new secretary it's nearly unwatchable. It's truly awful to leave a lady on the stairs during a fire drill because she's in a wheelchair.

I remember the bravery of the Tim and Dawn story, especially the moment when – behind the glass walls of a small inner office – Tim tells Dawn how he feels. I remember a discussion about the moment and the kind of silence it involved. Tim goes into the room with Dawn and we see him take his microphone off. In most of the episode we forget that this is a cod documentary and there's a crew involved, but here the fourth wall is well and truly broken, and the silence is absolute. It's brave.

It's certainly brave of the show to eventually sack its leading character and watch him break down and beg for his old job back. This sort of thing isn't normally done in a comedy. It's a tough watch but hugely well worth sticking through.

The performances of the whole cast are just great. Brent is a monster in Gervais' performance – self-loving, lazy and weak but desperate for approbation. There's an astonishing truth in his performance that comes close to self-loathing. He never lets Brent off the hook. How does he know the character so well? Where did Ricky find all that?

Gareth (Mackenzie Crook) is also a narcissist, but one who wants to lead, always, even though it's the last thing he should be doing. The assumed knowledge of military violence is spot-on, and reminded me of a floor manager at Granada who always claimed he'd been in the SAS but hadn't.

Tim (Martin Freeman), Gareth's nemesis, is the only one we really root for, though even he has his flaws. He just won't follow through. Selecting the man who would go on to play both Dr Watson and Bilbo Baggins shows taste, even if the creators of the show *didn't* know any actors.

Then there's Dawn, the down-trodden receptionist and would-be illustrator who picks 'the wrong guy'. She is played by Lucy Davis, the daughter of comic Jasper Carrott, and is a very fine actress in her own right. In the UK, her character's name was surely chosen so that Brent could do a line about 'waking up at the crack of Dawn'. In the US version her name was changed to Pam – which is apparently a non-fat cooking oil spray…no, me either.

The show sold everywhere and won a huge number of awards. It spawned a German version called *Stromberg* and a Swedish show *Kontorei*, in France *Le Bureau,* and many other versions in countries where they were all-too familiar with their own David Brents.

Around this time, on a visit to California, I met Greg Daniels who was setting up the US version, starring Steve Carell. When I met him he was very exercised about the need for oak tree branches to be hung outside the LA location of Dunder-Mifflin, their version of the UK Wernham-Hogg. He wanted to shoot through the windows and make the place look more East Coast. Producers have the same sort of worries and preoccupations the world over. I put him in touch with my therapist (see lesson above).

After the huge triumph of *The Office,* Ricky sold the TV version of his live show to Channel 4 rather than the BBC. This is a strategy that he and 'his people' have followed throughout his career. The philosophy that says 'these people helped make me famous so I owe them' can be countered by 'spread-betting pays more'. And of course – it looks as if everybody wants you.

After a brief pause, Ricky and Stephen came back with *Extras* which was a bigger and in some ways 'straighter' show. Ricky plays an extra or 'stand-by artist', the people in the background of every big movie and TV drama. The series involves a change of focus. The big stars are now the background artists – so *Extras* featured Kate Winslet, Samuel L Jackson, Ben Stiller, Robert de Niro, Daniel Radcliffe, David Bowie, Patrick Stewart, Ian McKellan and many more, but no longer centre stage. It was a very nice idea.

Stephen gives a hilarious performance as Andy's hopeless agent, and the wonderful Ashley Jensen plays Andy's sad and put-upon best mate Maggie.

Extras shares with its predecessor the idea that we're laughing at the joketeller as much as the joke. It takes us on a more straight-forward comedy journey than *The Office.* In series one, Andy Millman is desperate to be noticed, desperate for his moment in the limelight. In series two, he gets what he wants only to find that it's not all he hoped it would be. The comedy he'd written in series one is being made and watched in series two, but it's been vulgarised. Andy has been noticed, but not in the way he wanted. He finally gives it all up, after a breakdown live on *Big Brother.* He apologises to his best friend Maggie, who's also given up acting, and he disappears. It sounds serious and affecting for a comedy. But the very best comedy can be distilled to a simple statement of dilemma, crisis, quest. If a show isn't 'about' something, it won't have a life. Of course, in *Extras,* we're treated to vastly entertaining movies within movies, and the spectacle of famous folk laughing at themselves along the way. But these would be worth nothing without a serious idea underpinning the whole.

Extras was a co-production with US cable company HBO, and together with the success of *The Office*, this made it easier to get the stars to play ball (and to play nuns, cops and boy scouts). Charlie Hanson, the producer, was the guy who had to schmooze agents, particularly those whose clients hadn't seen *The Office*. This included Robert de Niro who was asked to do a small scene with Stephen Merchant. 'Thank God for his assistant,' Charlie says. 'She'd seen it and told de Niro he *had* to do it.' Hooray for PAs. Charlie and Stephen were not so lucky with Jude Law, who said 'Yes', but then had to pull out because the press were in self-righteous outcry about his private life. Tracey Gillham, the casting director remembers a sleepless night phoning agents in LA, trying to find *anyone* who would pick up. 'Hello, this is the *Extras* office in London. We're offering a set fee and a first-class return airfare and we were just wondering if by any chance George Clooney were free for our dates?'

He wasn't, nor others, but fortunately Sir Patrick Stewart was, and did a fine job. Incidentally, Ben Stiller didn't bother with the airfare bit of the deal. He just borrowed the Dreamworks private jet. Well, if you've got it, flaunt it (or at least fly it.)

If you want to see my old BBC office, you *can* at the end of season one. I let Stephen film there, but I'm not in it. A character who isn't me, but works where I worked and is supposedly head of comedy (it's OK, I just told you, I'm seeing a therapist; see Lesson above) says 'Yes' to Andy Millman and his sitcom. Me/he wants Andy to work with a staff producer who is nothing if not camp (I'm not saying a word). They don't see eye to eye and unfortunate things are said. He/me wants to make the show broader and to put in catchphrases and play it in front of an audience for BBC1. It's called *When the Whistle Blows* and is set in the works canteen of a northern factory.

I think the joke about doing Andy/Ricky's sitcom in front of a live audience may be a reference to us making the first series of *The League of Gentlemen* this way. Fun was being poked. I geddit. Or this may be total paranoia on my part, in which case I'll keep on with the pills.

Extras was a very good series, and a good character study. Gervais is an unusual comedian because he emerged 'fully funny' without having really done stand-up or radio or student revue. He came from the music industry, and that seemed to have given him a confidence and style that many comedians *develop* but which he appeared to have right from the start.

And I was wrong to get an audience in for *League*, OK? I've paid for my crime, OK? Get over yourselves.

23

Royston Vasey and Other Animal$_s$

'It's a wife mine now' – Papa Lazarou, 2017

I am in the Pleasance Attic, an Edinburgh Festival venue which, when packed as it is today, resembles the black hole of Calcutta. It is 1997 and I am watching three guys who are the talk of the Edinburgh Fringe. They are doing a sketch show in black tie and dinner jackets even though it's late afternoon. One of them, the tallest, is showing us round a cave. He is telling us about a boy who may have died down here, and it becomes clear that he, our guide, had something to do with it. It's funny but also strange and unnerving. They truly are different and, as the press keep saying way too often, 'in a league of their own'. Other characters I meet that day are severe Pauline and her restart class, salesmen Geoff, Brian and Mike, and Tubbs and Edward – who were soon to be the famed owners of a 'local shop for local people'. The

213

overly possessive shopkeepers are characterised by a strip of Sellotape between the tip of the nose and the forehead (try it yourself at home). There is no question about it. They are all bound for cult fame and the BAFTAs.

The person who'd brought them to my attention was a very good producer called Sarah Smith. She's now moved on from Royston Vasey to Aardman Animation (maybe that's not such a leap). At the time I was BBC head of broken comedy, and I was trying to develop the links between TV and radio. Maybe the League should start on radio. Sarah and the boys – Steve Pemberton, Reece Shearsmith, Mark Gatiss and the unseen Jeremy Dyson, had the brilliant idea that the sketches might work even better if all the characters lived in the same place. Sarah suggested Ambridge and *The Archers* as a model. Perfect. A number of characters and storylines linked by a location. Initially (when *The League of Gentlemen* was first broadcast on Radio 4) this place was called Spent, which apparently has some sexual connotation (I'm such an innocent). It worked well on radio, but Radio 4's best slots are at 6.30 in the evening. Some thought this was strong stuff for the early evening listener, but the show was popular. The puritan zealots won out, though. When we came back, fresh from TV success, for a second radio series – the series was, quite simply, turned down.

Amazingly, selling the *League* to BBC2 rather than Radio 4 wasn't difficult. It satisfied an appetite they had for the original and strange. On television, the name of the town changed from Spent to what the boys had learned was the real name of 'blue' comedian Roy 'Chubby' Brown. Henceforth they all lived in Royston Vasey. In the second series Mr Chubby Brown plays the local mayor.

I thought originally that the *League* should be made the way you normally make a sitcom. Film some scenes, and then do others in front of an audience. To be fair, the audiences in Leeds were very encouraging, given that our show was not standard comedy fare. We weren't even presenting it to them in the usual sitcom format. Stories went across the series and so the first 'episode' for the live audience was not the thirty-minute broadcast transmitted later, but rather the storyline of a particular set of characters. The antics of the toad-loving Dentons were played out in the Denton house sets on one night in front of an audience. So the next week the show took place in the shop with Tubbs and Edward. Whether it was because the four members of the *League* brought their own families or because the population of Hadfield (the town that stood in for Royston) hired a charabanc, the idea worked and the audience laughed.

Then there was a discussion. The *League* and their producer lobbied against doing series three with an audience.

Now, this subject has been debated as long as comedy has been made for television. Sitcoms were originally done in front of audiences because they were like plays in the theatre. People watching at home join in the laughter and vicariously enjoy the community of the audience. The laughter in the studio acts as a cue and tells them that it's OK to laugh. Another school of thought says that we don't want to share our sofa with 300 strangers who live somewhere near west London or the centre of Leeds. We'll decide for ourselves what's funny and what's not, thank you very much, and we don't need some 'bunch of braying ninnies' (a choice phrase from a viewer's letter) spoiling the show.

Yet another argument says that a studio audience can change the way the performers perform. Just as they make Rik Mayall feel less nervous and nauseous, and Jennifer Saunders less shy, audiences *can* make the comedy stars more theatrical in order to get a laugh, which won't suit the more intimate scale of a TV screen. It also tends to make the performers put more emphasis on 'jokes' and punchlines, which in some cases may distort the idea of the sketch.

There is no end to this argument. I can already hear the letters to the *Daily Mail* saying 'I thought comedy was supposed to be funny so if comedians don't want people to laugh at their work, then maybe they're just not doing their job right.' Well, no. Some comedy may be about creating an atmosphere, being wry, telling a comic story, not just telling jokes.

We had this argument, and the *League* won the day. They didn't want to perform the story of Royston Vasey in front of an audience. I conceded, I can do that sometimes, and we used the Leeds studio for filming without an audience. The *League* showed no signs of missing their 'braying ninnies'.

It is remarkable how quickly the whiff of an original idea reaches the nostrils of talented people. Gifted practitioners were attracted to work on the show just by the smell of it, and they stayed. We had an outstanding costume and make-up team who kept with us because they liked the challenge of making a suit and wig for Herr Lipp, or getting Pauline's lippy just right, or creating Mrs Denton's minge wig. They came back series after series because they knew that they were actually contributing to the creation of these characters.

The costumes were designed by Yves Barre, a man of cosmopolitan background, who created weird and beautiful things out of the air, and not expensive air either (that's the sort of deadly comment that only a producer could make). Yves was with us through *League*, and *Psychoville*, and *Inside No. 9*. He even tried to get out of some great big drama in order to work with the *League* in 2017. He followed the *League* into the Theatre Royal Drury Lane! We enjoyed the same loyalty from the design team, who relished making things look as strange and grim – but also as *believable* – as possible. That's tough when you're asked to create a local shop in the middle of the moors, which then has to explode, nearly get hit by a train and return in the latest series looking the same but tellingly different. What characters or places looked like was helped immensely by Reece's ability as an artist. It meant that we knew what Pop or his family looked like, well before Yves came up with actual clothes (or in the case of the Dentons, didn't have to).

The originality of the idea not only helped us secure a loyal team, it also helped develop a loyal audience. When the guys announced their reunion tour at the end of 2017, they sold out in five minutes flat. Every date. That's how loyal the audience are. There's obviously something cultish about the *League*, and try as you may, you've either got cult status or you haven't. When Papa Lazarou knocks on your door, you either shut him out or let him in. The audience has a thirst for an unexpected story, and the more twisted and strange that story is, and the more it sticks with a particular style and vision, the more likely it is that you'll attract steaming great cultists before anybody else. Bless their weirdly coloured hessian socks.

Filming in and around Hadfield was odd. Normally when you film, there are passers-by and questions are asked.

'What you filming, mate?'

'When will it be out?'

'Is there anybody famous in it?'

'Can me and my friend be in it?'

Here it tended much more towards:

'That vicar is a man dressed up as a woman isn't he?'

'Is that man blacked-up? Is he from the circus?'

'Why is that woman naked and holding a toad?'

'Why is that man with a paint pot making the town look like a shit-hole?'

'Is that butcher's open?'

The *League* was directed by the brilliant and mercurial Steve Bendelack. He did a very good job, maybe because he'd seen the same obscure Japanese horror movies the *League* boys had, and understood the references. He and I had met a couple of years earlier on *This Morning with Richard Not Judy* starring Stewart Lee and Richard Herring. This show was, frankly, obscure, surreal at times and for the executive producer (me) a real headache. It transmitted on Sunday lunchtimes when *children* could see it (child viewers are always a worry for a comedy producer). I think we were all saved by its obscurity. Anyone who watched it and wasn't part of 'the club' would have been baffled. Those who were going to make a fuss weren't in front of the box.

LESSON: The League and the Herring/Lee show teach us that if the talent is confident of the off-centre world they're creating, *let them go with it.* Follow the chutzpah. A diluted, half-baked cake won't work. Not that I'm recommending you should ever undercook or even dilute cakes. It's just a bad idea and Mary Berry would be straight after you with a turkey baster.

The *League* was a sketch show of grotesque characters tied together by a familiar location. After the first series the question was – what would happen next? In the most recent series – because of boundary changes and fracking deals – Vasey is nearly sucked up and absorbed by other villages. Local problems like this give the series a coherence, a unifying locus for the sketches. It's a very good device.

Royston Vasey and Other Animals

Reece and Steve, Mark and Jeremy have always had a very clear vision of how the show should be, from the look of the characters to the atmosphere of the settings. They know what they want and aren't afraid to say. This precision has not diminished with the years. For example, I have emails without number about the way the shows should be *publicised*, always a bone of contention with any production, but particularly so with the *League* and subsequent spin-offs. Their work is tricky to sell to a mainstream audience, but there's no point in just preaching to those already converted by Bernice. *The League of Gentlemen* should provide a rich source of inspiration to the people who make trails and invent PR japes. Too often they see them as an opportunity to showcase the makers' own talents for the weird and unexpected. Trails either give away too much or sail very wide of the *League*'s house style. This has happened to such an extent that we've often ended up making our own trails or (on *Inside No. 9*) commissioning our own film posters. These are reminiscent of the realistically drawn posters for Hammer Horror movies, also seen in the old Renoir and Academy cinemas (ask your grandparents) (or me).

Steve Pemberton and Reece Shearsmith next attempted a series where *story* became more important and a unifying mystery became the backbone of the show.

Psychoville.

Reece and Steve hadn't fallen out with Jeremy and Mark, though I'd love to tell you a bizarre story involving jealousy, cross-dressing and an axe. Sadly, no. Varying ambitions pulled them in different directions (*whatever* happened to Mark Gatiss?).

In *Psychoville*, the main characters all lived in different parts of the country and all received mysterious letters that read, 'I know what you did'. Eventually we find out that they'd all been in a mental hospital together and had all been partially responsible for the death of the matron, Nurse Kenchington. Doesn't sound much like a comedy. So what makes it so funny? Well, the grotesque people and the dialogue (for starters) but perhaps it is also the way the size of performance matches the size of the plot. It is gothic and psychotic and that's how it was played.

LESSON: In comedy, the world can be very strange and peopled by very eccentric characters. The *crucial* thing is that all these characters absolutely believe in this world and in themselves and in each other. So we do too. They are passionately bound up in this alternative reality. This is what makes the comedy *true*. And it's what allows them to create the strangest and most bizarre people and situations. Camp it up, wink at the audience – and everything is lost. Truly.

The script for *Psychoville* had appeared in the first instance because the writers wanted to create it, not because of me or the broadcaster or anything we'd suggested. We persuaded the channel to do what was essentially an early 'box set' of a show by staging a starry read of the first two episodes, with a few wigs and props, at a small theatre in Notting Hill Gate (where Laurence Olivier had undertaken his first professional role). This was partly the idea of an Australian called Justin Davies whom I'd taken on not long before. We needed to make it clear that this was an *event*. The *League* hadn't been on TV for a few years, so people were interested in what they might be doing next. We invited 200 people to see a reading of episodes one and two. The reading provoked the kind of reaction you'd expect for the Second Coming, and we had to be careful that the press weren't among the audience. The performance generated much excitement and the channel controller said 'Yes' to the first series there and then.

LESSON: Make your project seem un-turn-downable and show the people in charge that the world is already panting for it. We didn't need to do this, but, if necessary, pay for people to laugh and cheer and mob the actors afterwards.

It was the first time that a show from the *League* stable had needed and wanted other classy performers. Most took no persuading. Dawn French played Joy – a childless nurse who treats a pregnancy practice doll as if it were the real thing. Dame Eileen Atkins played the matron of the mental hospital, who may or may not have done terrible things to her patients. Well done the casting department and the boys for finding (early in his career) Oscar nominee Daniel Kaluuya to play Tealeaf. The altogether splendid Adrian Scarborough gave us Mr Jolly against Reece's one-handed Mr Jelly, and Jason Tompkins played diminutive Robert. I always felt that Reece kept the best character for himself, the Silent Singer, a character out of a nightmare (or a David Lynch movie) who appeared as a vision to librarian Jeremy Goode. He may not have had many words – actually, he didn't have any – but he certainly made a big impact.

The whole series had a big impact. Good ratings and very good reviews. I was a bit nervous about how it might be received. In the first episode a mentally challenged boy, David Sowerbutts, is part of a murder mystery group at a hotel. Early on in the episode he has to run into a room of guests and shout, almost incomprehensibly: 'Come quick, come quick, there's been another murder! ... Look! The murderer has written the words "Fuck Pig" in his or her own excrement!'

And indeed he or she has. We see the writing centre frame on a white board.

Now even I thought that this might prove strong meat for sensitive viewers. The day after it was broadcast, I went in early to check the Duty Log (the record of invariably irate telephone comments from viewers of the previous night's output). Surely there would be quite a number objecting to hearing the words 'Fuck Pig'?

Under *Psychoville* there was only one comment and it read: 'Do your researchers do no work? Don't they know that Bristol is *not* in the county of Avon?'

This referred to a caption we had used early on to identify the different places where characters lived. The character of Joy lived in Bristol. Sorry, we should have checked.

What does it take to offend people if 'Fuck Pig' written in excrement doesn't hit the mark? There's a discussion to be had about whether offending people is a bad thing. Do people have a right *not* to be offended? No they don't, but getting the counties wrong where they live – they *clearly* have a right to get offended about that. *Mea culpa, me paenitet.* Yes, it's Latin for 'I'll carry the can!'

The trickiest episode of the first series was episode four, a three-hander between Steve as the junior fruitcake David Sowerbutts; Reece playing Maureen, his entirely mad mother; and Mark Gattis as Detective Jason Griffin. It had to look as if the whole 28-minute story had been made in one shot by our brilliant director Matt Lipsey. In fact it was just two. Hitchcock aficionados will know that he shot his movie *Rope* without any cuts (though in fact in those days you could only get 12 minutes of film in a canister, so he had to cheat and make cuts when the camera was behind stationary objects). We did the same but with one 18-minute take and one of ten minutes.

In the scene there is a murder and the body is then hidden from the detective. Accomplishing this in only two takes meant that the crew had to work some magic. They wore soft shoes to make no noise on the studio floor. They had to rehearse camera moves as they would for a live show, and 'boom' moves to keep the booms out of shot, but the sound constant. The scene-shifters had to move in and out, not just to manoeuvre props but also to make sure that the main props (like the trunk with the body in it) didn't get in the way of the cameras. At one point the body was hanging on the back of a door, and the crew had to silently unhook it with only seconds to spare. Of course, all this had to be done while Steve and Reece, and then Steve and Reece and Mark are moving around acting their socks off. If they forgot a line 15 minutes into a take we had to go back to the beginning and start the whole thing again.

It was much more like a play than a television episode, except that you might rehearse a half-hour play for the best part of a week. We had given ourselves two days to rehearse the actors, one day to rehearse with the crew, and then a final day to shoot it. I think that the first take was finally done to everyone's satisfaction on the fourth attempt, though bear in mind – that's 48 minutes of tape (there's the producer again... 48 minutes of tape, we'll have to cut back on biscuits and tea, except I don't think it was tape). It was like doing a live episode of the series. People remarked afterwards that it was like watching a ballet – the graceful interplay of actors in front of the camera, and crew behind. It had its own beauty. So, well done to everybody who had anything to do with it. If you want to see what was entailed, we had a camera recording actors and crew on a big wide shot. It's available as an extra on DVD or Blu-ray, at good shops and websites everywhere. Worth a look!

It was an expensive series with a few big spectacular sequences. It was all shot on film sets and locations. The look was weird and detailed. It had a large cast, though we could schedule them to our advantage and film 'in blocks': a Dawn French block, a Mr Jolly block, a Lomax block, a Robert/ Blusher block.

The second series looked as though it would be even more expensive. We persuaded the channel they could afford it, by throwing in a Halloween special gratis and for nothing. Buy six, get one free. We made the special as cheaply as we could and still had enough money for the telekinetic dwarves and beanie baby collectors of series two. Steve and Reece made the special a portmanteau show, where a number of terrible tales are told by two characters: a researcher from the Psychic channel for *Dale Winton's Overnight Ghost Hunt,* and Phil, who has a strange connection to Nurse Kenchington's past. It was the first Halloween comedy special on British television. Who knew?

For the second series, the writers opened a whole new box, or possibly coffin, of tricks. The wonderful Imelda Staunton joined us. She played the manager of a cryogenic storage facility where the head of Ehrlichman, a Nazi and father of Kenchington the matron, is kept. Bringing Steve Pemberton's severed head back to life was one of the big challenges for our team, as well as constructing Hoyti Toytis toy shop (a front for the sale of Nazi memorabilia). The designer reported back that this memorabilia was worryingly easy to get hold of.

Psychoville is a thing of beauty and a joy forever, unlike most TV. Where else will you see a decent clown funeral procession except in Jodorowsky's *Santa Sangré* (so I'm told), or observe distinguished Hollywood director John Landis playing a part not much bigger than an extra? The plot is wild, the details are precise and wonderfully well achieved. Of course, I would say this, wouldn't I? But after some years the shows still look amazingly good. And I'm not easily pleased.

Psychoville was both a new genre – a *horror-com* – and an old one – a mystery serial delivered to the viewer over six weeks and then another six weeks. The next thing that its creators wanted to make was a 'throwback', a return to the single play. *Inside No. 9* was (and is) a series of entirely separate stories told in very different ways. It has a different cast of characters each week, and each story has an unexpected twist at the end.

Meetings with controllers are always difficult. They're quite hard to set up, and when you do manage it, it always seems you're on their doorstep, selling them something they're not at all sure that they need. This is especially true when you're selling a show for BBC2 that isn't a guaranteed hit (which is most shows). After *Psychoville*, the controller wanted something more cheerful from the guys, 'Something a bit more "Alan Ayckbourny", perhaps?'

Reece and Steve are really interested in *horror* rather than the strains and tensions of suburbia. But, of course, the two of them can be very funny. So the way to sell the new series was maybe as a series of pilots. Let us make six shows, then the controller could see if there was *one* that took her fancy among the six and develop that into a series. This was my strategy. If she settled on one, then 'Hooray!', if she didn't, then we and the viewers will have had a helluva ride producing the selection.

How to Produce Comedy Bronze

Inside No. 9

The first series of *Inside No. 9* clearly showed what wonderful writers Steve and Reece had become. Their range was extraordinary: a group of people stuck in a wardrobe; two burglars silently robbing a house while the couple who live there are having a row; a theatrical dressing room during a production of *Macbeth;* the house of a family with a sick child being visited by a pop star; a flat where a tramp gradually turns a teacher into another tramp; a girl who is asked to babysit a strange old man who turns out to be more dangerous than he first appears. Pretty good for a first series, and that's before you see the twists in the tale. They also decided to give themselves challenges like the ones they faced in the Halloween episode of *Psychoville.* So, in series one there was a silent episode: no words are spoken during the burglary: the owner of the house listens to Rachmaninov as Reece and Steve duck and dive to avoid being discovered. In series two there was a drama with seven people, set in a train couchette travelling across France. A crime is committed and solved within the couchette before it reaches its destination. In the most recent series it was an episode written entirely in iambic pentameter.

It was a challenge for the producer, the brave but resourceful Adam Tandy, not least because he had to make this range of settings within the BBC's budget. There were a few things working in his favour though. He could use more than one director per series, and the production could secure very good actors because the commitment was only for one week of filming. The advantage of discrete stories.

We were very pleased to have made a bit of a discovery with one of our directors. This was a man who had mostly made low-budget Spanish horror movies, but thought that the Spanish horror movie market might be a bit limiting. His name was Guillem Morales and he did us proud.

> **LESSON:** When you employ a director who draws well and does storyboards for each day's shoot, it saves everyone a lot of anxiety (and you end up with very attractive Christmas cards for the cast).

Six one-off films are demanding for everyone involved, but especially demanding for directors and designers. How do you get 12 actors into a wardrobe? (You have a wardrobe brought down from Scotland for shots looking into it, and you build an interior version that is slightly bigger and allows you to manoeuvre cameras and booms.)

How do you build a believable couchette and allow the camera in to shoot all the angles that you need? (You build a realistic four-walled couchette, then put it on springs so that it mimics a train moving, as soon as people get in. You also make it possible for each of the walls to be removed when needed.) Then you set the designer and director new problems to solve for next week. Can you recreate (please) a 16th-century barn for a witch trial? (Well, that's actually a location manager's job and it has to be said that the barn he found somewhere near Chalfont St Giles, where we filmed David Warner, now in his eighties, was bloody cold in January.)

We've only made one seasonal special – 'The Devil of Christmas'. For this, Adam dusted off some period cameras and a period director (sorry, Graeme). The script was a spooky ghost story shot in the style of a 1970s TV special. It called for the 'smears' – those brief trails of light on the screen as an old tube camera tracked across a light source. Thankfully we found some old tube cameras in a collection in Yorkshire. We then went to the British Film Institute and asked if there was anybody still around who knew how to work them. They recommended a man called Graeme Harper. So we booked him and hoped. The cameras, for the geeks out there, were Ikegami 323s – the last generation of this sort of equipment, and they achieved just the right kind of smears. Elstree studios gave us a gallery that could still cope with these cameras, and a cast led by Rula Lenska in a thick fur coat did the rest.

As I've said already – an astonishing attention to authentic detail. But really. All this just to scare people!

The first series did not yield the 'funny' Ayckbourn-style show that would be a hit for BBC2. The nearest we got I suppose was 'Last Gasp', a title typical of its authors' work, about the mother of a terminally ill child who persuades a pop star to visit her bedside. It was set in suburbia and Tamsin Greig played a charity worker bringing the celebrity to a house where, for complex reasons, he has a heart attack and dies. The set-up suited the controller's request for comedy, but the content was dark. Yet somehow, by the time the series finished going out, there was no more talk of pilots.

Everyone, from the controller down, appreciated that the six shows were remarkable achievements in their own right. The audiences did what audiences do, they *found* the show over time, but then liked it once they had found it and came back for more. Some particularly enjoyed trying to guess the twist before the end of the show. They rarely got it right, and we know this because the BBC monitored Twitter for us. Most comedies generate a certain amount of chatter as they go along:

'Always liked him since he was in that thing with that girl'

'I bet she goes like a rocket, and she's got a mouth on her and look at that hair'

'That's the guy who used to do "suits you sir", Paul whatshisname'

With *Inside No. 9*, it was different. There wasn't much chat during the show, but at the end – an explosion.

'I didn't see that coming, did you?'

'So he murdered him before it all started? Clever.'

This seems like a better use of Twitter than, say, using it to sack your secretary of state if you're US president. So far Trump hasn't tweeted about the show...

'#Trump. It's very funny. So funny. Funny, funny. And weird. And fired. It's fired.'

Since the early days of working with them, I've noticed that Steve and Reece really see the point of social media. They go out of their way to use it and respond to it and make special items for it. Reece tweets profusely to publicise shows, sometimes ahead of official announcements. This can ruffle feathers in the BBC publicity department, but it's only natural that he should want the world to know. Particularly because it's a show that falls between comedy and drama when it comes to publicity and awards. They dream up more ingenious ways of using the internet. For example there's one prop that finds its way into every episode of *Inside No. 9* – a small brass hare. It's there on a shelf, or in a corner of the shot, just to be spotted and discussed on social media. Apart from the title and the authorship, it's the only thing that has linked all 24, soon to be 30 episodes.

I take no credit for the *League*'s success, or for *Psychoville* or for *Inside No. 9*. It's happened because the creators are original and good. I eased their passage onto the telly and made the odd suggestion here and there and tried to keep people off their backs. In the most recent series of the *League* I suggested that maybe we shouldn't listen too hard to the editorial policy department. They were saying that Pop could not refer to or show the Picnic chocolate bars he was about to put up 'Ricky's shit-pipe', because it would give the bar 'undue prominence'. Advertising by the back door? I don't think so. I suggested ignoring the note.

Steve and Reece are really good at writing within the boundaries and budgets of the show. Most episodes take place within one setting and, in the case of the one that they directed themselves, from one camera position. Only once have I had to back the producer when he said that we couldn't make an episode. It was an *Inside No. 9* set on a *real* ghost train at a *real* funfair, just because it would be too expensive and take more than the five days we allow ourselves, but whole episodes on European trains or in architect-designed houses to be filmed all night over five nights in July? No trouble.

As I conclude this chapter, a man dressed as a scarecrow, carrying a volume of *Wisden*, has appeared outside my window. He has started to laugh, and is pointing at a heraldic emblem I've never noticed before on the door lintel. It is a strange mythical beast, and as I stare at it – it starts to howl. It is…oh God…it is…my accountant!

Aaaaahh.

24

Beautiful People

O f all the shows that I've had something to do with, this is the one that I feel warmest about.(Apart from all the others.) This is partly vanity, because it's a show where I did what you're supposed to do as an executive producer. I read the book, bought the book (more accurately got the BBC to buy the book), found the best person to adapt it, and then got it made.

The book was originally called *Nasty*, which felt a bit, well, nasty for a comedy, so we got the author's permission and changed the title. The author was Simon Doonan and the book tells the story of him growing up in the 1960s, as a teenage gay kid in Reading, Berks. Home life is pretty good. The household features a wonderful warm mum, and his dad and his dad's homemade wine, and a slightly older sister plus a blind aunty/lodger. There's also a great singing and dancing best friend. This is a happy, crackpot existence in working-class England.

Simon aspires to be with the beautiful people of London's glamorous celebrity world, but when he gets there, it's all slightly disappointing. In fact, the real Simon went on to be, not just a writer of note, but also the creative director of Barneys department store in New York. It was Simon who decided what went on display in the most glittering store windows in the city. He went from a suburban street in Reading to 660 Madison Avenue. Quite a rise! What interested *me* most was the first half of the book, the Reading years, because it seemed funny and warm and happy. Many of the comedies I've worked on have been – what? – sharp, acid, just a little bit savage. This wasn't anything like that, and maybe that's why it appealed to me.

The person I asked to adapt the book was Jonathan Harvey. I'd known Jonathan since I was the exec on *Gimme Gimme, Gimme*.

DIGRESSION: *Gimme* was a show that played to the loudest audience laughter of anything I've ever been involved with (but then it was a relatively small studio and the audience were very close). We sometimes had to do re-takes because the sound level of the audience was overpowering the sound of the actors, including the not-always retiring but ever brilliant Kathy Burke and James Dreyfus.

Jonathan's ability to write camp and funny was not in doubt. He and I went to see Simon Doonan at a rather rococo hotel where he was staying, in Euston Road, London, to talk about our approach. We found the most affable and amenable man you could hope to meet.

Beautiful People

US: So Simon we're thinking of moving the main action of the thing to the nineties rather than the sixties because we think it will capture more of the... *(burble on with artistic thoughts when what I really mean is that it would make things cheaper and easier to film.)*

SIMON: Yes, that'll be fine. You should do anything you think will make it work.

Wow. At this point I am completely in love with Simon Doonan and offering to pay for all the fattening cakes that we're currently eating, and to order seconds. I'm not picking up his hotel bill, but the cakes, fine.

Jonathan H went away relieved and created something wonderful that reinvents Simon's world in nineties Reading. It's that rarest of animals: a witty script. Its characters are sharp and funny from the outset because you quickly understand their context, which lets them 'take off'. The various characters are established early in episode one when Simon reads out a school essay describing his family. Mum drinks too much, Dad's a plumber, Aunty Hayley is blind and overweight, Ashlene (his sister) has snogged all the boys in the street and his best friend Kyle/Kylie lives across the road. Done. Five minutes in and we can move on.

As you might imagine, our casting director Jo Buckingham and producer Justin Davies auditioned more than 100 kids for the two leading boys. We gradually narrowed it down, getting those we liked to read in pairs so that we could see if they were believable as best friends. Then we asked them to read with the actors who were going to play Mum and Dad, to see if they felt like a family. We also asked them to sing, because we knew that we wanted a lot of music in the show. Partly as a mood-altering substance and also because these boys wouldn't just know songs, they'd also know who performed them, the shows that they came from, and how to sing the harmonies.

We finally offered the main role to a boy called Luke Ward-Wilkinson, and his friend Kylie to an extraordinary guy who had been the first non-white Billy Elliot in the show of the same name (let's face it, he was hardly likely to have played Billy Elliot in *Annie,* unless it was a very odd production). This was Layton Williams and that boy could *jeté* to die for. Among those who nearly played Simon but didn't was Will Poulter, later to star alongside Leonardo di Caprio in *The Revenant.* It just shows. (Quite what, I'm not sure, but it definitely shows it.) Olivia Colman – about whom the casting department had rightly said 'Get her while you still can' – was our mum and Aidan McArdle our dad. Meera Syal played blind Auntie Hayley. It's no exaggeration to say that when they were together as a family, you could have centrally heated Reading from the warmth of the cast. They bonded. Oh boy, did they bond.

Not always the case. I once did a pilot with a *very* well-known actress in the lead who was frosty and difficult with everyone. Many of the team suffered ice burns. As you might expect, the pilot show didn't work, so there was no further risk to our health.

Jonathan structured the show with Simon Doonan's older self played by Sam Barnett in a shop window in New York introducing each episode. We did a tiny bit of filming in New York – there-and-back in a day and no sightseeing. Otherwise we were (only slightly less glamorously) in a cul-de-sac in Bushey near Watford for most of our locations. They included one day when (with the blessing of the locals) we used a huge crane to film a medley of numbers sung by three families as their kids head off to audition for the school play.

Beautiful People

The school should be so lucky. The songs were 'Tomorrow' from *Annie*, 'Take That Look off your Face' from *Tell Me on a Sunday*, 'Don't Rain on my Parade' from *Funny Girl* and 'Walk on Down the Road' from *The Wiz*. Who knew Reading could get this camp?! *Reading!*

If you haven't seen it, this may sound like *Glee,* but it definitely wasn't. It was suburban England and not a hint of tinsel for miles. Well, maybe just a little – but it was honest-to-goodness, slightly tatty, *British* tinsel, and no number in *Glee* ever included dance moves for an overweight, seeing-eye dog.

The school play, *Joseph and his Amazing Technicolor Dream Coat*, provokes a slanging match between Simon's dynamic mum Debbie Doonan (Olivia) and its teacher/director. How dare he only cast Simon as a quivering palm tree when Debbie's spent all night making him a dream coat from the lodger's hippy skirt! She smells nepotism and grooming! She's wrong, but she smells it nonetheless, and is going to fight hard for her boy. Olivia Colman has a good left hook.

Later, in a different episode, we find Debbie and her neighbour Reba exchanging blows in a boxing ring at one end of the street, bells, gloves, the works. Thank God most of the householders went out to work during the day.

It's also the only show I've ever done that had a soundtrack album. We had a musical director – Ian Masterson – who is a maestro of the recording studio and managed to get us Dan Gillespie Sells of The Feeling to do the title song. He also persuaded Kylie Minogue and her sister Danni to work together on an Abba number. I'm not saying that the two were in the same studio at the same time but they duet on the track. He also got us permission to use all sorts of music in the show, so that (for instance) there is music for Kylie (the 14-year-old boy, not Minogue) to hairbrush sing to with a feather boa, while Simon is trying on a dress he's stolen from Kylie's mum. An album, currently available on an eBay site near you, was inevitable. Sadly, it didn't include Olivia Colman's rendition of 'Papa Can You Hear Me?' from *Yentl*, but you can't have everything even though she was kvelling naches for her son.

Our family Doonan were a joy to work with. If there were problems they involved our guests. In one episode, Simon gets obsessed with all things Eurovision. It is the year that Israeli trans singer Dana International was the winner. Jonathan, our writer wanted to use the relatively famous gap of time that occurred in reality between the announcement of Dana winning and her appearance onstage. He did so by imagining that our heroes, Simon and Kylie had smuggled themselves into the loos of the contest venue during the dress rehearsal and that this is exactly where Dana wants to change her frock before her final appearance. All good, Justin Davies, the producer got permission to use backstage at Wembley arena. He persuaded Dana to come over from Israel. However when she arrived she had the wrong paperwork and would not be allowed to work in the UK. The valiant producer, Justin, then had to persuade Dana and her manager to take the Eurostar to Paris for the day before our shoot and to return on the same day but with different entry papers. She is tired, she has come from Israel, she doesn't want to go to Paris. Only a bit of spending money for Paris and an extra day or two in London do the trick and she goes, but even more importantly she comes back just in time.

With Irish actress Brenda Fricker, who plays Andy Doonan's mum, the problem was more physical. She fell down the stairs at her London hotel and broke her arm.

We are halfway through filming with her and now she is

in A&E. It is decided that she will return home to Ireland to recover. The problem now is persuading her that, once recovered, she has to come back to us to 'complete' her scenes. Equally tricky is that Jonathan Harvey now has to rewrite the episode to account for her character's arm being in a sling. He does this by inventing a scene where she has to go into the Doonan kitchen and put a can of baked beans into the microwave. There is an explosion which injures her arm! You bet it does! Anything else would have severely injured our budget and plot.

LESSON: Expect the unexpected and cope with it.

If the show has a message then it's probably best summed up by Simon, when he's given a purple tracksuit by his Aunty Hayley. He learns two useful lessons.

SIMON: Never wear nylon, and never wear nylon picked out for you by a blind person.

Good advice.

If the show was trying to do anything (apart from be funny) it is summed up best when Mum and Dad are having a late-night discussion about Simon, who wants a Spice Girl doll for his birthday. Andy, his dad, says, 'I love the bones of him. We always said that we'd do things differently to the way our parents did. I just won't bully our son into being something that he's not.'

They agree Mum will make the doll for him and Dad will try to 'butch' him up a bit.

It's a show that is very merry, very upbeat (when so many

shows are the opposite) and unreservedly gay. It's also a show that is very tolerant. The world is as it should be, not as it always is. Nobody at the BBC ever suggested that we should calm the show down or 'butch' it up. Maybe no one in power ever saw it.

I'm glad I read the book.

25

People Like John Morton

'To write comedy is to report on life as viewed
through a special lens, one that shows us and
reminds us of all that we share in common, and all
that we refuse to admit we do.'
– Larry Gelbart, writer of *M*A*S*H* and *Tootsie*.

People Like Us

L ying in the bath one Saturday morning, it must have been
1996 or 1997, I chanced across a radio series called
People Like Us. I wasn't quite sure what to make of it at first.
Was it a serious if naïve look at people's professional lives
conducted by a genuinely naïve interviewer, or was it an
interesting if oblique comedy? I realised, as the credits *didn't*
run at the end, but the name of Chris Langham and others
'emerged', that it *was* a comedy, and a bloody well-written
one at that. I got out of the bath and looked into it a bit further.
The programme, not the bath.

How to Produce Comedy Bronze

It was written by former schoolteacher John Morton who, unlike many comedy writers, had found his own unique writing voice. His style is meticulous and enjoys the rhythms of speech. It particularly enjoys subtle linguistic misunderstandings. Once you've tuned into the voice and begun to share John's view of the world, it is hilarious and like no other. It specialises in 'phatic communication'. No – not a typo – we all do it, every day. Phatic communication is the 'bits in between', the language that lubricates everyday conversation but doesn't *say* anything: 'Yeah well, er, now then', 'what I mean is', 'Before we go any further what I'd just like to say is, and I really mean this...'. The words have meaning but don't really amount to anything; they just get us to the next bit of real substance. John created the character of Siobhan Sharpe in *Twenty Twelve* and *W1A*. When starting a discussion she is inclined to kick off with words that simply fill in time and don't get us anywhere...

'OK, OK here's the thing, OK. Here's what it is. OK? No one watches TV any more like no one.'

When confronted by the idea that this might be a bit over the top her answer is: 'It's not an overstatement, it's an uberstatement, OK.' Language as Polyfilla, meaningless and pointless.

For John Morton's characters, the English language always seems to be lying in wait for them. It's always ready to throw a curveball at Roy Mallard, the interviewer in *People Like Us* (inasmuch as language can lie in wait or throw anything at anybody). Here's an example. Roy is talking to a farmer with whom he's spending the day:

MALLARD: Can you remember this farm without a tractor?
FARMER: Oh yes, I've got a good memory I don't need a
            tractor.

People Like John Morton

It's a simple enough joke, but if played right...

Here's another example from the day Roy spends with an estate agent. It's from the first ever episode of the show and he is introducing an interview:

MALLARD: Mark and Sarah are both in their late twenties and have been going out together for a year and a half, since they met on an orienteering weekend in Andover, Salisbury, Devizes, Salisbury and Devizes. Since then they've been living separately in a one-bedroom flat, Sarah in the mornings and Mark late at night. Now they're looking to buy their first house together. If they get it right it could be one of the most important decisions they ever make, if they get it wrong it could be an even more important one, of course.

As John M said to me, 'It's only a few degrees wrong. The cadences sound right and if you were listening casually, in a car say, you just wouldn't notice.'

It is precise and perfect, even at the start of his writing career.

Having admired *People Like Us* on radio, I persuaded John to bring it to TV. He brought his radio producer Paul Schlesinger with him and he directed it himself, which worried me slightly because of his lack of experience, but he was not to be dissuaded and I'm glad. Of course, TV and John M gave us the extra problem of what to do with Roy the interviewer. It was decided never to show him. He is glimpsed briefly reflected in windows and shop doorways but otherwise stays behind camera. It's a great device not least because it allows the brilliant cast who are being interviewed to shine – and what a cast! Tamsin Greig, Bill Nighy and David Tennant played the Mother, the Photographer and the Actor in their respective episodes. People Like Jessica Hynes and Vincent Franklin, Rebecca Front and Robert Webb added comic weight to the mixture. It's even possible to spot John Oliver, now a huge star with his own show in America. Getting a cast like that assembled now would need Agatha Christie to come back from the dead and write a celeb-filled Christmas Day special called something like *And Then There Were One or Two Left Over at the Vicarage*, and only then if it was for Comic Relief.

For radio, John Morton went on to develop a 'newspaper of the air' called *The Sunday Format.* Sketches were different items in a newspaper. They began, stopped halfway through, and moved on, in much the same way that articles come and go as you flick through a paper.

For TV, he and co-writer Tony Roche came up with *Broken News*. This was a show that laughed at what John described as 'The Babel of News'; the increasing number of less and less capable stations that often put style over substance. John and Tony's show featured 'Walking News', in which the interviewer in the studio is attempting to keep pace with the reporter who is walking and talking at the scene of the story. The story itself is more often than not a non-event. Reporters being talked to in faraway places know less about what's going on than people in the studio back in Blighty. Then there are local newscasters ambitious to move on to that bigger more important network job, they read undue significance into a parade of boy scouts, or patronisingly josh with the local weatherman. Who might or might not be called Josh.

Smaller stories came and went through the coverage of a main story each week. The main stories included the disappearance of a small island/rock in the Atlantic, the spread of tomato flu and the celebration of 'Half-Way-There day', the day in the middle of the Second World War that was halfway between the beginning and the end of the war. We had a huge cast of nearly 100: different faces for different stories. God knows how we afforded that size of cast! What the hell was the executive in charge thinking about? I can only assume that we didn't feed them, or perhaps we just didn't pay them all.

Once again, John Morton leant on me to let him direct the show, and he turned out to be very good at it. Writers know more about their shows than anyone else, but can't, or don't *want* to direct their work, either because they think it's 'not the done thing' or because they think someone else will do the job better. Often true. Mr Morton was undaunted. John brings to directing a knowledge of the thought behind the line. He is able to give actors precise notes about how or why or in which of a huge number of different ways a moment might be played. John's comedy comes from playing the right inflection and hitting the right rhythm. It is more akin to ballet, where the performers might be given 'corrections' rather than 'notes'.

LESSON: If the creator wants to be part of the process then just remember that you wouldn't have a job without him or her – so don't endanger the project. Listen carefully, be sympathetic, admire his or her sagacity and insight. *Then* say no.

How to Produce Comedy Bronze

Twenty Twelve

Now we arrive at the Olympics. When it was announced that London was going to host the Olympic Games in 2012, I thought that we couldn't let this momentous event go by without laughing at it. It would be an organisational nightmare. When else would the world get a chance to see us fail so spectacularly? I was sure that other people would have the same idea and I was determined that they wouldn't get to the Gold ahead of us.

I rang John M because he was about the only writer I could think of who knew anything about sport. After all, he played five a-side football every Wednesday night, didn't he? What greater qualification was needed?

Then – oh dear me, then – dear reader, I fucked up. I made the mistake of talking to some Australians about how they had made *The Games,* a satire about the Olympics in Sydney in 2000. They took it that this meant that we wanted to make a UK show with them in Australia. No! Stop! Forget I even mentioned it! I shouldn't have approached them at all, because it landed us in all sorts of legal tangles which, it should be said, the BBC lawyers were very good at resolving. When the UK legal team saw that the Australians were making a fuss in public about things, they said, 'Great, that means they've been told they don't have a legal leg to stand on.'

LESSON: This is a further illustration of how a producer's life is made up of anxiety, ulcers, and panic. Not to mention the phone calls at 3 a.m. from people who haven't bothered to work out what time it is in London.

People Like John Morton

Once over the Aussie bump, John started writing *Twenty Twelve*, a show about how a huge event like the Olympic Games is nevertheless put together by the sort of people who work on *much* smaller projects. They are just like us, not especially good, not especially bad, not totally incompetent but certainly not the opposite. At the centre of *Twenty Twelve* is Ian Fletcher – head of deliverance – who tries constantly to corral a group of people obsessed with their own corner of the project and who seem incapable of looking beyond it. There is Siobhan Sharpe, the jargon-filled head of brand (in the stage directions John Morton said 'She turns most sentences up at the end as she really wishes that she had been born American'). Graham Hitchins is head of infrastructure and is very sure that infrastructure is the *only* thing that deserves anyone's attention. Kay Hope, head of sustainability, is forever at odds with the head of legacy Fi Healy (what *exactly* is the difference??), and there's Nick Jowett, a no-nonsense money man from Yorkshire. They make up the main team bringing you the greatest show on earth. Ian's PA Sally Owen appears to be the person who actually runs the Olympic Games from her small desk in the corner of Ian's office.

When we first broached the series idea to BBC4 they didn't really 'get' it. The channel controller, Richard Klein, said: 'I don't think people this incompetent would get to run the

Olympic games. They'd never have got this far, they need to be more ruthless and Machiavellian.'

NOTE: Ruthless and Machiavellian eh? A glimpse there into what a controller thinks he needs to be, to have got where he is. Maybe he just thought we should have been giving him *The Thick of It* in running shorts, and was pissed off that we hadn't.

He was also worried about what he considered to be an excess of narration, apparently not in fashion at that time in the documentary world. Of course, David Tennant's narration has some of the best jokes in the piece and allows John to add or remove commentary when he's editing it together. David always seemed to be doing a film in some far-flung corner of the world just when we needed him to record for us. John Morton took to directing him over the international phone. Thank heaven also for the interweb. It gets script to actors like David, even if they're on location in Tristan da Cunha (or perhaps was he *playing* Tristan da Cunha)…Whatever, I know he was very good and added authenticity.

So after the first difficult pitch, we went through the usual placatory formalities, and changed a few small things and got the channel controller and the commissioner for comedy into a small room where we managed to convince BBC4 that life (Machiavelli) and comedy (*Twenty Twelve*), though related, aren't always the same…and we finally managed to get it commissioned.

To make the show, we hired one of those short lease offices facing the Games site in a Canary Wharf office block. This meant that every morning the receptionist for International Investment and Mercantile Holdings (London) watched as a camera crew, sound crew, wardrobe and make-up artists, electricians, scene painters, actors and John Morton walked past her desk on their way to a day's filming. Our team was more casually dressed than the regular inhabitants of this Docklands block, and a deal noisier. It made for an unusual meeting of art and life but was educational for both sides. One side was dealing with multi-million-pound contracts, whilst the other appeared to be fielding phone calls from Seb and Boris, then lounging around between takes.

One of the actors looked like Lord Grantham from *Downton Abbey*. Was it? Could it be? Yes, it could! We were very lucky to secure the services of Hugh Bonneville for the role of Ian. He had a vast amount of John Morton's linguistically meticulous meeting-speak to learn, and it was the others around him who quite often had the gags. His discipline and concentration were wonderful to behold. Breaks in the *Downton Abbey* schedule were the only times that we were able to get Ian Fletcher behind his desk, but it was worth it. How he switched from one world to the other is beyond me.

Life echoed our art. In episode one, Ian unveils a clock that will countdown in reverse to the Olympics. The fact that it is counting backwards in a world where time is counting forwards leads to inevitable problems. The real countdown clock was unveiled by the real Olympians on the day following our first transmission. It was presented to the world in Trafalgar Square and then promptly stopped. Comparisons were drawn with events in *Twenty Twelve*, much to our advantage.

A later episode tackled the problem of visitors not knowing where the stadium was or how to get there. In our version, a bus with a delegation of visiting Brazilian dignitaries gets horribly lost on its way east, despite the presence of Ian and head of infrastructure, Graham and a translator onboard. In real life, some of the earliest athletes to arrive in London got similarly lost somewhere around Tower Hamlets. I gather there is a Samoan high jumper still struggling to find his way to – or more likely from – the stadium.

Our relationship with the real LOCOG (the organising group for the actual games) wasn't very close. A few things we gathered about them proved useful. We heard from the friend of a friend whose neighbour was a secretary there, that they mostly didn't wear ties to work, so our guys didn't either. We knew that their offices had huge posters with motivating words like 'Win' and 'Endeavour' and 'Deliver' on the walls. We copied that. Otherwise we only knew for certain that we were fiction and they were non-fiction.

Yet sometimes we wondered. Just before we started, LOCOG said that we couldn't call our show '2012' because they had copyright issues with it. Hello? How do you copyright a year? They had *apparently* copyrighted 'London 2012', both the place AND the year. Surely we are entering the world of Siobhan Sharpe here? Isn't that something we discussed for episode three but decided was too far-fetched? We eventually reached a compromise. We were allowed to call it *Twenty Twelve* in letters but not in numbers.

Lawyers again. Hooray!

I personally had a strange encounter with Lord Coe (chairman of LOCOG) when we previewed the second series. We thought that good relations might be served by inviting the LOCOG high-ups to a screening. The first episode of the second series dealt with Algeria threatening to pull out of the Games when they discover that the Shared Belief Centre in the Olympic Village does not face Mecca. France then threatens to pull out if a separate mosque is built to placate the Algerians.

People Like John Morton

We only had time to show LOCOG the first episode of a 'two-parter' which ended with Algeria saying that they're off. It's a cliff-hanger. As the lights came up, Lord Coe turned to me with a genuinely worried look on his face. 'It does turn out all right, doesn't it?'

He had not only been watching it but living through it. He was busy thinking, 'Now, what would I do?' The Greeks called this *catharsis* (but then they also called their children things like Odysseus and Splatapetonia.) (I *know* that last one's not an actual Greek name, because actually it's Albanian).

I reassured him that a solution is found in the next episode. His worry was a compliment, I suppose, but I didn't get free tickets to the opening ceremony and neither did John Morton or the producer Paul Schlesinger or Hugh Bonneville. Suck it up, guys.

Twenty Twelve was generally regarded as a hit.

'There is surely no other country in the world that would laugh at itself in this way' said the *Independent* newspaper, and seemed to think that this was a good thing.

Jessica Hynes (Siobhan Sharpe) was especially well liked. A character who invents phrases like 'let's nail this puppy to the wall' when she means 'let's get on with it' is surely going to be loved. Siobhan Sharpe (rather like Edina Monsoon) was an archetype of PR rubbish-speak, a terrible warning about the power invested in people whose job it is to make things *look* good. She understands nothing, she only knows how to sound radical. She has no roots, she is entirely random, her stupidity is her USP. And she is shockingly funny.

So 2012 (surely I can write it in numbers now) came and went. Some people came from abroad and chased each other round a track and other people threw long pointy things or rowed things and even rode things, and then it was into the hands of the Legacy and Sustainability Departments, and it was all over.

The receptionist at International Investments and Holdings (London) was left in peace to check her emails, paint her nails and answer the phone. That's unkind. She may have been reading *War and Peace* and studying for a masters in philosophy for all I know.

W1A

The BBC was going through changes. The BBC is *always* going through changes. Now they included completely insane notions such as the open-plan office and hot-desking. Let me put it more selfishly. When I was head of comedy at Television Centre and even when I was head of comedy entertainment at the same address, I had an office and a secretary. She was called Fiona and then she was called Julia. Of course, they actually ran the departments.

Sometime back in the days of director-general Mark Thompson, who is now head of everything at the *New York Times* and has an office with its own restaurant, it was decided that secretaries were a luxury and that production offices were so last year. Everybody should grab the best seat they could find when they arrived for work (a bit like sunbeds in Benidorm). First come, first tanned. As a fellow comedy producer remarked of the BBC in this iteration, 'It's a great place to come and meet people, and talk through ideas, but it's a terrible place to work.'

Gradually, the august organisation was becoming a news organisation, with a few ancillary bits that competed with the independent sector and the outside world to provide the programmes that people actually watched. Gradually, most programme-makers were being moved to New Broadcasting

House, where they could have meetings in rooms called Enid Merryweather or Arthur Askey and float balloon-like around the news-gatherers, for whom the building was initially designed. Satire was urgently required and not just to save the inmates, but who could provide it?

There was a lunch just after *Twenty Twelve* to say 'thanks and well done' to J Morton, Esq. It took place in an inexpensive restaurant (honest) in Holland Park and was undoubtedly paid for by one of those present, who *didn't* then set it against expenses (because it was probably over the agreed BBC rate for lunches – then about £1.20 per person). We discussed the future and whether it might be possible to bring Ian Fletcher and the rest of the group back to life. Various suggestions were tossed about the table. Surely, having sorted the Olympics, Ian would get another really big job. Could he run the British Army and our diminishing defence forces? Could he bring the ailing NHS back to life? Should he organise the next World Cup? Or was that rather like his old job but with bigger bribes?

'Those all feel rather like what we've already done...' said John, 'but the one place I *had* actually thought about for Ian – though I'm sure it would never be possible – was the BBC...'

A howl of 'YES!' and 'OF COURSE!' and 'WHY NOT?' went up from around the table. All imaginable barriers were immediately swept aside in our enthusiasm. No one quite took on board that the BBC might say 'no' or that John had never worked at the BBC. 'For', but not 'at'.

We ploughed on regardless and didn't ask anyone's permission. *When in doubt, don't ask.* The education in all things BBC that I organised for John consisted of long lunches with important people. We lunched the head of radio and news, we lunched the head of editorial policy (who had also been head of sport and editor of the *Today* programme), we

251

lunched the head of programme compliance and we even had lunch with a much feared former DG.

We didn't lunch with, but we did *meet* Alan Yentob, who showed John M around some of the more obscure bits of New Broadcasting House. These included a lift that calls at floor three of Broadcasting House (Radio) before calling at floor three (Television) where the lift doors open on the other side because the other door is now between floors. It's where old Broadcasting House and New Broadcasting House don't quite join. There was a moment when we passed a telephone on a researcher's desk, and John asked innocently if he could use it to make a call home,

'You can try,' the lady of the desk replied cheerfully, 'But it doesn't work any more. None of them do.'

Alan hurried us on. Everyone we met had good stories about things going wrong, or how they'd been frustrated by the organisation. It was fun and it was convivial and even fattening, but finally it wasn't what was needed.

'It's not about dramatising other people's after-lunch anecdotes, good and funny though most of them are,' John said, 'That won't quite do. We have to make up our *own* for our own characters.'

So John M went away to work. As previously remarked, he is painstaking and exact, so rarely works super-fast. Usually about a month per episode once he has the overall format sorted. Hugh and Jessica were on board: thank God. All I could do was…among other things…gather examples of the more bizarre BBC memos that I received on a regular basis in case they were useful to John. These two are both real. Well meant, I'm sure but…

Good morning,

People Like John Morton

Please be aware we are fitting the new toilet roll and soap dispensers in all of the toilets throughout New Broadcasting House tomorrow Tuesday.

For the implementation of new Toilet Roll dispensers –

SmartOne Toilet Roll Dispenser Benefits:

The main benefit of SmartOne is reduced consumption of toilet paper due to the unique dispensing method, which means;

- *Reduction in the amount of paper used. Which is good for the environment*

- *Reduction in the amount of cases that need to be delivered. Less deliveries, less CO2 emissions*

- *Reduction in cases used. Less packaging to throw away*

- *Reduction in the amount of toilet paper in the system. Less possibilities of drains getting blocked*

- *Less time spent by your cleaners filling dispensers, more time spent keeping the site maintained.*

Also please find attached a PowerPoint presentation on more of the benefits of the toilet roll dispensers.

If you could please spread the news that all the toilets will be out of action at different times throughout the day tomorrow and all of the positives that will come from the new products.

Vital and important. No question. Especially as the BBC is almost always – through no fault of its own – in deep shit.

A friend in News sent me this other titbit that I passed on.

I was in NBH today & saw all the blinds pulled down around the vast windows overlooking the news room. The blinds are used when they do rehearsals of sensitive subjects such as Royal obits. Everyone is routinely warned not to report this on social media, but in this vast building, lots of people are either not on the news email list or otherwise could not know that this was just a rehearsal. *(Anyway this place leaks like the proverbial.) Hence there was indeed a tweet to the outside world about the Queen's health worries – the fictitious basis of the rehearsal. First it was picked up on the Guardian website & then it started to go viral. A denial/clarification followed from the BBC.*

Our proposed show was already acting as a kind of group therapy for staff.

A story that came to me from the personnel/human resources department did finally make it into the show, not as a joke but as a character. A few years earlier, they'd found that there was an intern who'd been working for 15 months on a daytime show, but who had *never* been *paid*. When HR finally brought this to the attention of the producer for whom the intern was working, her response was, 'Oh that's OK, it's saving the BBC a lot of money – and anyway he's my cousin!'

So not only breaking employment law but also clearly nepotism! It was at that moment that Will Humphries, intern of *W1A*, was born.

New Broadcasting House was very generous, letting us film extensively within it. They moved a subdivision of a department to give us a production area, and let us roam around mostly unfettered. They even let us confuse everybody by renumbering the floors for a day or two. Filming in the main reception area was trickiest because it was always busy. It meant that a rare thing happened: those being sent-up met those doing the sending-up at the closest of quarters. It meant, for example, that when we were just going for a 'take' with Will the intern, the genuine newly appointed chairman of the BBC came straight up to him with a cheery, 'Good to see that they've given you a proper job, at last!'

Life and art, I love them both!

In the interests of saving money (that old thing!) we shot what couldn't be shot in the real NBH in our own version of NBH over at the recently vacated White City building. This proved to be an error. The White City building that we were allowed to use had been decommissioned by the BBC some time before, so we had the run of it and were able to put up sets that made it look like the real place. So far so good, and so cheap. Except that because the building was out of use, there was no running water, and no running water meant no loos. This meant that whenever make-up needed to be applied or nature's call had to be answered, those involved had to go down in a goods lift with a security guard, out into the cold (it was winter) and into an adjacent building. Where, I'm sure, the toilet roll holders were of the most environmentally friendly, ergonomically efficient, and economically sound variety. It wasn't so much the inconvenience, though it *was* inconvenient, it just seemed so primitive.

For the next series we went to Pinewood Studios instead. It was more expensive, but had much better sanitary facilities.

As head of values, Ian has a very wide brief. This helped the show address many different BBC issues, especially with Charter Renewal looming. It wasn't just 'what to do about the BBC Swing Band', or 'are there enough Cornish people on the air?', but will there still *be* a BBC after these problems have been sorted? It may not have always seemed so, but Renewal had the tension and urgency of the Olympics. It was the ticking clock that gave a sense of drive to events in *W1A*.

Is the show accurate?

Well, lots of people who work at the BBC told us it was more of a documentary. Do Alan Yentob and Salman Rushdie arm-wrestle every day? No. Is there a director of better? Not yet. Has *Britain's Tastiest Village* made it to the screen? Not yet – but check the daytime schedules. Is BBC ME a reality? Not as such but it's in development. Is there something like Syncopatishare making lives a misery across the organisation? You betcha. Has the BBC News caption service called the current (at time of writing) prime minister, Tweezer May? Almost certainly in the wee small hours. Do heads of this and that suddenly up-sticks and go to work in the US? Yes indeedy. Might Evan Davies appear on *Strictly*? Don't rule it out. Might Ian's salary become public knowledge and lead to all sorts of confected outrage which eventually means he has to take a self-inflicted cut? Ask John Humphries.

Since our show was broadcast, we *have* heard that when a meeting in the real BBC seemed to be heading for the self-important or the jargon-filled, someone would say, 'Is this all getting a bit *W1A*?' Memos to the staff have been known to begin 'I know this sounds a bit *W1A* but...' Not often, not always and not enough, but maybe we've helped the BBC (and many another big corporation) – what? – calm down, cut the crap, save time.

LESSON: Encourage people to write about what they're living through. It might even help make things better.

People Like John Morton

> **LESSON:** Remember that comedy plotting is really about giving your characters a problem (like closing down bits of the BBC or dealing with dodgy captions) and seeing if they can solve it. Sometimes they might not be able to but quite often, that's what's funny.

At the end of the series the real DG, His Tonyship the Lord Hall, agreed to get lost inside the Tardis. I shall say no more.

26

I'd like to be in
Am-er-i-c_a

(Apologies to Leonard Bernstein)

*'The USA is a foreign country they do things
differently there'*
(Apologies to LP Hartley)

On a couple of visits, I've been lucky (or unlucky) enough to observe how shows are made in America. Over there, it's much more a question of supply and demand. The demand is for 22 episodes a season (in the UK it's six) so the way they're supplied has to be structured differently. The model is changing both here and there with the arrival of Netflix and Amazon, but the basic model is still very different from ours.

In the UK, we make six episodes at a time because that's what we've always done. Six is what you offer, and then six of some other show, so the viewer doesn't get bored and the writer of the first show has time to go away and write some more. In America there's a very different attitude. If they find something that works they want to exploit it.

'Let's make four or five seasons of the damn thing, then we'll have enough to sell the show into syndication, dagnabit'.

But what the sweet bippy is syndication?

(Sorry about 'bippy' and 'dagnabit' I was going for local colour.)

Syndication means, after your first network showing, that you can sell your 110 shows to smaller TV stations across the country, and that they have enough to show them Monday to Friday, every night, without repeats. Syndication is where you can really make *big* money. There is a story, probably apocryphal, that when *Cheers* first sold into syndication, Ted Danson gave a party to reveal to all his guests the huge cheque he'd received, in a nice way. It had eight zeros on it even back then, I gather.

The lure of getting to 100 shows, which is what you need to get into the world of the 'S' word, proved such a lure for Charlie Sheen that he set up *Anger Management* with the aim of getting to syndication as quickly as possible. They made 45 shows a year and got to 'S' land in just over two years. They had to employ a large number of writers, and an archivist to help them avoid repeating plots! The whole set-up for the writers simply became: 'Who is Charlie going to shag this week?' Nothing more subtle than that. The show was picked up by Cable channel FX and its transmission was: series one (ten episodes, running June, July, August 2010) then series two (90 episodes, running January 2013 to December 2014). Pile 'em high, sell 'em cheap... well, not so cheap actually.

I first went to 'the coast' (that would be the *West* Coast) to observe working practices as part of a group of European producers who were on an exchange programme. In the

I'd like to be in Am-er-i-ca

UK we had just made *The Office,* which was already being downloaded and watched by US writers and producers in the know. Copies were changing hands for serious money. Plowman suddenly had a modicum of status! As a result, people from BBC Worldwide kept pulling me out of meetings between the Europeans and the Americans: 'You mustn't meet them in a group – you're too important – we'll sort out private meetings for you.'

Really.

But as a result of this I was able to sit in on some writers' sessions for *Will and Grace* to see how it was done without any interruptions from Dutchmen. (There were several Dutchmen.) The show was 'run' by the very tall Jeff Greenstein, who has subsequently become a good friend. I saw on day one that the operation of an American comedy is a truly elaborate piece of engineering. There wasn't a producer in sight who wasn't a writer. So – just to be clear – every one of the 12 writers on the show is also a producer or executive producer. On the walls round the office were hundreds of Post-it notes showing the characters' direction of travel through the series and story points to help them get to their destination. The notes also had episode concepts for the next week and (God help us) the next few months. For example, Grace gets pregnant (*'Don't tell anybody!! This is top secret!! Swear on your copy of Jack Benny's life story'*) so this means a change of shape for Grace, new characters, lots of new jokes, visits to gynaecologists etc. Also BIG story developments for the other main characters: Will tries to get a boyfriend, Jack gets a job and so on.

Individual episodes are 'pitched' by individual writers. On *Will and Grace* there were 12 of them – men and women, young and older. Story ideas are kicked around, and then one of the writers is assigned the episode. For the next week or two that writer goes away from 'the room' to produce a basic script. A core group from the team will then work on the episode when the writer brings it back. It is taken apart and rewritten in an almost surgical way, a line at a time.

As much of this process as possible is done before the season starts (that is – the shows begin to go out on the channel) because once that happens, life gets very busy indeed. The showrunner takes that week's episode to 'the floor' where the director and the actors do a reading at which 'the network' (in this case NBC) is present. The network give notes to the writer(s), the actors go home and then the writers take the script away to be re-engineered yet again. This is done by putting the script onto a large computer screen in front of which sits the team, rewriting it – again a line at a time – usually well into the wee small hours.

Imagine.

Head writer says to the group, 'OK, as we open, she's wrestling with a machine in the kitchen area, clearly having a bad time. He comes in. She turns and says, "I'm going mad. I can't make this juicer thing work." That's our opener, but has anybody got a better reply than: "Never forget, no juice is good juice"?' (These are **not** real lines of dialogue, you'll be glad to know).

Back in the room several other, much better lines are pitched and the head writer is the final arbiter.

Of course, it takes a long time to work through an entire script like this, and then they're going to be doing it *again* tomorrow night when tonight's version of the script has been rehearsed and found wanting and they have to take it back to the workshop to be improved. This goes on for four or five days before the recording. Rewrites even happen on the floor on the day of the show, in front of a warmed-up audience who haven't laughed enough at the old line. New lines are pitched by a small group of writers in a cabal on the studio floor. Then these new lines are given to the actors, who must now forget all that they'd carefully learned and learn a new version of the scene in five seconds. Eventually something will be found that works.

Spare a thought for the actors who have to take in so much and then replace it. But not too much of a thought. At the end of the first season of *Will and Grace*, the network gave each of the main actors a new Porsche. While the poor old writers just got nice leather binders. The binders had each writer's name engraved on the front, but on closer inspection, their names were engraved on labels that covered up the names of other writers on an old show that hadn't worked. Sad, but true.

I was invited back by Jeff Greenstein to take part in this process on a different show a year or so later. He had written a pilot for one of the main networks called *The Rich Inner Life of Penelope Cloud*. It starred Oscar-winning actress Marisa Tomei and was the story of a once great, now unproductive writer (Penelope Cloud), stranded as professor of creative writing at an unnamed university, who regains her inspiration – partly with the help of a much younger male student. There were four or five good writers helping Jeff for no money, in the expectation that they might be taken on to the writing team if the show was 'picked up'. *Penelope Cloud* was doubly unusual in that a) it had an older-than-usual female lead and b) it had *something to say*.

My first day was the network read-through. Not just the network that had commissioned the show, but also the network with which Jeff had a deal, who had 'lent' him to the first network. The cast was there and the main people working backstage on the show, but there were also – maybe – 45 others. These were people from the two networks, and the cast's agents, and their business managers, and PR people and lawyers, and the people employed to make sure that nothing in the show will get the network into trouble (from a department known as Broadcast Standards and Practices), and a few casting directors, and PAs, and gardeners and probably a few stray Marisa fans as well. Quite a crowd.

The script was read. Marisa Tomei was very nervous because she had never starred in an audience sitcom before. This didn't help. The laughs tended to come for the lesser/ funnier characters who had distinct comic turns. One of the larger parts still wasn't cast and was read by an assistant. At the end of the read the writers and I retreated, but Jeff had a meet with the network. Their one note to him at this stage was: 'Wow, you got Marisa Tomei!'

No notes about the script or the performance, just delight that their famous leading lady, whose name was on the invitation, got in the limo, and came to the read.

So. We go through the rewrite process that I outlined above. It very quickly becomes clear what the different skills of the different writers are, and how they pitch material. There is Bob, a full-on guy – LA born and bred, always ready with a good gag. His lines are sometimes brasher than the tone of the show but he's good, and up for it. He's worked on *The Simpsons* and *3rd Rock* and *Malcolm in the Middle* – and he will go on to write *Way to Go* for me, and he will also help bring back *The Muppets* to TV. He's fast and funny.

There is Alexa Junge. She is a quieter figure, slightly more thoughtful. Unsurprisingly, she has worked on *West Wing* and *Friends* and, as I write she's working on *Grace and Frankie* with Jane Fonda and Lily Tomlin. She doesn't pitch as quickly as Bob and tends to work inconspicuously in the corner. Austin Winsberg is the third guy in the room, young and more like me, in that he spends as much time watching the process and learning as he does pitching in. He's also nearer to the age of the younger characters in the show, which is useful. We are also helped by a guy called Ari Posner who had been Jeff's writing partner years before (and had also once interviewed various Russian leaders for *Newsweek*. No really, not much use to this show but true).

Jeff is the driving force. *Penelope Cloud* is his baby and besides, a guy who is an imposing six foot eight is always more likely to lead than follow. As the week goes on he keeps having to take calls from the network who are worried about Marisa, and think that with the pilot due to be recorded on Friday night, it would be a good idea if on Tuesday she and the cast performed it in front of them. NO! It would NOT be a good idea. The actors need time to settle in and the script needs time to settle down. The last thing that a slightly nervous actor needs is a group of 'important' people being nervous about her and making her more nervous with their nervousness. Anyway she's really good. If she's allowed time.

The director of the piece is a veteran genius called James (Jimmy) Burrows. He absolutely knows what he's doing – after 203 episodes of *Will & Grace*, 237 of *Cheers*, and lots of *Taxi* and *Frasier* and 10 years of *Friends* and – well – everything else in between. He is great with actors and good on plot and dialogue, as you might expect. As a technical director he couldn't be more different from a UK TV director. At the BBC, a director of live comedy works out a camera script that will let the vision mixer cut between cameras as the show happens, so that he/she – the director – has to do as little as possible in the edit. Mr Burrows knows that in the US, the showrunner and the network will want to have as many different options as possible in the edit. They will want the output of *all* the cameras available to them. So the director's job is to provide them with all that material, and only to cut the show as it progresses for the audience in the studio. James Burrows does this by ear. As far as I could see he listens to the show *very hard*. He sometimes walks up and down behind the cameras and just occasionally he kicks a camera, never a cameraman, into a slightly different position. Not because he can *see* that the shot isn't quite right, but because he *knows*. He can feel it.

I can think of no other TV comedy director who has had a two-hour tribute show made about him on US TV. We were lucky.

The show went well but wasn't picked up. The highlight of my evening, apart from just being in a studio in Hollywood, was my encounter with a leather-clad woman who was from Broadcast Standard and Practices, or the Gestapo or possibly worked in development at the network. There is a point in the script where we learn that Penelope Cloud has had a lesbian fling with her best friend. The length of the affair isn't stated but it's not important. So I am part of the rewriting huddle when this leather lady comes up to Jeff and says in no uncertain terms: 'That'll have to change.'

'What?'

'The lesbian affair – we need to make clear that it was *very* short. We need her to say "brief" or something like that.'

It seems to me that, firstly, this is interference by someone we've never seen before, secondly, it's something that should have been said and sorted earlier – they've had the script with this in for a while – and thirdly, this is something where my alien status might be useful.

'Hang on a minute,' I chip in, 'Are you saying that a leading lady's lesbian affair has to be short or non-existent in your country? What happened to lesbian equality? What happened to the eighth amendment?'

I'd like to be in Am-er-i-ca

She is a bit floored by this and frankly so am I.

'I don't know, I'm just telling you that's how it has to be' is her 'I'm just following orders' reply.

I think I won on moral grounds. But of course we changed the line.

The entire experience was a good one for me and a great learning curve.

27

These you may have Missed

ANNOUNCER: And Now a Brand New Com—
(Sound of audience switching channels)

Hard to believe, but there are a number of shows that I helped look after, which it's *just* possible you may not have seen. Unlike the olden days you haven't necessarily missed them for ever. BBC iPlayer and DVDs and channels like Gold and Dave, or if you're in America, Crackle and Squark, TV Land and Adult Swim, Fearnet and Shock, all regurgitate comedy like so much acid reflux. Nothing has gone for ever.

NOTE TO BROADCASTERS: Does it tell you something about the importance of comedy that there are all these outlets for past shows but not so many for long-gone documentaries about say, the history of the garden shed? Think on.

How to Produce Comedy Bronze

This is a survey of programmes I had something to do with, which I'm traumatised and grief-stricken that more people did not watch (that isn't really true). I hear tough, right-leaning readers say, 'Get over yourself. I watch what I want to watch and the market decides if something works or not, so pull yourself together.'

Yes but. You might not have seen the trails, or you might have hated the way it was promoted. Thursday may be the evening you go to tango lessons, or it could be your night for Bridge, or Latin prose translation, or oiled-up Japanese Wrestling, or reading up on Teach Yourself Autopsy. I cannot know. I'm just saying that if you had a spare half hour at some point in the future and didn't then vomit as you watched the first half minute, then these shows might be for you.

The Robinsons

Consider if you will the quality of the cast on offer here. I give you Martin Freeman and Hugh Bonneville, Anna Massey and Richard Johnson, Amanda Root, Abigail Cruttenden and Amanda Abbington. And, as if all that wasn't enough – Olivia Colman! Our new Queen on Netflix. Really. For chocolate lovers, that's the equivalent of being given a box of Knipschildt Madeline truffles. Really.

It's about the Robinson family (the clue's in the title). The recently divorced reinsurance salesman son of the family is played by Martin. His brother, played by Hugh, is a high-achieving, highly-organised time management consultant, married with a six-year-old son but haunted by being bullied as a boy. He is the sort of guy who – in pursuit of another child – works out exactly when his wife will be at her most fertile, and makes a note in his diary to be available that week (unless a conference comes up). By the way, if you want to see Hugh – dressed in a red bra and panties – reliving his childhood experience of being bullied, then this is the show for you. Go to episode three, not far in.

Martin's family are desperate to see him married again but he isn't keen, though he will go to singles bars. His sister hates men and is pedantic. His mother and father have grown to dislike each other. I like that it's not afraid to do short scenes for the sake of a good joke. Example:

ED ROBINSON
(Martin) voice over: *I am the grandson of Cyril Robinson, who as legend has it, was the youngest person in his street to sign up at the outbreak of World War One.*

Onscreen in black and white, we pan along a queue of young men signing up. The camera eventually comes down to a very small six-year-old, with cap and moustache. This is Cyril.

It's a treat. Martin's delivery is dry and matter-of-fact. And the show has bothered to recruit extras in costume and film the whole thing in great period detail. They even found a six-year-old willing to wear a moustache.

Why didn't people watch? Why didn't the BBC give it a second chance? Ah...It was what?...'probably seen as too middle-class and middle-brow'. It's not, I promise you.

For me it had the flavour of *Arrested Development* about it. It wasn't afraid to throw its characters backwards and forwards using flashbacks, or to interrupt its narrative line for a good aside. The cast were superb (as you would expect) but they and their extended families were obviously too busy to watch.

If, on the other hand, you were one of the select group who bothered, then thank you and well done. If not, then catch it if you can. It's available, at time of writing, on Amazon.co.uk (and other good book retailers, I'm sure!) at £17.99 (a snip!). It was written and directed by Mark Bussell and Justin Sbresni, who also wrote a show called *The Worst Week of My Life*, and they know what's what.

Hyperdrive

You have to get used to me assuring you that shows are FUNNY. I know, I know. I was paid to make them. One man's hilarious romp is another man's slough of despond. But I'm talking to the rompers here. Did you watch *Hyperdrive*? No? You missed a treat.

This was a British sci-fi comedy. It was set aboard the HMS *Camden Lock* – a British spacecraft in 2151. Its crew are on a mission to convince aliens to base their businesses in Milton Keynes. *Hyperdrive* is really a 'work procedural' comedy in the unlikely context of a sci-fi adventure. It was shot in a shed in Bolton. The problem with getting viewers to it was partly that it wasn't *Red Dwarf,* and partly that it wasn't *Star Wars*. Fans of the George Lucas epics didn't believe that the BBC had enough money to make the sci-fi effects impressive enough (those who remember the TV version of *Hitchhikers* may understand this fear – and we had even less money than they did). *Red Dwarf* fans are usually in a world of their own so competition was always going to be difficult. Anywho, it was written by Kevin Cecil and Andy Riley (no slouches), and it stars Nick Frost, Kevin Eldon and Miranda Hart. Wonderful. Another platter of posh chocs – maybe a choice selection of Leonidas this time.

It's possible that I didn't push hard enough for it to be

more satirical. 'Brits in Space' certainly feels like it might be a microcosm of the country and its ambitions. I could have urged the writers to send up the whole sci-fi genre more comprehensively, as in the glorious *Galaxy Quest*. Isn't that what executives are supposed to do? Isn't my job to push shows to be one thing or another? It may be but I wasn't sure enough and I didn't.

Whatever. It's good. It had two series, and all the right production values for the story it tells. John Henderson was the director and both he and the special effects team did an excellent job. Just watch the shots of HMS *Camden Lock* being attacked whilst carrying a huge British weapon. The effects are every bit as good as anything you'd see in a first series *Star Trek*, and at least a tenth of the price. If the spaceship is a tad undermanned, then we were just being careful with your licence fee, and you can't say *that* happens very often.

P.S. Kevin Eldon is brilliantly funny too. And so is Miranda Hart and so is Nick F. Just thought you ought to know what you missed.

Way to Go

This is a show that's very close to my heart. Right. Deep breath. It is about three guys who attempt to set up a business to help people kill themselves. Yes – it's a comedy about euthanasia. An entertaining drama about suicide. OK, so I can see why it might not be to everyone's taste.

It was written by an American called Bob Kushell, whom I mentioned earlier and who I liked very much. He was one of the writers on *3rd Rock* and he helped bring the Muppets back to US TV, so you can see that he's not just a ghoul. It starred Blake Harrison (the tall one from TV's *Inbetweeners*), who plays Scott, a medical student who has dropped out and now works as the receptionist in a 24-hour veterinary clinic. Ben Heathcote, a bright young actor who should be better known, plays Scott's step-brother who's in deep debt to some very dodgy gangsters. Marc Wootton, (Mr Poppy from the *Nativity* movies – sorry, Marc) plays Cozzo, a guy who repairs machines in fast-food restaurants. It was darkish, of course, but the dialogue was great.

Near the beginning we see Scott and his girlfriend who've been making love. He suggests that they go for a curry later.

LUCY: Sorry, I can't, I'm seeing someone else.
SCOTT: What d'ya mean? You've been seeing someone else? How long have you been seeing this other bloke?
LUCY: About two weeks, but there hasn't been a good time to tell you...
SCOTT: So how about before we had sex. That would have been a very good time!

A neighbour who is ill asks Scott to help him commit suicide. Scott gets Cozzo to build a machine that can pump a fatal drug into the neighbour. Scott obtains the drug from the vets where he works (the vet sharply played by Melanie Jessop.) Cozzo unveils his machine. He calls it 'The McFlurry of Death.'

No, we didn't get sued by McDonalds (but maybe I will for mentioning that).

Then there's the late great Warren Clarke performing 'Mad Dogs and Englishmen' in a hotel restaurant (a sight for sore ears). He's another volunteer for Scott's services.

Thankfully, we got some nice reviews (the *Telegraph* called it 'Absurd and very funny'). So – yes – it sounds dark and in places it *is* dark, but it's really worth a look, even if you're terminally well. It's daring. It takes a risk. And comedy works by surprising you, by presenting you with unfamiliar situations, by suggesting events that you never thought could happen, by challenging you to take a look at something different. It even makes you think. Always a worry.

I think the show has real élan and imagination. It takes the rugged philosophy that says young people should get on their bikes and make opportunities for themselves, and pushes it to an extreme. In a world much in love with free enterprise, it asks whether enough attention is paid to morality. What would they say on *Dragons' Den* if someone came up with Cozzo's machine? Would they know why it was just a wee bit iffy? *Way To Go* is maybe not for all tastes, but the pace, the style and the performances should have an appeal for a larger crowd than first watched it.

Marc Wootton thinks that scheduling cowardice saw it consigned to the (very unhelpful) slot that it had. And I can't help but agree with him.

It's on DVD, dig it out if you can, before they dig you in.

Flashmob The Opera

One day a man came into my office called Steven Wright. He had the idea that the comedy department and the music department should combine to produce a Flashmob opera for BBC Three.

> **NOTE: A flashmob is a group of people who agree that they can be contacted at not much notice to take part in a spontaneous and unrehearsed artistic happening. They have to gather together in a specified place where they will be given instructions about what is needed of them.**

In our case, the place was Paddington Station at 8 p.m. one evening, and participants had to arrive ready to sing some English lyrics to *Nessun Dorma*. We didn't know if anyone would show up. The idea was that if enough arrived then our opera's hero would be able to go back to our heroine. The whole event included the Metropolitan Police choir and a gospel choir, with the BBC Concert Orchestra, and soloists conducted by Robert Ziegler. This would all take place on Paddington station concourse – live on BBC Three.

Train announcements were silenced for an hour. Commuters were perplexed and bemused, but many put down their bags, postponed their journeys and were royally entertained.

The plot involved a young man having to choose between going to a football match and going out with his girl. *She* has to choose between getting on a train (about to leave Platform 8) with a handsome stranger, or staying on the platform just long enough for her boyfriend to show up, having decided to miss the game. The story featured well-known arias, choruses and duets cobbled together to tell the story. The argument between boy and girl that kicks the whole thing off happens at home and on a tube train, and was filmed earlier, to the consternation of tube commuters.

A huge amount of work had been put in by others, not me. As I recall the idea was developed with the BBC head of music, Peter Maniura, me as some sort of comedy doctor, Tony Bicat who wrote the libretto and the head of BBC Three – which transmitted it. It was produced by the Frances Whitaker of *Wogan* fame. I then turned up to watch. It was extraordinary. The wonderful thing was seeing people who were not in on the event respond to it, and watching people who *were* in on it, suddenly bursting out of the crowd of commuters and into song! Until the climactic arrival of the

These you may have Missed

Flashmobbers, we had no idea whether anyone was up for this thing or not. There were about 80 in the end.

Somehow, cameras and sound and the director, the late great Phil Chilvers, all kept up with the action. The camera crew often worked on football matches so they knew how to cover the unpredictable. A number of luggage trolleys with speakers on them meant that the orchestra and the singers and the sound department kept in touch and in time. The singers watched the conductor via these trolleys.

It's the only show I've been present at – live – where I have found myself ringing friends to encourage them to watch along with me. That's how good it was. The channel controller we dealt with, Stuart Murphy, has just been appointed head of the English National Opera. He got it all from us.

LESSON: Always answer the door, it may be someone with an idea so mad that it has to be done. When in doubt, do it!

28

Fifty-Seven Million Coke Can$_s$

By the time we made our film in 2015 there had in fact already been an *Ab Fab* movie. It was French and therefore called *Absolument Fabuleux* (I think) and in my view it wasn't that *fabuleux* at all. That's not really fair, or rather *ce n'est pas juste,* because we saw it at a special screening with the UK cast and it was like a bizarre dream in which people you know are played by people you don't, and there seem to be punchlines without set-ups, and set-ups without punches. It was also in French and had been especially subtitled for us, so I'm not the best judge. *Je ne suis pas le meilleur magistrat.*

Cut to: ten years later: Day.
I am once again in the office of Maureen Vincent (you *must* know by now – Jen's agent) (still), being introduced to Damian Jones. He is the producer of *Iron Lady, The History Boys* and *Goodbye Christopher Robin* (among many others). These are the films for which he's best known, though to me

he will always be *best* known for his very short emails. He just *does not do* email small talk. 'Yes', 'Tomorrow', '8 p.m.' these are some of the longer messages I have had from him.

Maureen is introducing him to me because Jennifer has had an idea! For a movie! We've been waiting for this – oh – for a while. A number of different studios have been pitching to help us make it, ever since Jennifer let it be known that it might be the vaguest of possibilities, somewhere around 1992.

The big difference between a film and a TV sitcom is that you have to have a proper beginning, middle and end for a film. A sitcom can just 'be', but a film has to have a *story*, a structure, something that keeps an audience in their seats and is worth 90 minutes of their time. It needs a BIG IDEA that can command our attention and develop excitingly over an evening's entertainment. It needs to be longer than a sitcom. And it's equally important to have a script, not just a blank page with 'Patsy and Eddy have a row, don't worry – I'll put some jokes in later' on it.

Damian and Maureen and I seem to get on. He makes the sort of noises that a man who's made a lot of films makes, but a film of *Ab Fab*? I keep telling Damian that he doesn't know what he may have got himself into, yet he presses on regardless.

Cut to: Jennifer's house a few weeks later: Afternoon.
I am listening to Jen's ideas and we are kicking them around (this is useful, rather than destructively cruel and violent). We are much encouraged that Jen's main idea is good but short. It will have a good 'inciting incident', as film students say. In the middle of the movie Edina will be responsible for pushing Kate Moss into the Thames. Then Pats and Eddy have to escape the law. Of course, Kate has to survive. So do our heroines. Where things might go after that, or indeed before

it, is not quite clear yet, and will depend not just on thoughts that Jen has, but also what the film company has to say, and all the other people who may provide finance and support. Oh and we also know that Patsy and Eddy are going to flee the country, and head for the South of France

Cut to: BBC Radio studio; two weeks before New Year's Eve. Dawn and Jennifer quite often record shows for Radio 2, to be used on high days and holidays. On one such, at the end of 2013, Dawn asks Jennifer on-air how the film script is going. Jen mutters something of a non-committal nature. Dawn says –

'I bet you £100,000, Jennifer Saunders, that by this time next year you won't have done it. The listeners are my witnesses. This is a *one way* bet…'

Twelve months pass. Another radio show.

DAWN: How's the film script Jen? The one which I bet
            you £100,000 that you wouldn't finish?
JENNIFER: Actually, Dawn French, it's here, would you like
            to read it?

Sound of paper being passed across desk. They play a record, probably Honor Blackman and Patrick Macnee singing 'Kinky Boots'. We return to the studio.

DAWN: Well I've read your script, Jen, and it gets
            particularly good after page 27, I thought.

This, I realise is code for *it doesn't go past page 27*, but Dawn later told me that in fact they'd refined the bet to allow Jen to finish it by New Year's Eve, when the radio show would be broadcast. At about five to midnight on 31st December, Dawn says, her printer whirred into life and the first version of the script arrived. Jennifer did not want to part with £100,000.

Cut to: 20th Century Fox: Day.
We have decided to go with Fox Searchlight as the principal production company for the film. They've made lots of good films over the years, and they're prepared to let the BBC in on the deal. Without the Beeb, they wouldn't have a project, and we need to have the BBC onside so we can access archive (and maybe the odd wig). Finally, it's because Fox seem to know what they're doing.

So it will be (mainly) a Fox Searchlight and BBC Films production.

This is our first meeting with a proper film company and they are making real 'film noises' (so different from the noises you get out of a TV channel). They talk about the great commercial opportunities they're going to line up. *Ab Fab* has always felt like it would be a wonderful show to hang 'product' on, but it hasn't been because of the BBC's distance from advertising. The show's never been available to the world of commerce before, and commerce is *excited*. We hear about possible sponsorship from Coca-Cola, who might put Pats and Ed on 57 million Coke cans. How do we feel about appearing on Cadbury's Amaze Bites? (Not sure, I've never tasted them... Oo – now I have, that's fine.) They also already think that *Absolutely Fabulous The Movie* will read better on a poster than *Ab Fab The Movie*, which they worry looks like an odd jumble of letters. They're right.

We've never been asked these things before and who knew that all this starts even before you have a full script? They're optimists, these film folk. They are also talking about who Jennifer might like to be directed by, and designed by, and costumed by, and who should compose the music for her magnum opus. Better yet, two very good people called Katie Goodson-Thomas (from Fox) and Christine Langan (from BBC Films) are giving Jennifer script thoughts and notes, and she seems to be taking them on board! (Something that she's never done with *my* notes.) They talk to her about how important the beginning is, and how it's good not to assume too much audience knowledge of what's gone before, and about how there should be 'clear water' between the TV show and the movie. It shouldn't feel like a glorified Christmas special.

Everything should be *bigger*, and already it's decided that the whole film will be shot on location, not in a studio. It must look like a film and feel like a film. It must also, they say, have a good ending. Well, they can't have everything!

But no, stop. Just a moment. I must record that Jennifer worked *very hard* on the script. She really did. The proof is on the screen.

Cut to: Production offices Ealing: Day (and Night).
Now when I say Ealing, you may fondly be imagining the home of *Kind Hearts and Coronets* and *The Lavender Hill Mob*. No. Wrong. We are not at Ealing Studios, we are in offices that used to be the offices of BT, its Ealing Telephone Exchange. Glamorous, it *ain't*. It makes me pine, just a little, for hot-desking in Shepherd's Bush....well, a smidge.

Damian has an office down the corridor; another office contains the design department led by Harry Banks, busy drawing set plans; and along the corridor, where personnel used to be, is the wardrobe department led by the remarkable Rebecca Hale who works costume miracles. Next to her is an office occupied by the most important person on the film, the financial controller, Trevor. He stands up most of the time and his desk is perched on top of another desk because he has back problems. Actually, I think it's also so he can get out fast when things turn to shit, without having to get up from a chair.

I sit in a corner of the main office, humbly realising that these people actually know about Film, whereas I only know about film-ing. ('Film' is what *Citizen Kane* is, 'film-ing' is what you do for a studio insert on *One Foot in the Grave*.) In the other corner is the organisational wizard, the co-producer Mark. He actually *does* things (weird) like hiring crew and locations and French people. We need Gallic types because we will be filming in reverse order. The last third of the action is in the South of France and we need to get that done first. We'll start filming in October, and we want the Riviera to look warm and glamorous, still in its summer glory. No problem. Mark has found an English guy who runs crews out there and who can also vouch for the climate. He's good.

I spend time talking to Alex, our casting director, who is having a *great* time because people are actually saying yes to her! This is the power of our brand. It must be, because we're not offering the cast vast amounts of money. There's a standard guest rate per day, and that's it, take it or leave it. Fox Searchlight influence the casting, I can't deny it. They think that a few American names would do no harm to the box office over there. They negotiate with stars who want to work with them on bigger projects, suggesting mildly that they might like to work on ours first: 'We'll let you star in the remake of *Moby Dick* if you help us out with *Ab Fab*, and anyway you *like* London and your wife *loves* Harrods.'

I realise that so far I've not mentioned our director, Mandie Fletcher. She is perhaps best described as a 'horse-loving, game girl', first famous for directing *BlackAdder 2* and *Hamish Macbeth*, as well as *Roger and Val Have Just Got In*, on which she was great. She has all the enthusiasm required for the film and is Jennifer's first choice, having directed some of *Ab Fab* on TV, as well as *Jam and Jerusalem*. So we set off with our faces towards the sun and the ordered chaos that is both Film and film-ing.

Cut to: Monday 12th October: Villefranche-sur-Mer: Early morning, street.
It's our first day of filming. We begin with a slightly greyer day than we'd hoped, but it gets better.

My schedule tells me that we're shooting Scene 94 parts 1–4. *'Patsy and Edina whizz along past restaurants on the front, causing a waiter to jump into the water.'*

For a chase sequence to work you need lots of shots for the editor to play with, and a *great* deal of patience. Start with some slapstick; start as we mean to go on. The idea is to get everyone in the right mood for the next seven weeks.

Cut to: Wednesday 14th October: Coast road towards Cap Ferrat in Rolls-Royce: Cannes – the Croisette.
This is more like it, one of several 'money shots'. This is what Patsy and Edina wanted to escape to – the glamour, the wealth and a very expensive car. It requires Joanna to wear a moustache and we have to do a drive-by twice because we've got our leading ladies in the car the wrong way round, so their position won't match with other shots. A couple of days after this we move into full bling mode with a huge yacht that we've been lent as long as we pay for the petrol (not cheap) and a helicopter from which we can get good shots of the yacht.

Cut to: Thursday 22nd October: Ext. Palais Bulles, Cannes: Camera Crane Day.
This is an extraordinary location. The Bubble Palace. It's on a headland with a fantastic coastal view and until recently

was the holiday home of Pierre Cardin. Everything is round. The windows are round, the 12 bedrooms are round – and it's all made of terracotta coloured stone. The place was on sale recently for a mere 350 million euros. We are using it because nobody can afford that, but mainly because it serves well for our denouement. Patsy and Eddy are being chased by the police and are driving one of those really small French vans called an Apé (pronounced Ap-A as in 'I want to be 'appy, but I can't be 'appy', *not* as in monkey). At the climax of the chase the van has to fly over a hedge and land in the swimming pool of the Palais Bulles and then sink slowly over a couple of pages of dialogue. The crash will be handled by a visual-effects team, and the gradual immersion by a crane slowly releasing the van on wires into the water. Both the crane and the wires will be painted out in post-production. That's the plan.

Jennifer and Joanna are inside. Gulp.

Incredibly, it works! I mean I *know* it's not up there with SpiderMan meets Thor, but we *haven't* got their budget and the girls just *would not* look good in those costumes. Trust me. So hooray for us! Nobody is drowned and the effects look good, and the acting is magnificent. I say *chapeaux* off to the French crew and the British effects crew. See what we might lose with Brexit? The ability to lower people into swimming pools slowly, in the name of comedy.

Cut to: Monday 2nd November: Thames Embankment: Night.
We have returned to London. We have already filmed guest artists for tiny scenes in tiny locations that we hope will look like tiny corners of up-market French hotels. We've also shot a scene with Graham Norton and Mark Gatiss in which Edina goes to a publisher to try for an advance. We are being fitted *very* snugly into other people's schedules. Mark was filming

something else on the day we were using him, and Graham Norton had come to us by motorbike from his three-hour Radio 2 show, and was going on to another function later in the afternoon. It's a tough life, show business.

Continuing our reverse schedule tonight, we are shooting the reaction to Kate Moss's fall into the Thames before we shoot the fall itself. We have Kirsty Wark telling viewers that police are urging onlookers to move away. We also have respected foreign correspondent Orla Guerin reporting from the Thames Embankment on shrines that have already been erected for Ms Moss.

Getting Orla is a bit of a coup. She's actually based in Cairo and sends reports from there and many another Middle Eastern trouble spot. She lends a sense of impending doom to any event she's reporting. I ask her why she said yes to our bizarre request?

'My two boys said that they'd never speak to me again if I didn't do *Ab Fab.*' The power of comedy and a good brand.

She has flown in from Cairo the night before, popped home to have a cup of tea and, after doing our film she will be flying back to Cairo. The following evening, I see her reporting from the site of an air crash in the desert. And we think making a film about a fashion PR is tough.

Cut to: Monday 9th November: Power plant, East London: Night. This is Huki Muki day. The big event that Patsy and her magazine editor have organised, to celebrate Huki Muki – the fashion designer of the hour. It is the event at which Kate Moss will 'accidentally' be pushed into the Thames by Edina Monsoon. There are a lot of beautiful people at the event played by glitterati such as Jon Hamm, Lulu, Chris Colfer, Bruno Tonioli, Celia Imrie, Gwendoline Christie, Kathy Burke and obviously Janette Krankie as Huki Muki herself.

Now can I just clear something up? When we were making the film we were accused of 'Yellow Face' because Janette was playing a character called 'Huki Muki'. Casting Caucasian actors as Japanese characters is wrong, I agree. But at no point did we identify our celebrated designer as any particular nationality, Eastern or not. I *can* confirm that Janette is Scottish and that neither we nor she meant any offence to be caused.

> **NOTE: I'm not actually sure that there's anything wrong with causing offence and sometimes offence should be caused to some people. But it should be to individuals rather than groups. OF COURSE. For example, not all blond, shaggy-haired folk are as tactless and egocentric as Boris Johnson. But that's a whole other can of maggots.**

We were all dreading this part of the schedule. We had to keep a crowd of major artists happy and it was a big action day. Many shots would be needed to tell the story clearly. Patsy lures Jon Hamm away from Kate's side and Edina moves in to recruit Kate as a client, just as a rival PR person, Claudia Byng, does the same. In the resulting tussle, Ms Moss falls to her watery doom. I'm sure it will come as no surprise to learn that at the crucial moment, our supermodel is replaced by a super-stunt model who falls onto a lot of empty cardboard boxes acting as a crash mat and then later into a tank of water deputising for the River Thames. It *looks like* a watery death.

The Huki Muki party takes three days to film. That's something like 30 hours of filming/partying.

Fifty-Seven Million Coke Cans

Cut to: Monday 16th November: Vauxhall Tavern: Day
The Vauxhall Tavern just south of the Thames has been famous for many years as a helluva drag. It's a place where you'll find men dressed up as glamorous women most nights of the week. Our movie has a sequence in which Saffy is looking for Edina's hairdresser Christopher because he alone will know where Eddy and Pats have gone post-Moss-plunge. The drag queens who are hosting the evening persuade Saffy to sing Janis Ian's sad-and-haunting song, 'At Seventeen'. We suddenly learn that Julia Sawalha has a *lovely* singing voice. Why didn't she let us know in the 20 years that we've been making the series?

The scene involves approximately 80 drag queens who have all fought, wig and nail, to be in our film, since far more applied than could be fitted into the Tavern. An extraordinary sight greets commuters as they exit the tube station opposite for the start of their working week. Standing outside the pub, groups of young men are putting on lipstick, adjusting bra straps, checking eyeliner – all in a state of great excitement.

The gay community has always welcomed Patsy and Eddy with open arms. Why do we like these characters so much? It may be that they represent such grotesque versions of the opposite gender that we feel safe. Or because they're only just clinging on, but doing it with style and panache. (It may just be that we envy their frocks.) In any event, when we get to the end of filming that day, the drag queens line up like 'gorgeous girls in gooey gowns' to get Jennifer and Joanna's autographs. No other group of 'walk-ons' would ever do that, and well done Jen and Jo for coming to the Vauxhall Tavern on a day when they weren't strictly needed.

How to Produce Comedy Bronze

Cut to: Tuesday 17th November, Edina's house: Day.

Our first day filming in Edina Monsoon's house. After the decision not to build this in a studio, as before, the team has been scouring London for something suitable (and available). This has not been easy. It's quite a particular look. We need it to be like the kitchen in the TV series, but bigger and better – oh – and it needs to have a wall where the studio audience are normally seated. The rooms need to be big enough to accommodate a film crew as well as our actors. Most houses like this are now in the possession of Russian oligarchs or absentee landlords.

We eventually find somewhere in Harlesden. Gosh! I've always thought that Harlesden was a rather down at heel north-west London suburb, but it turns out that I'm wrong. Who knew? Round the back of the main bit is an up-market area with some very large houses (I can do estate agent prattle pretty well, can you tell?). The one we're using is not only a large house, but it has stairs down to a very grand basement kitchen, with a garden opening on one side, and a large indoor swimming pool on the other. It's all very Edina, and, with some help from the art department, it can become more so. This is where we are today and for the next seven days, shooting scenes that mostly involve the family plus old friends Fleur and Catriona. It's quite like old times and the end of the shooting schedule is at last in sight.

At the end of one of our days in the house, we rush off to a car park in Cricklewood to shoot a 'pick up'. This is not something sleazy involving men in limos, but a section of a scene we have already filmed most of, but not all. Stella McCartney couldn't make the evening on which we were filming the Huki Muki fashion event but she can make one of our Harlesden shooting days. We no longer have the Huki Muki location and are therefore in the drizzle in the corner of a depressing car park trying to make it look like the dazzling entrance to a very glamorous party. All Stella has to do is get out of a car, sweep past a (very small) crowd, and then engage in dialogue with Patsy about the time that Patsy may have spent with Stella's dad and the other Beatles. All that we have to do is make this 'match' the Huki Muki event, so we place a green screen behind Stella by which means we can substitute the South Bank and the Thames at night for the slightly less charming east side of Cricklewood Broadway.

TECHNICAL LESSON: For those who aren't acquainted with green screen this is a flat solid colour (doesn't have to be green) put behind a scene. The scene you are filming mustn't have the same colour as the screen anywhere in it. Once you've lit the scene correctly and in line with the scene you want to cut it into, then you key out the colour of your screen and it magically disappears and the background of the scene you're cutting it into magically appears. If you've done it right. So suddenly a car can be driving on the moon.

Sorry if a) this is too technical b) too boring c) wrong. There is a story which relates how an enthusiastic young director was explaining the subtleties of green screen to the splendid actress Irene Handl – then considerably advanced in years. After a few moments she stopped him, saying 'I'm sorry, young man, but I think you're confusing me for someone who gives a fuck.' Apologies if you feel the same.

How to Produce Comedy Bronze

Cut to: Friday 27th November, airfield: Day.
This is our last official day of filming. We spend it on an airfield in Buckinghamshire where our location and design teams have found an aircraft that doesn't actually fly, but does spends its days as a film location. With one arrangement of seats it can be a budget airline, with another the president's private jet. For us, it's a budget plane to Nice, whose crew consists of a loud and wonderful Australian (Rebel Wilson) and the winner of the 11th series of *Celebrity Big Brother*, Rylan Clark-Neal. Rebel tells us that she's a huge fan of the show and indeed, like many others, she's squeezed us into an impossibly tight schedule. Rebel's character rebukes Patsy for smoking, and tasers her. Patsy enjoys this: 'You don't get that on British Airways!'

I'm sure that BA are planning to add it in as an extra feature for all passengers any day now.

That's it. Our last day of filming, apart from the odd one or two shots that have been forgotten, (it does happen). Our scene now moves to the world of post-production. Editing, special visual effects, dubbing, music and so on.

Cut to: mid-January, editing house: Day.
Mandie (our director) and the editor have put the film together remarkably quickly and it really does look like a film! The story works and it's the right length and, although everyone can see that there's work to be done, we seem to be heading somewhere. None of us are quite sure where, but definitely somewhere. We all begin to see opportunities to move scenes around, and change the way in which a line is said or received, by using a different take. It's a dangerous time, because suddenly everyone has an opinion. It must be tough for Mandie.

There is now talk of when the film will open. Fox favour a date in June when it won't clash with other premieres.

Fifty-Seven Million Coke Cans

Especially films that may be for the same sort of audience. Apparently this includes the all-female *Ghostbusters*. Yes – I can see the similarity. They've both got women in them.

> **TECHNICAL LESSON: Lots of films use ADR.**
> **This is the process whereby actors can re-voice**
> **lines that are muffled or unclear or missing.**
> **Jennifer wants to use it as much as she can. She**
> **has realised that it's an opportunity to make**
> **characters say funnier/sharper things than they**
> **did in the first place. Of course these lines can**
> **only be dubbed by characters who have their**
> **backs to the camera . All you need is a sound**
> **studio, the actors whose backs we were looking**
> **at, and some better jokes. If you have a look at**
> **the film again you will see several examples of**
> **this. Actually if you have another look at the**
> **film, you are perhaps in need of a life.**

Cut to: Monday 15th February, Wimbledon Cinema.
This is not a happy night. It is our first test screening. Fox do these a lot, so if you're near Wimbledon on a Monday night, you may be asked your opinion of a new movie. Don't give it, don't go.

Test screenings are an opportunity for the studio and the production team to see how a film plays with a test audience. The audience are given score cards, and some of them are asked to stay behind in focus groups and discuss what's wrong with the film. They do this with the producers and the writer and director listening in. It's the nearest thing we have in modern times to Christians being fed to lions.

293

The film this focus group has watched is NOT FINISHED YET. It hasn't been 'fiddled with' in all the ways that films need to be fiddled with. The picture hasn't been refined, the sound isn't precise, the music isn't all in place. There is *some* laughter from the audience at the big gags, not quite so much at the smaller ones.

Then comes the worst bit. The audience have been given score cards and they are going to give us a score out of a 100. It seems to me that this is not going to be helpful. They are not an audience who have come to see *our* film, they have come to see *a* film but they don't know what it is until it starts. So the scores and comments are not from fans of the film or the show. Of course, I understand that we want *everybody* to come to the film, but *Absolutely Fabulous* is an entertainment that people will already have a view about. Obviously, I can see why the process is done but it doesn't make it any nicer.

We get the scores and they're not quite as high as they might be. We listen to the focus groups and there are clearly plot developments that they don't understand and 'intentions' that aren't quite clear. These can quickly be fixed. Some of the jokes can be made clearer. There is a general air of disappointment *but* we still have time. The film opens in three and a half months. Everyone sets off with a will to make the movie as good as it can be.

And we do something quite radical. After much thought, we recruit a second editor who is known for his 'doctoring' skills. In other words, he's a new pair of eyes, who hasn't been staring at the movie for months, and who really understands his craft. What does he bring to the movie? He can calm a scene down and let it breathe. Sequences that felt too rushed are given room. The audience is allowed in.

We also recruit the skills of a second composer. Jennifer

(especially) feels that musically the film has become rather safe and middle-aged. A bit like all of us. The score needs to feel more contemporary. So Damian gets in touch with Jake Monaco in LA. He will be just the guy to achieve this. We never meet Mr Monaco. The music is the one part of the movie that can be done 6,000 miles away.

Cut to: 15th June, World Premiere, Leicester Square, London: Evening.
Dawn French has just introduced me to Rupert Murdoch and to his wife Jerry Hall, who is in our film. Dawn says to Mr Murdoch: 'I'm so glad you married Jerry. If you hadn't, I would've had to marry her myself.' Dawn then fades gracefully away into the crowd. We are standing in the very busy foyer of the cinema where the first of our premieres is taking place.

'And thank you for paying for the film, Mr Murdoch,' I continue (because he does still own most of 20th Century Fox, doesn't he?).

He has the look of a man, let alone a fish, entirely out of water. Australian royalty he may be, but he seems uncomfortable around showbiz. The foyer and the street outside throng with stars, cheering fans, and a parade of Vauxhall Tavern drag artistes. It doesn't seem to be his natural home. I make social noises and leave him with Jerry.

We are having two premieres tonight, one immediately after the other, because we can't get all the cast, creative team, producers, Fox executives and their wives, marketing people and their wives, distributors and their wives, our crew and friends (some of whom have come over from France especially), into the same cinema. One of the other cinemas in Leicester Square has been hired – principally for crew and friends.

All goes well. The film has been trimmed and tidged and

music has been added and new jokes have been inserted and it's generally much better than it was on that ghastly night back in Wimbledon. And it's being watched by people who WANT TO SEE IT, and who may have had a drink or several beforehand. Not the normal audience, but hey.

Afterwards, everyone adjourns to Liberty's in Regent Street, who have given us their store for a first-night party. A large amount of Bolly is drunk, nibbles are nibbled and a good time is had by all (I hope). Certainly the store is closed all the next day so that they can tidy up and recover. They are still pulling glitterati out from under piles of expensive fabric days later.

Time passes.

The marketeers have done their stuff. We have been on 57 million cans and bottles of Diet Coke, and all over Amaze Bites; we have tube ads and newspaper ads and mostly nice reviews. The cast, in various states of sobriety, have been pictured in the press. In its first weekend the film takes $4.2 million and to date it has taken over $12 million in British cinemas alone. Altogether it has certainly made many times its budget. This is regarded as good.

Several things have helped. The EU referendum result helped *(apparently)* in that it made people want to see a *British* film. More to the point, it helped because it led to the resignation of the prime minister, and there was a general air of doom, gloom and foreboding. People were desperate for a laugh and we were it.

A slightly older crowd than might go out to (say) *Fast and Furious 7* made an effort to see our film and then told their friends. This is exactly what our director kept telling us. It was a Tuesday afternoon picture as well as a weekend movie.

I am both proud and pleased.

Fifty-Seven Million Coke Cans

Ten Movies that Make me Laugh

I know it's an obvious list but funny is funny and good writing and playing are always loved!.

Some Like it Hot: The best. Nothing else to be said and nothing can beat it.

Ferris Bueller's Day Off: You may need to be of a certain age but the death of a very expensive car is completely worth the cost of a download and repeated viewing, as is Matthew Broderick beating his sister and parents back home.

Bullets over Broadway: For the performances of Jim Broadbent and Dianne Wiest. Jim getting fatter through tricky rehearsals is both funny, daring and accurate.

Trains, Planes and Automobiles: Another film from John Hughes inspired by a short story in National Lampoon. Has anyone else made driving the wrong way down a freeway so funny? John Candy is a great loss. Steve Martin never better.

Monty Python's Life of Brian: Funnier and sometimes at least as wise as the Bible. I apologise that this is the only mention of the brilliant and ground-breaking Monty Python team.

Love and Death: Woody Allen's movie with the highest joke count and the end of his 'funny' period: is there a better period to be in? Or a better parody of Tolstoy?

The Birdcage: Mike Nichols' version of *La Cage aux Folles*. Where else can you see Gene Hackman in drag to such great effect? Nathan Lane and Robin Williams are perfect partners and Hank Azaria was never better than when falling over.

The Producers: Mel Brooks is a god and I'm not even Jewish. The earlier Zero Mostel version is the best and it takes a simple premise and runs with it. The casting is superb as is the writing and staging

Dr Strangelove: Kubrick showing that comedy and pessimism

can walk hand in hand. Peter Sellers does what Alec Guinness did in *Kind Hearts and Coronets*, and plays multiple parts to great comic effect. Surely the film should be playing on a loop in the Trump White House?

The Philadelphia Story: Katharine Hepburn, Cary Grant and James Stewart showing yet again that in comedy, character is everything. All three are wonderful but this brilliant screenplay also has casting in depth. Ruth Hussey is great as James Stewart's smart-talking sidekick and Virginia Weidler is wonderful as Hepburn's smart-alec younger sister. Director George Cukor was a genius.

29

Ending$_s$

How to finish?

In comedy this can be by looking forward – 'Oh no, Norman! Don't walk under that ladder *again!*' (*Run credits.*)

Or with a sense of tying up – 'Phew! Well I'm glad that ladder's gone, come on, Norman, let's all go home and have tea.' (*Wide shot as they hold hands and walk off.*)

If you're Shakespeare you can end with a dance.

'Strike up Pipers': *Much Ado About Nothing.*

'But come your Bergomask': *A Midsummer Night's Dream.*

If you're *The Sopranos* you c....

Endings are tricky for TV sitcoms because you rarely know if you're ever going to come back. You can't often end the war like *M*A*S*H* or kill off your main character like *One Foot in the Grave* or marry her off as we did in *The Vicar of Dibley*. Mostly comedies end with an average episode and then never return.

Quit while you're behind, leave them wanting less!

How to Produce Comedy Bronze

Movies have it easier because they're one-off events. The end of *Some Like it Hot* is perfection. Marilyn Monroe has just managed to jump into the launch of multi-millionaire Osgood Fielding III to tell Tony Curtis that she doesn't care if being with him will only get her the 'fuzzy end of the lollipop'. In the front of the launch Daphne (Jack Lemmon) is explaining to Osgood (Joe E Brown) why they can never be married. Osgood will not accept her excuses so finally Daphne rips off her wig and throws the supposed clincher, 'I'm a *man!*', to which Osgood coolly replies 'Nobody's perfect!' Pull out. The end. Bliss. I hope that we paid it proper homage at the end of our movie.

Almost as good is the end of *The End*, a 1978 movie starring and directed by Burt Reynolds with Dom DeLuise and Carl Reiner. Burt has been diagnosed with a terminal disease and spends most of the movie trying to find ways to commit suicide. None works but he meets Dom DeLuise in a mental hospital to which Burt, wrongly, and Dom, rightly, have been committed. Burt makes Dom's character swear that even though he, Burt, may beg him not to, he, Dom, will kill him. (Trust me, it makes sense.)

Inevitably in the last reel Burt's diagnosis is turned on its head and he can live. He is intensely happy until suddenly Dom appears from behind a rock with a huge knife and murderous intent. 'Surprise!' he shouts with wonderful comic energy and chases Burt down the beach as the credits roll. It truly is, as the best comedy should be, a surprise!

Rent it! Download it! Buy it! Steal it! It has some good gags and is worth it for the finish which I've now spoiled for you. It's funny, I promise.

So, as we nearly said as homage to *Dad's Army*, at the end of each *Dibley* episode, 'Bless you for *reading*.'

And bless you for watching any comedy on any channel

Endings

ever. I hope it made you laugh and that if it didn't, you didn't take it out on the cat. I hope that I and everyone I've ever worked with, and a good few that I haven't, will continue to make you laugh long into the future. Thank you to all the people, way too numerous, who ever made me laugh.

The End
Roll Credits/Sorry, roll Acknowledgements

Acknowledgement$_s$

There are way too many people without whom... Here are the main ones, or rather here are the ones that I can remember and have helped with this book:

The BBC, Adam Kay, Adam Tandy, Sophie Clarke-Jervoise, Helen Boaden, John Morton, Cathryn Summerhayes, James Farrell, Eirwen Davies, Justin Davies, Peter Maniura, Dawn French, Charlie Hanson, Tracey Gillham, Jo Buckingham, Shane Allen, Paddy O'Connell...and my editor Joel Simons... and above all Francis who has read, reread and corrected every word, sentence and anecdote except those read, reread and corrected by the copy editor.

Further acknowledgements to those without whom I wouldn't have a career to write about:

André Ptaszynski, Peter Bennett-Jones, Maureen Vincent, Caroline Chignell, Steve Morrison, Sandy Ross, Sita Williams, Johnny Hamp, Jim Moir, Paul Jackson, Roger Laughton, Michael Appleton, Jill Sinclair, Frances Whitaker, Richard Curtis, Dawn French, Jennifer Saunders, Joanna Lumley, Bob

How to Produce Comedy Bronze

Spiers, Paul Mayhew-Archer, Ruby Wax, Tom Webber, Lucy Lumsden, Peter Fincham, Jonathan Harvey, Simon Doonan, Ade Edmondson, Stephen Fry, Hugh Laurie, Alan Yentob, Michael Jackson, Jane Root, Phil McIntyre, Janice Hadlow, Roly Keating, Paul Schlesinger, Charlotte Moore, Alex Walsh-Taylor, Anil Gupta, Sarah Hitchcock, Julia Cottrell, Fiona Neill, Bill Dare, Ed Bye, Sue Vertue, Clive Tulloh, Phil Bowker, Phillippa Catt, Jo Sargent, Cheryl Taylor, Ian Critchley, David Liddiment, Steve Pemberton, Reece Shearsmith, Gareth Edwards, Damian Jones, Stuart Murphy and Chris Sussman.

And all the others who know who they are, even if I don't.

A Chronology

This is partly so that you know the order in which I did what. Also so that I do too. This is just the 'main' stuff. I'm sure there were some things I've forgotten. Sorry.

Royal Court Theatre (assistant director): 1975–77
Absolution movie starring Richard Burton (assistant to director, Anthony Page)
Granada Television (researcher then producer): 1978–82
BBC (producer)
Russell Harty: 1983–84
Pop Quiz including Spandau vs Duran Duran: 1984
Wogan (three times a week): 1985–88
A Night for Comic Relief: one of several producers: 1989–91
French and Saunders: (producer then exec prod): 1989–2018
Absolutely Fabulous: (ditto): 1991–2012
Talkback (producer)
Smith and Jones: 1987–88–89
Murder Most Horrid: (producer then exec producer): 1991–92

How to Produce Comedy Bronze

BBC (producer)
Fry and Laurie: 1994
Bottom: 1995
Tiger Aspect TV (producer then exec producer)
The Vicar of Dibley: 1994–99

Somewhere around 1994 I was asked to be head of comedy entertainment at the BBC. I did that until 2005 when I became head of comedy. This means that on most of the shows after 1994 I'm executive producer. I should here and now thank all the producers who let me fiddle with their work. In June 2007 I stopped being head of anything, and went back to making shows for anybody who would have me, mostly the BBC. It's just more fun than deskwork. I also helped make *Absolutely Fabulous: the Movie* (as you may have already read…).

These are some of the shows I had something to do with. If you wrote or starred in or produced one that I've left off the list, I'm really sorry, it's memory not malice.

Alexei Sayle's Stuff: 1998–2001
Gimme, Gimme, Gimme: 1999–2001
The League of Gentlemen: 1999–2017
People Like Us: 1999–2001
Grass (Simon Day on the run): 2003
The Office: 2001–2003
15 Storeys High: 2002–2004
Dead Ringers: 2002–2005
Little Britain: 2003–2006
Absolute Power: 2003–2005
The Thick of It: 2005–2007
The Robinsons: 2005
Hyperdrive: 2006–2007
H.R. (one-off): 2007

A Chronology

Extras: 2005–2007
Broken News: 2005
Jam and Jerusalem: 2006–2008
Taking the Flack: 2009
Beautiful People: 2008–2009
Psychoville: 2009–2011
Roger and Val Have Just Got In: 2012
Twenty Twelve: 2010–Guess
W1A: 2015–2017
Inside No. 9: 2014–2018
Absolutely Fabulous: the Movie: 2015